LEGENDARY LOCALS

OF

LAKE COUNTY

FLORIDA

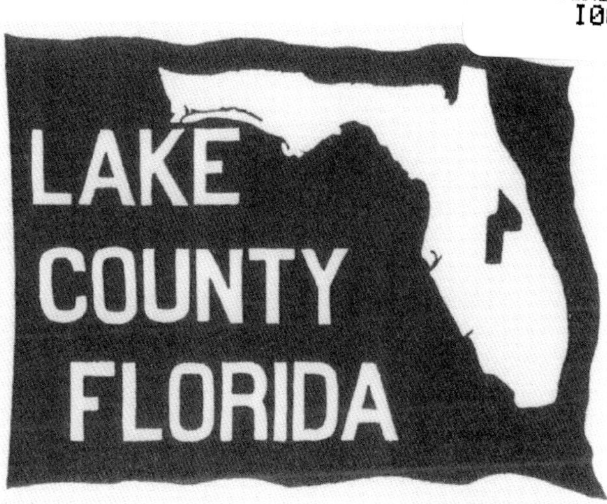

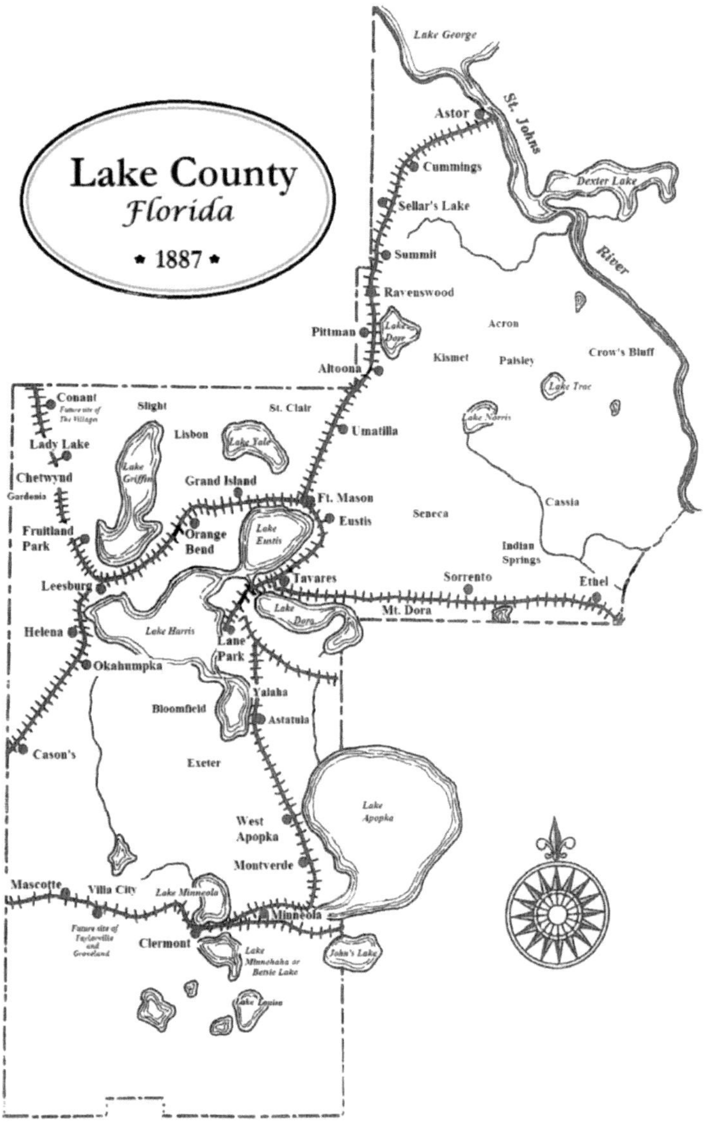

Map of Lake County c. 1887

This map provides a glimpse of sprawling Lake County at the time it was created, on May 27, 1887, from portions of neighboring Sumter and Orange Counties. Lake County has 1,400 lakes and covers 1,156 square miles. The population in 2011 was 301,019, about 30,000 more people than lived in the entire state in 1880.

Page 1: **Lake County Flag**

Lake County was the first county in the nation to have its own flag. It was designed by Karl Lehmann from Montverde to celebrate the county's 50th anniversary. Lehmann, known as the "human dynamo," led the Lake County Chamber of Commerce for 30 years. Under his leadership, the chamber was one of the largest in the nation. He was a tireless promoter and generous philanthropist. (Courtesy of the Lake County Historical Society.)

LEGENDARY LOCALS

OF

LAKE COUNTY

FLORIDA

DORIS BLOODSWORTH AND
CONNIE FLEETWOOD

LEGENDARY LOCALS

ISBN 978-1-4671-0025-0

Legendary Locals is an imprint of Arcadia Publishing
Charleston, South Carolina

Printed in the United States of America

Library of Congress Control Number: 2012932885

For all general information, please contact Arcadia Publishing:
Telephone 843-853-2070
Fax 843-853-0044
E-mail sales@arcadiapublishing.com
For customer service and orders:
Toll-Free 1-888-313-2665

Visit us on the Internet at www.arcadiapublishing.com

To the dedicated members of the historical societies across Lake County and to our wonderful families, who supported this labor of love

On the Cover: From left to right:
(TOP ROW) Ann Dupee, journalist (Courtesy of Ann Dupee, page 94); David Walker, astronaut (Courtesy of NASA, page 52); William J. Howey, founder (Courtesy of Lake County Historical Society, page 82); Virgil Hawkins, attorney (Courtesy of University of Florida, page 87); Marian P. Duncan and Henry H. Duncan, pioneers (Courtesy of Harryette-Anne Duncan, page 41).
(MIDDLE ROW) Jess Thomas, soldier (Courtesy of Ila Mae Thomas, page 116); Nathan Trowell, founder (Courtesy of Evelyn "Sis" Allen Sebree, page 72); John Philip Donnelly, mayor (Courtesy of Mount Dora Historical Society, page 67); Harold Schwartz, founder (Courtesy of The Villages, page 35); Bob Grenier, historian (Courtesy of Bill Casey, page 48).
(BOTTOM ROW) Dr. Olive Worcester Swan, physician, and Orpha Worcester, artist (Courtesy of Lady Lake Historical Society, page 27); Lacy Day Edge, legislator (Courtesy of Lake County Historical Society, page 107); Millard Coggshall, beekeeper (Courtesy of the Coggshall family, page 123); Albert Sharp Matlack, merchant (Courtesy of Lake County Historical Society, page 76); Norma Hendricks, journalist (Courtesy of Leesburg Heritage Society, page 10).

CONTENTS

ACKNOWLEDGMENTS

From the start, the people who contributed to this book understood the importance of passing along the history of Lake County. The generosity of those who so willingly shared their time, photographs, and memories cannot be measured. We are grateful to all of you for your support.

Contributors include: Scott Amey, Randa Anderson, Susan Stanfield Ball, Ric Baysinger, the Barwick family, Toni Bell, Thomas Benfield, Clayton Bishop, Donna Bott, Vivian Bruns, Clark Blake, Betty Burleigh, Dr. Susan Glenn Caddell, Louise Carter, Bill Casey, Linda Charlton, City of Fruitland Park, City of Groveland, CDC of Leesburg and Vicinity, Peggy Beucher Clark, the Coggshall family, Aurelia Cole, Cooper Memorial Library Association, Charles and Eileen Costigan, Kimberly Couch, *The Daily Commercial,* Norma Delaney, Rupert Deleveaux, Diane Disney, Rebecca Bryan Dreisbach, Harryette-Anne Duncan, Ann Dupee, East Lake Historical Society, Jeanette and Ernie Edmundson, Eustis Historical Society, Glorianne Fahs, Gloria and June Fairchild, Florida Citrus Hall of Fame, Gee Gee Franklin, Garst Museum, BettyAnn Gray, Greater Altoona Society, Greater Umatilla Historical Society, Bob Grenier, Groveland Historical Society, Catherine Hanson, Kitty Arnold Herzog, Historical Society of Tavares, Holy Trinity Episcopal Church, Holyoke Public Library, Howey Historic Preservation Society, Olive Ingram, International Society of Weekly Newspaper Editors, R. Eugene Isted, Glen Jones, Shirley Kimmons, Howard and Dodie King, Lady Lake Historical Society, Lake County Historical Society, *Lake* magazine, Mary Jane Lange, Ken LaRoe, James Laux, Julia Law, Leesburg African-American Museum, Leesburg Heritage Society, Bruce Lee, Ruth Lockett, Sally Luther, Gary Maitland, Betty Slaven McClellan, Bristo McGregor, Shirley Meade, Bill Milton, Milwaukee Brewers, Minneola Schoolhouse Library, Montverde Academy, Tatty Morgan, Lavonda Morris, Mount Dora Historical Society, Mary Helen Myers, Merideth Nagel, Micki Blackburn Nagel, NASA, National Sculpture Society, Northeast Black History Committee, Bernice Odums, Vivian Owens, Marie Padgett, Mary Page, Pastfinders of South Lake County Genealogical Society, Wanda Payton, John D. Pease III, Emmett Peter Jr., Melanie Peter, Greg Phillips, James Pitt, Judy Hux Rainey, the Ramirez family, Franklin Reaves, the Roberts family, Jane Robbins, Britt Runion Photography, Barbara Busbee Sealy, the Oakley Seaver family, Evelyn "Sis" Sebree, Peggy Parrish Sloan, Evelyn and John Smith, Kemp Smith, South Lake County Historical Society, State Archives of Florida, Karen Bolin Strawbridge, the Stokes family, Ila Mae Thomas, B.E. Thompson, Johnny Thunder, Roy Tremain, Jo Tucker, W. Glenn Tyre, The Villages, Dolores Gano Walker, George Warren Jr., Kristin Warren, Jimmy Watson, Eloise White, Sheryl Williams, the Wynn family, and John Zweifel.

The following publications were invaluable to our research: *Lake County Florida: A Pictorial History*; *Through Schoolhouse Doors: A History of Lake County Schools*; *The Other Leesburg: Johnny Thunder*; *History of Lake County Florida: Narrative and Biographical*; *Lake & Sumter Counties: Florida's Heartland*; *Central Florida* magazine; *City of Leesburg Sesquicentennial Celebration*; *Clermont: Gem of the Hills*; *Lake Today*; *Lakeside Inn, Mt. Dora, Florida: A Short History*; *Okahumpka Florida*; *The Story of Lady Lake*; *Clermont* (Images of America); *Groveland* (Images of America); *Howey-in-the-Hills* (Images of America); *Eustis* (Images of America); *Tavares* (Images of America); *The History of Astor on the St. Johns, Astor Park, and the Surrounding Area*; *The Villages: Then and Now.*

INTRODUCTION

In many ways, Lake County holds the same attraction today that it did when the Timucua and Seminoles inhabited the land many centuries ago. The county has more than 1,400 lakes and a year-round comfortable climate. No wonder many residents think living here is like being on vacation 365 days a year.

Well, almost, anyway. There are snakes and alligators and bears. And early pioneers faced many hardships, such as yellow fever.

Still, they came. Pioneers like Thomas Robertson, who arrived in 1843 to homestead south of Lake Griffin, arrived in what was truly a frontier land. He and other early settlers had to be self-sufficient, living off fish, game, and the crops they grew.

In 1862, the Homestead Act offered 160 acres of land to any US citizen who stayed on the land for five years, built a dwelling, and filed for a deed.

After the Civil War, many Confederate veterans, and some former Union soldiers, took advantage of this chance to start a new life in Florida. Former Confederate soldiers—such as Daniel Sloan in present-day Groveland, and Melton Haynes in what is now Tavares—put down roots. Clermont started as a planned community, the brainchild of four former Union soldiers.

Some communities in the north end of the county were originally settled by a group of wealthy, well-educated, young British men who wanted to learn the citrus trade.

With the introduction of railroads in the 1880s, Lake County's population grew. The rugged land beckoned hearty souls, such as Dr. Olive Worcester Swan. "Miss Estelle" lived near present-day Lady Lake. She traveled in her buggy, treating patients, delivering babies, and caring for the dying—no matter the time of day or the weather.

In 1880, an ambitious Orlando lawyer changed the face of Lake County forever. Maj. Alexander St. Clair Abrams traveled to present-day Tavares and was inspired. He sought to make his new home a railroad hub, county seat, and state capital.

St. Clair Abrams worked with legislators Henry H. Duncan and George M. Lee, from Tavares and Leesburg respectively, to pass a law creating Lake County out of portions of Sumter County to the west and Orange County to the east. On May 27, 1887, Lake County was born. Duncan chose the new county's name in recognition of the more than 1,000 lakes within its borders.

Leesburg had been the county seat for Sumter County. The new courthouse was temporarily established in a two-story house in Bloomfield, near Lake Harris and present-day Yalaha. Tavares and Leesburg leaders engaged in a tug-of-war over where the new county seat would be permanently located. St. Clair Abrams brought hundreds of African American workers to vote for his city and threw an extravagant barbecue. It took three votes before Tavares won. The opposition went to a DeLand judge to prevent removal of the courthouse records. Duncan had been tipped off and moved the records to Tavares, putting an end to the struggle.

New communities flourished, including Villa City in south Lake County. The founder, George T. King, a wealthy Baltimore Colgate salesman, envisioned a town of European-style villas. Sidewalks were lined with pineapples and roses. King started a steamship line.

In Eustis, Umatilla, and other towns, citrus was becoming an increasingly important crop. Clermont was making a national name for being Florida's tomato capital.

A few days after Christmas Day 1894, a freeze settled across Central Florida. January 1895 was warm and wet, which encouraged the surviving trees to produce new growth and to be filled with sap. On February 7, Lake County went from a balmy 80 degrees to a rapid freeze of 14 degrees. Eyewitnesses said citrus tree branches and fruit exploded throughout the night, sounding like cannon fire. More than

90 percent of Central Florida's citrus was gone. Clermont's prized tomatoes froze and rotted. Chetwynd and Villa City became ghost towns overnight. Those who could afford to do so, fled, leaving food and china on the tables.

As Lake County entered the 20th century, communities regained stability. Newspapers sprang up. Developers promoted residential properties to northerners, touting Lake County's healthy climate. Winter visitors, such as Wild West sharpshooter Annie Oakley, began making annual treks to the area to enjoy the weather and outdoor recreation.

By the 1920s, Lake County was experiencing a land boom. In Clermont, more than $2.5 million in real estate was sold in one month. The J. Ray Arnold sawmill, the county's largest employer, was running practically around the clock, with a payroll of more than $70,000 a month.

During the Roaring Twenties, east Lake County drew some of the most powerful and wealthy people in the country, who developed a 5,000-acre winter resort called the Mount Plymouth Golf Club. The resort boasted an airstrip and the largest dining room in the South. Tons of coquina rock were used to build the unique fountains and chimneys designed by architect Sam Stoltz in surrounding homes.

As the country slid into the Great Depression, Lake County's land boom became a bust. Mount Dora's bank was one of the few that did not fail. By 1939, Clermont went into bankruptcy, with the highest bond indebtedness per capita in the world. Citizens worked out a plan that allowed them to pay off most of the taxes owed by the following year.

During World War II, Lake County citizens bought war bonds and enlisted in the service. Some never returned, such as Robert McTureous of Altoona, who earned the Medal of Honor for his bravery.

From the 1940s through 1980s, citrus was king, driving the economy of most communities. William J. Howey opened the state's first citrus juice bottling plant and was one of the first to use pasteurization. Minute Maid, Blue Goose, Lake Region, B and W, and Golden Gem became iconic names in the citrus industry along with the families behind them, such as Crittenden, Langley, Herlong, Nelson, Micheloni, and Kuharske.

The 1960s started off with historic Hurricane Donna pounding Lake County. It was a decade with many changes, including the Cuban Missile Crisis, integration, and the Vietnam War. People like Virgil Hawkins, Ruthie Ann Watson, and T.H. Poole helped ensure opportunities for all people.

The 1960s and 1970s also were a time when proms and Friday night football games tied the communities and schools together. It was a time when legendary coaches gained prominence, such as Shaw Buck, Tom Perrin, Hubert Dabney, Dan Spear, and Clark Blake, to name a few. They put their towns on the maps with winning athletic programs. Buck and Dabney were inducted into the Florida Athletic Coaches Association Hall of Fame.

In 1983 and 1985, Lake County citrus owners faced devastating freezes. Each time, fewer growers were able to make a comeback. During Christmas 1989, a hard freeze knocked out electricity and dealt a death blow to Central Florida citrus, from which most growers never recovered.

New developments sprang from the barren land. Active retirement communities and championship golf courses brought new voices to Lake County. Visionary Howard Schwartz turned a mobile home park into The Villages, redefining retirement.

There is an undeniable spirit of optimism and neighborly concern that runs through the county and always has. An anecdote from Okahumpa's past says much about Lake County folks. There was a boy nicknamed "Catfish." His family was poor and struggled to make ends meet. Every morning, Catfish would get up early and go fishing to catch food for his family. Other people in town never fished in Catfish's fishing hole, to ensure that he always had a good catch and that there would be food on his family's table.

Simple acts of kindness—they're legendary in Lake County.

CHAPTER ONE

North Lake County

Leesburg, Fruitland Park, Lady Lake, and The Villages

The north Lake County cities of Leesburg, Fruitland Park, Lady Lake, and The Villages often serve as a welcome station to tourists traveling on the Florida Turnpike and on US Highways 27 and 441. Each has a different history and personality and offers a unique experience for those who enter the city limits.

Lake County was carved out of portions of neighboring Sumter and Orange Counties. Leesburg had been the county seat of Sumter County. Until recent years, it was the largest city. In its colorful past, it drew the likes of Annie Oakley and famed outdoorsman David Newell. Fruitland Park has a charming, small-town feel with a storied past and just enough quirky characters to make life interesting. Its historic Holy Trinity Episcopal Church is awe-inspiring. Early settlers were wealthy, well-educated Englishmen who enjoyed polo and steeplechase. But after the Great Freeze of 1894–1895, those who stayed were more like their hardy, pioneer neighbors. Fruitland Park's next-door neighbor, Lady Lake, with its oak-lined streets, has a history replete with resourceful characters, such as Jim Dudley, "the hitchhiking cop," who had to thumb a ride to catch speeders. Town folklore also includes tales of gangster Ma Barker's last stand, as well as the heroic sacrifices of some of its native sons.

And then there is The Villages, a community—many say a phenomenon—that redefined retirement. Founder Harold Schwartz was a true visionary who anticipated the active lifestyle that would define the baby-boomer generation in retirement. The collection of "villages" is home to celebrities, avid golfers, and others who worked hard and now enjoy their golden years—playing on the links, dancing in the town squares, joining one of the more than 1,800 clubs, or volunteering to help others, such as in the 700-member hospital auxiliary.

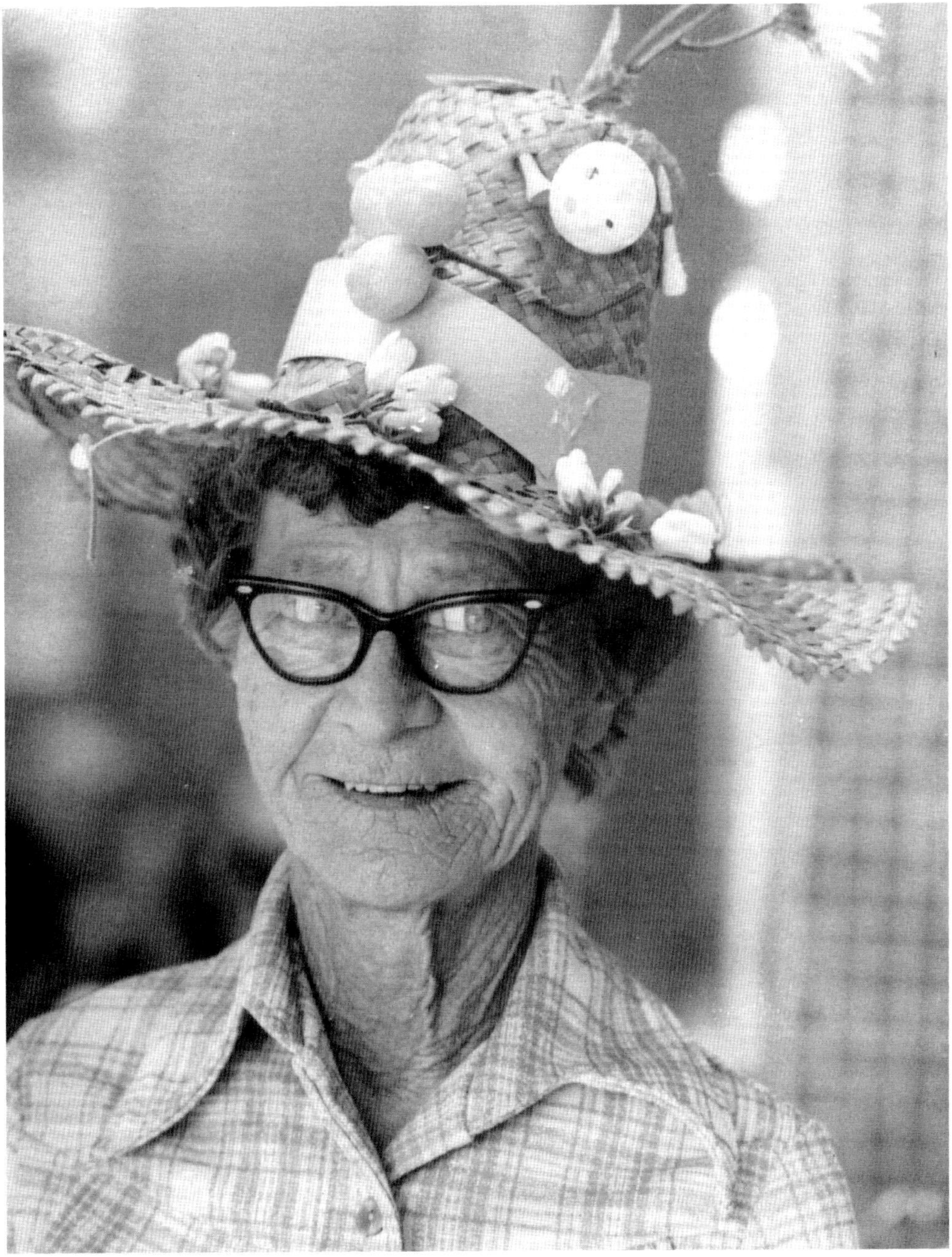

Norma Hendricks
Remembered for her heart and humor, Norma Hendricks became known as "the Hat Lady" for the themed hats she wore in photographs that ran with her popular columns in *The Daily Commercial* until her death in 1990. An award-winning city editor, radio broadcaster, and farmer, she was president of the Lake County Historical Society. Hendricks served on Leesburg's city commission and was the city's first female mayor. (Courtesy of Leesburg Heritage Society.)

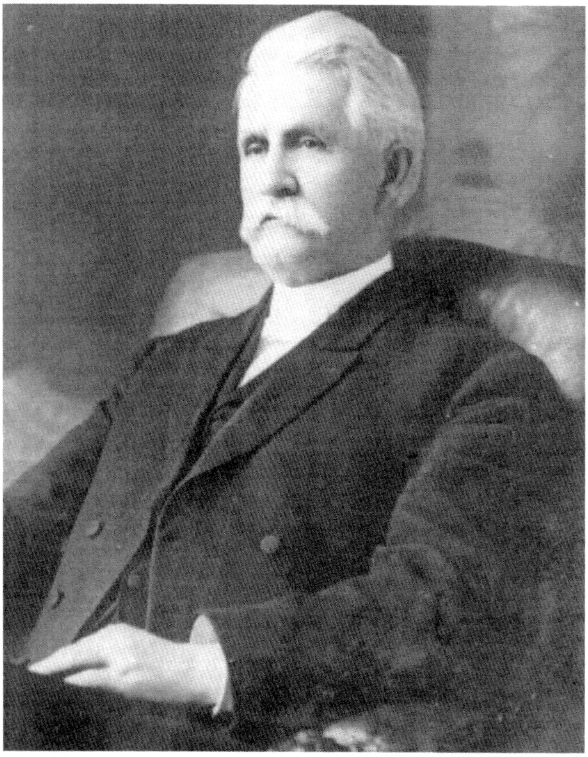

Bishop Henry Clay Morrison
A former Confederate chaplain turned eloquent evangelist, Bishop Henry Clay Morrison is the pastor for whom Morrison United Methodist Church in Leesburg is named. He served large congregations throughout the Southeast before retiring to the Mote-Morris house in Leesburg. He is credited with more than 8,000 conversions. His son, Dr. H.K. Morrison, delivered 3,000 Leesburg babies. (Courtesy of the Leesburg Heritage Society.)

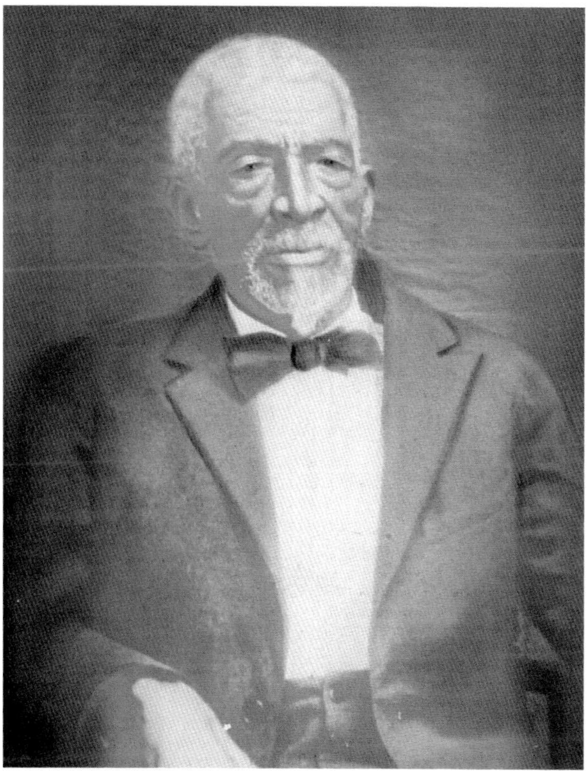

Dennis Mike
In 1860, Dennis Mike, a freed slave from South Carolina, came to Leesburg with his wife, Priscilla, and bought an orange grove. He helped found St. Paul AME Church and was a fan of the historic Negro Baseball League. Mike lived to be more than 100 years old. Mike Street, home to the Leesburg African-American Museum, was named for this beloved pioneer. (Courtesy of Leesburg Heritage Society.)

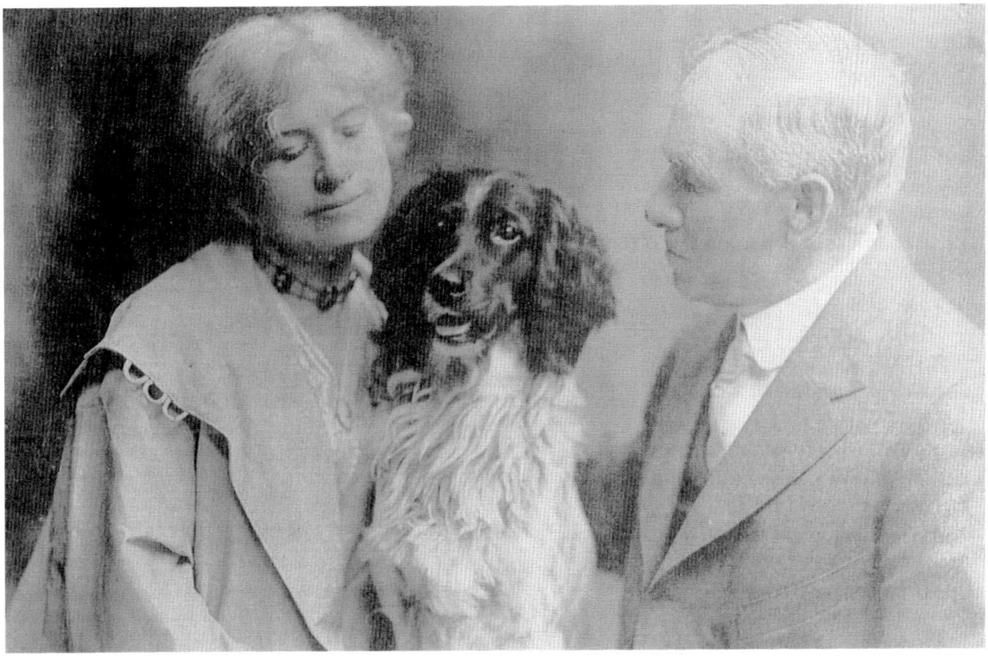

Annie Oakley

World-famous sharpshooter Annie Oakley was one of Leesburg's most famous "snowbirds." She and her husband, Frank Butler (above, at right), and their beloved dog Dave spent many winters at Leesburg's Lake View Hotel between 1911 and the early 1920s. Oakley gained fame performing with Buffalo Bill's Wild West show, amazing crowds with impossible trick shots. To help Leesburg residents raise money for the town band, she and Dave put on an exhibition. During a 1923 visit, Dave was struck and killed by a car. Oakley's request to bury him in Lone Oak Cemetery was turned down. She buried Dave at the home of hunting friend George Winter. A bronze statue of her and Dave at the Leesburg Public Library (right) shows her in her younger days, when she was known as "Little Sure Shot," a name given her by Chief Sitting Bull. (Above, courtesy of the Garst Museum; right, courtesy of Doris Bloodsworth.)

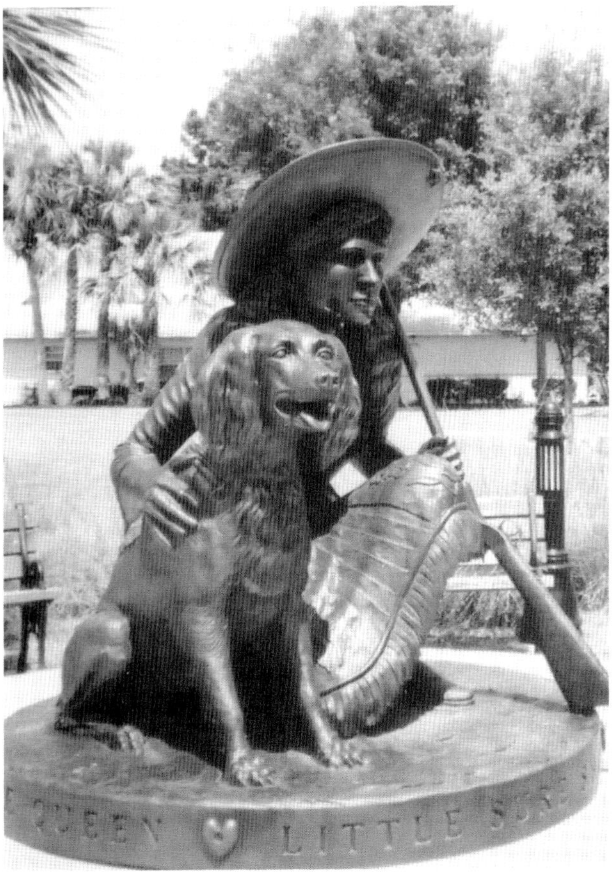

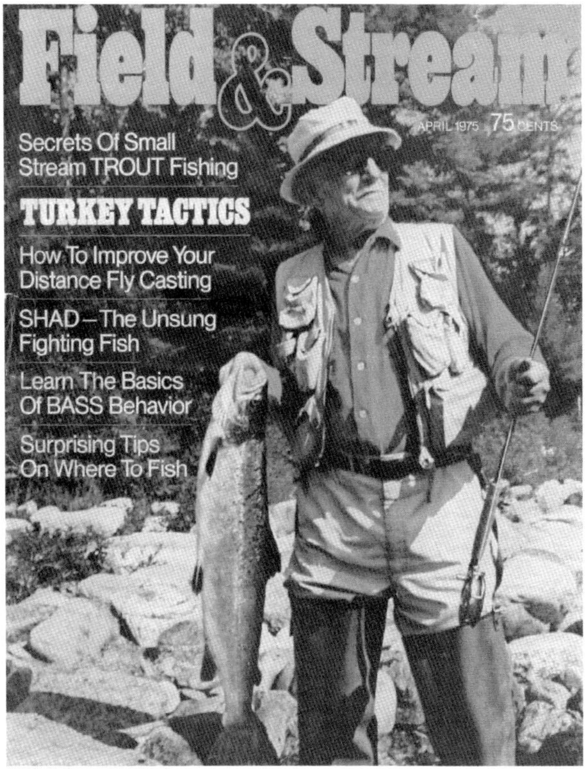

David McCheyne Newell
Leesburg resident David Newell loved the outdoors and spent his life sharing that passion. The talented storyteller was editor of *Field & Stream* magazine and reported for the *New York Times*. He wrote books and produced hunting and fishing shows for network television in the 1950s. An ardent conservationist, he was instrumental in the formation of the Florida Game and Fresh Water Fish Commission. (Courtesy of the Leesburg Heritage Society.)

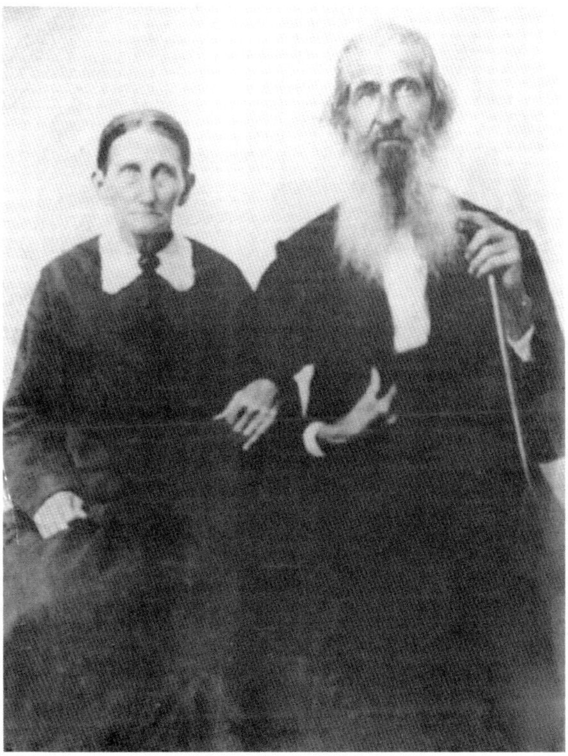

Evander and Susannah Lee
Pioneer Evander Lee (right) and his wife, Susannah, moved to present-day Leesburg in 1857 along with their eight children. He and his younger brother, Calvin Lee, opened a store and gave their new community the name Leesburg. Evander Lee was an early citrus grower who shipped his fruit north to New York and Philadelphia. (Courtesy of the Leesburg Heritage Society.)

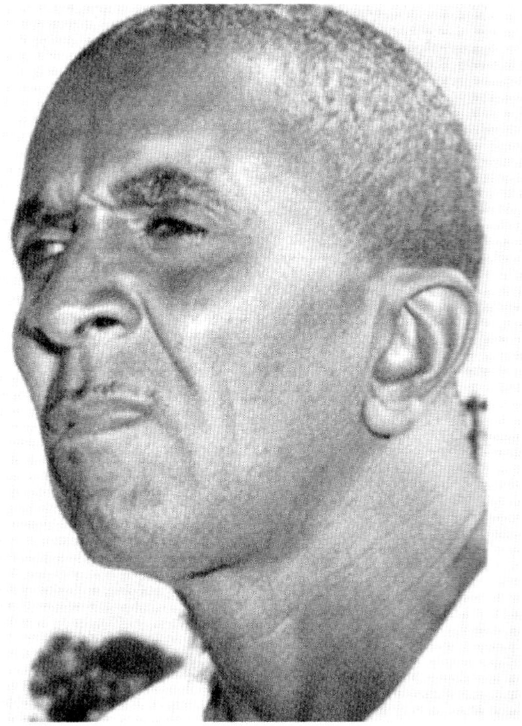

Coach Hubert Dabney
Known affectionately as "Coach," Hubert Dabney taught and coached youth for 50 years. He was inducted into the Florida Athletic Coaches Association Hall of Fame in 1982. Leesburg High School's stadium is named in his honor. His grandfather was the first African American to settle in Leesburg; his father was the city's first African American teacher. Dabney had a 207-45 career record in football. (Courtesy of the Leesburg Heritage Society.)

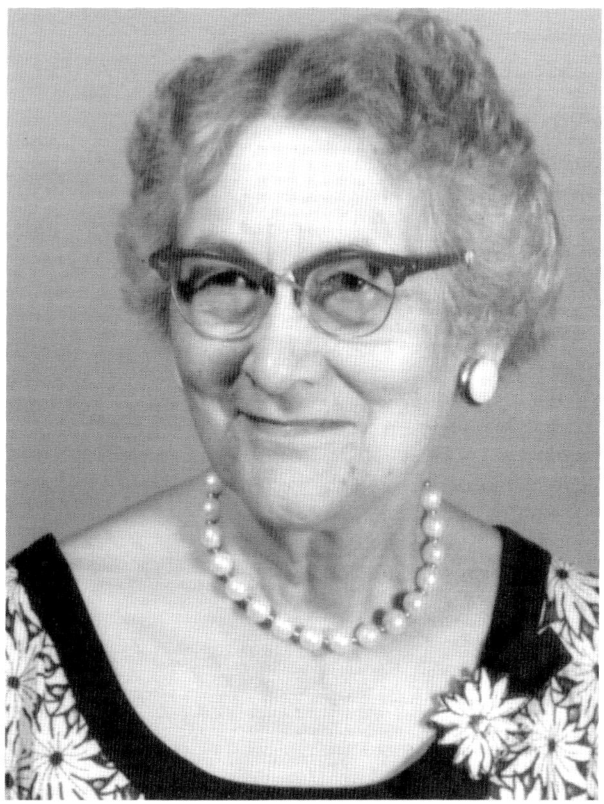

Nelle Conley Skeen
When Nelle Skeen died, a local columnist noted, "We do not believe we have ever known a person more universally loved and admired in Leesburg, or with a larger capacity to make people feel good about themselves and the world." Skeen was a teacher and principal at Leesburg Elementary School from 1914 to 1954. Skeen Elementary School was named in her honor. (Courtesy of the Leesburg Heritage Society.)

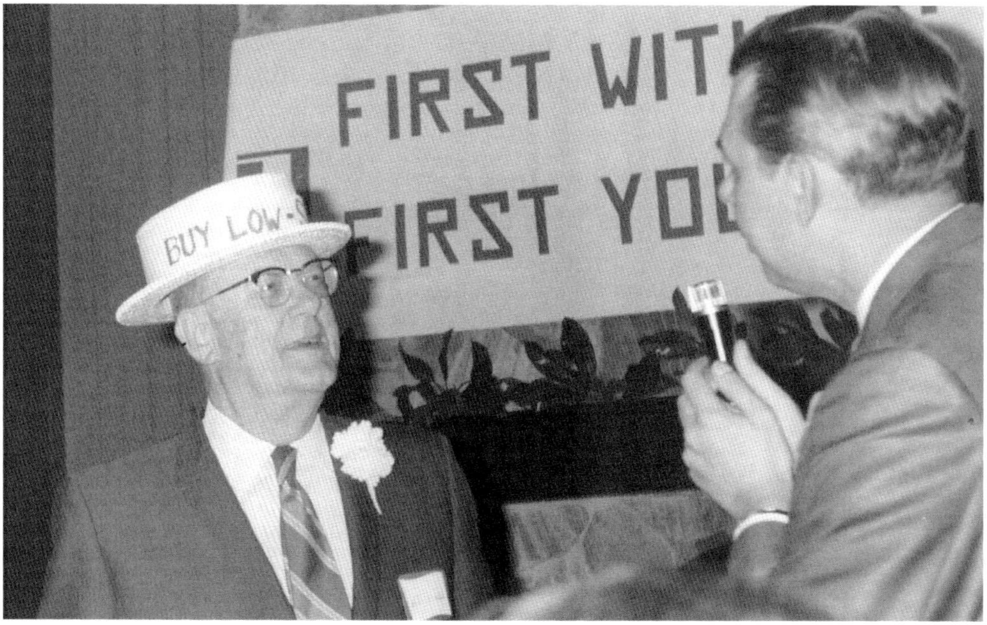

John Fahs, Banker
First National Bank of Leesburg chairman of the board John Fahs (left) was honored at his retirement party by Robert Carle. Fahs was a former state legislator, Leesburg mayor, and director of the Internal Revenue Service's Florida district. He was president of the Leesburg Rotary Club in 1936 and a Mason. The sign in the background reads, "First with us you are. First you always will be." (Courtesy of the Leesburg Heritage Society.)

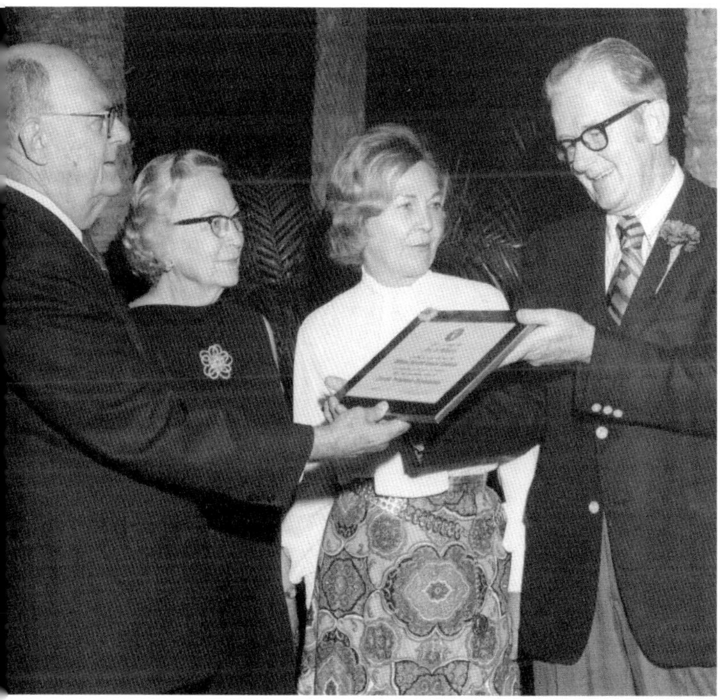

Max Wettstein, Telephone Pioneer
Max Wettstein served as president of Florida Telephone Corporation for 22 years. He was the son of the corporation's founder, Otto Wettstein. Under Max Wettstein's leadership, the phone company introduced direct-distance dialing and doubled in size. He was founding director of Citizens National Bank. Shown here are, from left to right, John Fahs, Mary Fahs, Joy Wettstein, and Max Wettstein. (Courtesy of the Leesburg Heritage Society.)

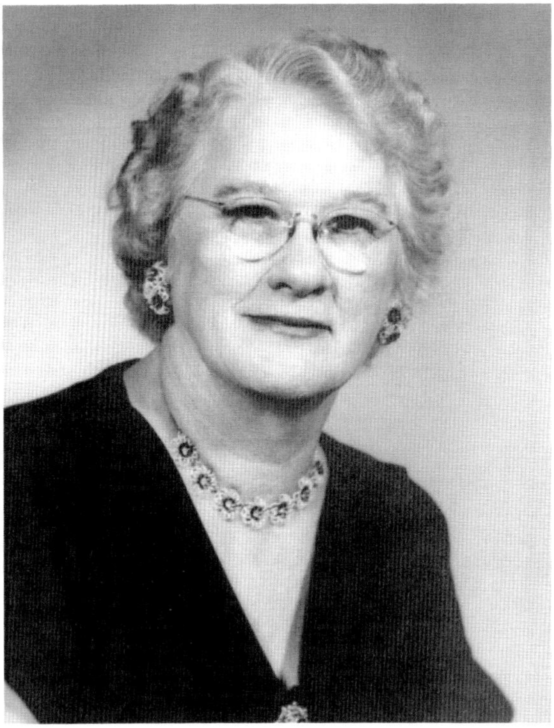

Elisabeth Watts Hunter Abney Geiger, Historian

In the 1970s, longtime Leesburg resident Elisabeth Geiger started a movement to form a historical society. Her vast collection of local history books, rare pamphlets, photographs, and memorabilia remains a significant part of the Leesburg Heritage Museum's and Lake County Historical Society's reference libraries. Geiger recruited more than 100 signatures of interested residents to help establish the Leesburg Heritage Society. (Courtesy of the Leesburg Heritage Society.)

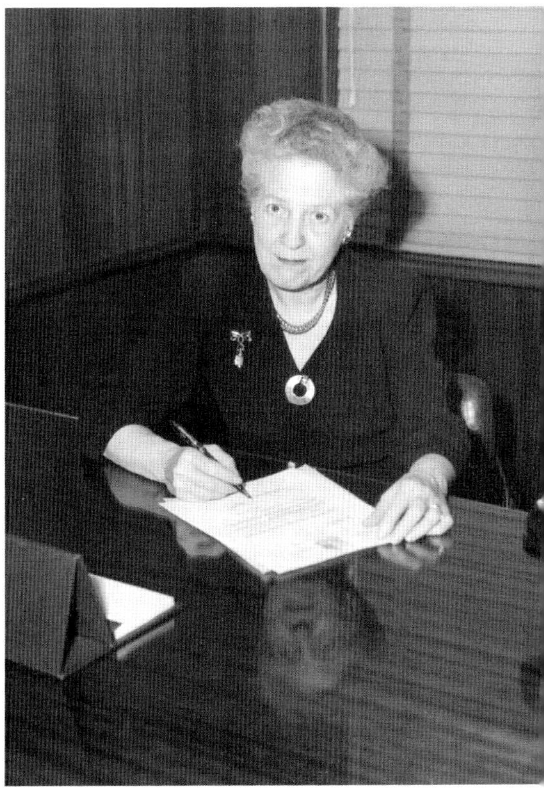

Belle Inez Sechler Hamilton, the Tell-Tale-Teller

Bank secretary Belle Hamilton started the "Tell-Tale-Teller" as an advertisement for First National Bank of Leesburg. The advertisement grew into a regular Leesburg newspaper column. Hamilton combined everyday events with historical news, and wrote radio scripts about the bank. She created a humor column about the banking industry. Over 19 years from the 1940s to the early 1960s, she wrote 945 "Tell-Tale-Teller" columns. (Courtesy of the Leesburg Heritage Society.)

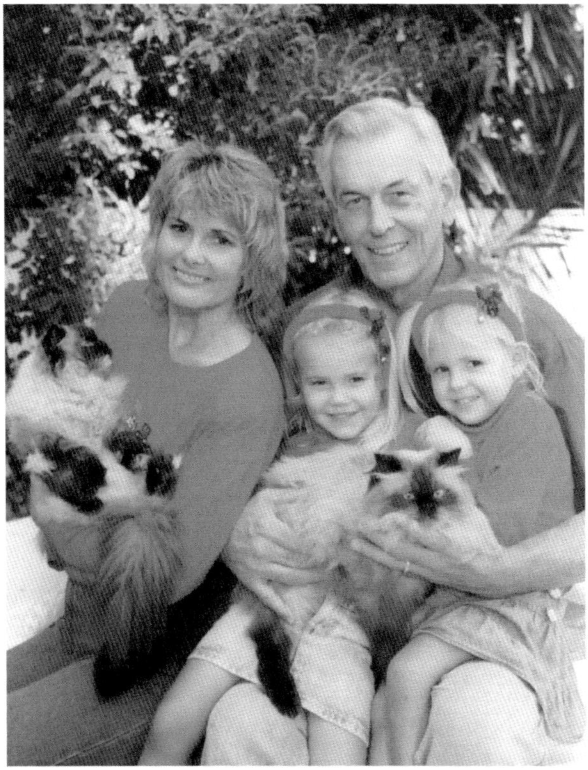

Vince Fechtel

Leesburg native and Leesburg High School football star Vince Fechtel served in Florida's house and senate before spending a decade as a federal parole commissioner. His daughters grew up to be beauty-pageant winners. Elizabeth is Miss America's Outstanding Teen 2012. Mary Katherine was Miss Florida Outstanding Teen 2011. Shown here are Dixie Fechtel (left) and Vince Fechtel, holding Elizabeth (left) and Mary Katherine. (Courtesy of the Leesburg Heritage Society.)

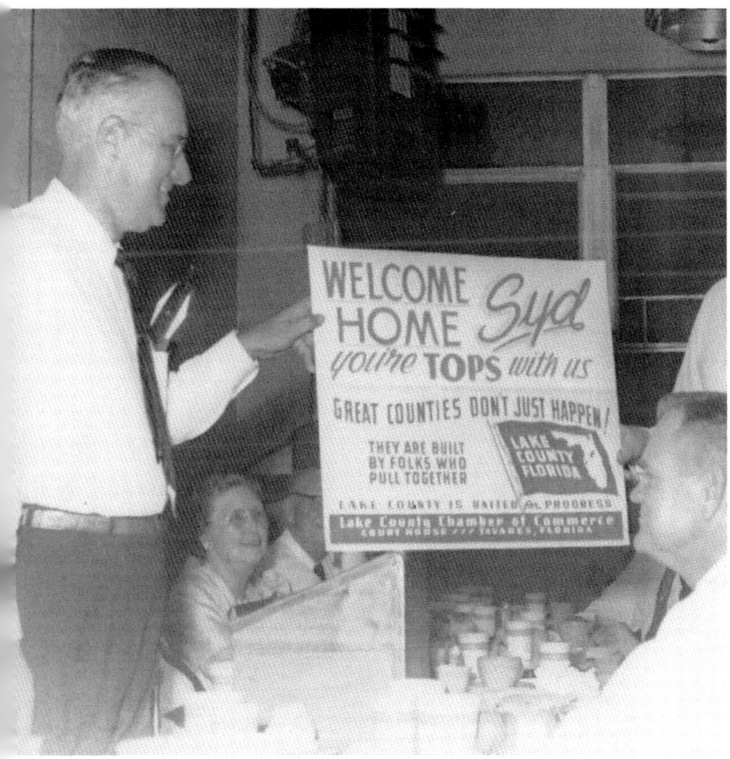

Albert S. "Syd" Herlong

Representing Florida's sprawling fifth district, Syd Herlong was one of the most powerful men in Washington, DC. After graduating from law school, he served as Leesburg's postmaster, then became one of Lake County's youngest judges. As a US legislator, he promoted construction of the Kennedy Space Center. He served on the Securities and Exchange Commission before retiring to Lake County until his death in 1995. (Courtesy of the Leesburg Heritage Society.)

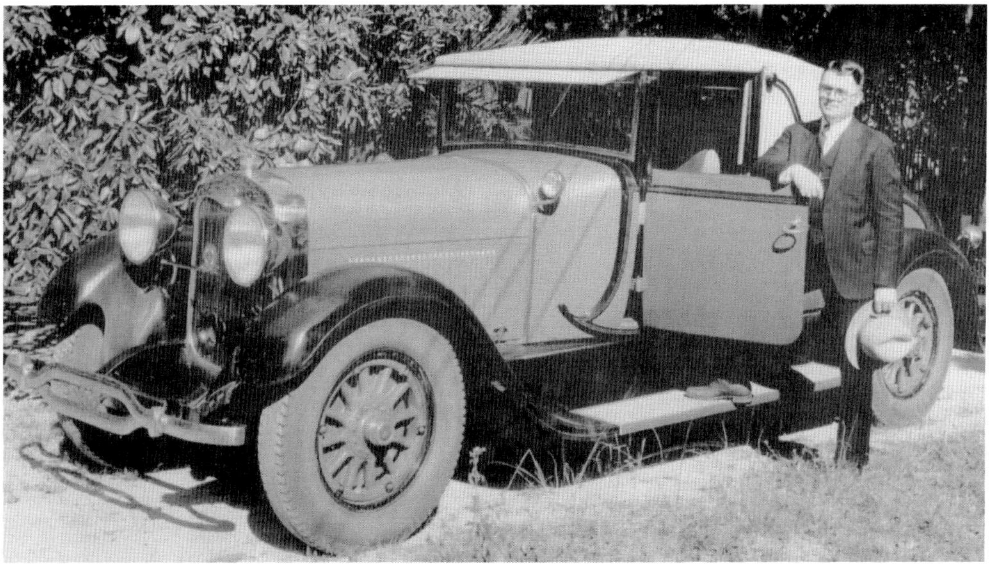

Dr. Howard Holland

Standing beside his 1928 Lincoln is the colorful, beloved Dr. Howard Holland. After earning his medical degree at Emory University, he came to Lake County and converted a house into Leesburg's first hospital. He was Leesburg High School's athletic teams' physician and gave a dinner for the players each season. He was said to be "the best friend Leesburg ever had." (Courtesy of the Leesburg Heritage Society.)

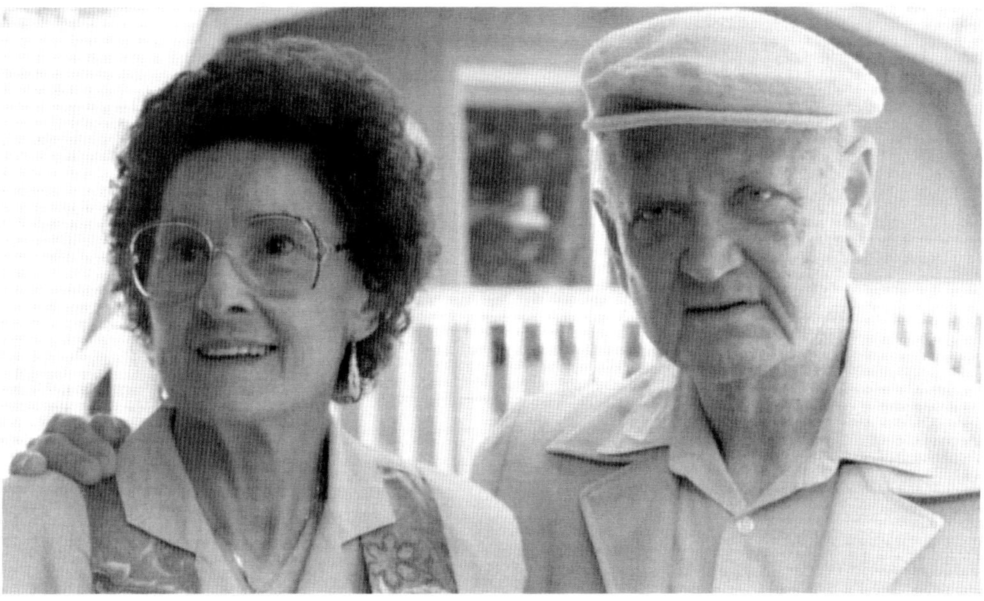

Emmett Peter Jr., Journalist and Historian

In 1940, Emmett Peter Jr. (right) became the nation's youngest newspaper editor at age 21. He later worked for the *Tampa Tribune, Orlando Sentinel, New Republic,* and *Daily Commercial.* Peter, son of a citrus pioneer, also served on the national commission to help desegregate land-grant universities and wrote histories of Orlando and Lake County. His wife, Marjorie, was an active member of Leesburg's art community. (Courtesy of Melanie Peter.)

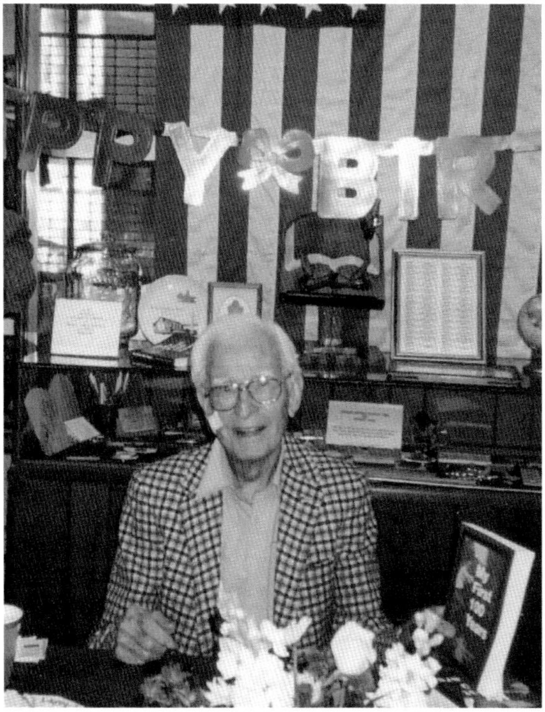

George Rast, Mr. Leesburg
George Rast made the most of his 102 years. He became known as "Mr. Leesburg" because of his many contributions, which included raising millions of dollars during World War II through war-bond drives, and heading the city's Watermelon Festivals and centennial celebration. The banker and historian helped get a football stadium for Leesburg High School, and he helped found the Leesburg Heritage Museum. (Courtesy of the Leesburg Heritage Society.)

Edwin and Lillian "Ping" Merrill
The 1928 wedding of Edwin and Lillian "Ping" Merrill was a beautiful start to their 65-year marriage. Edwin was a civil engineer with J.D. Manly Construction and served as Leesburg's mayor and as a city commissioner. He also helped found Leesburg's Boys Club. The Merrills were uncle and aunt to popular Leesburg mayor Sanna Henderson. (Courtesy of the Leesburg Heritage Society.)

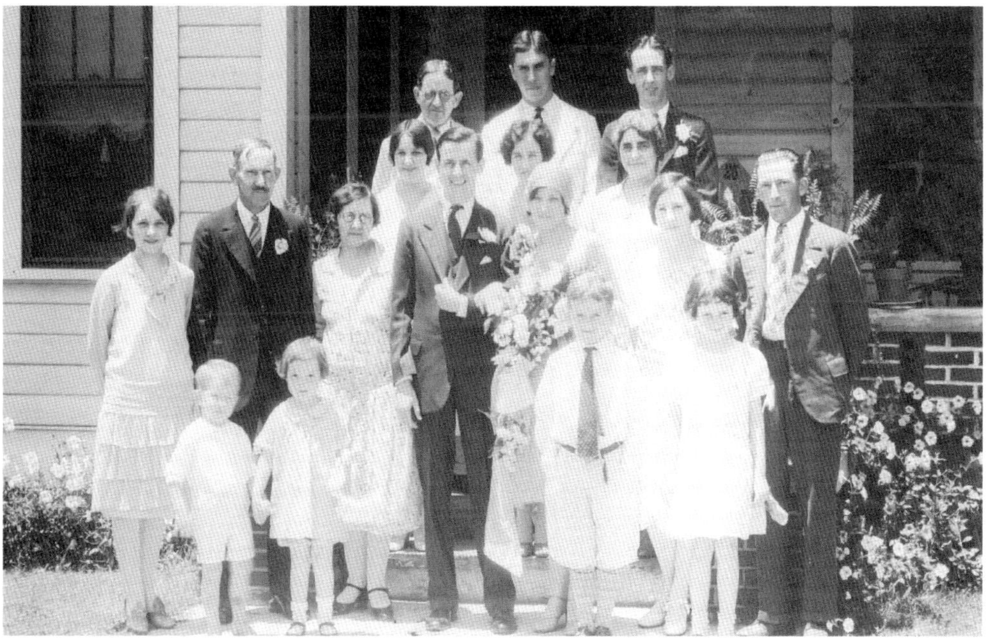

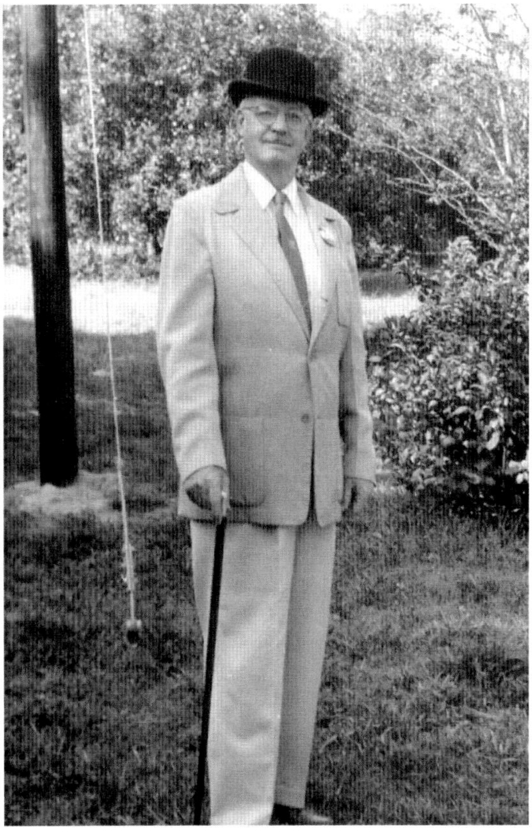

Henry Pringle, Developer

Henry Pringle arrived in Leesburg at the height of the Great Depression. He practiced law and helped found Florida's farm bureau. He was active in Kiwanis, serving as the organization's statewide lieutenant governor. He is remembered for donating land for the Leesburg airport, his charity work, his love of dancing, and for developing prime Lake County properties, including Silver Lake and other golf communities. (Courtesy of the Leesburg Heritage Society.)

Lloyd "Clyde" White, Civic Volunteer

At the Florida Department of Transportation, Clyde White received two awards for dedicated service. That dedication extended to Leesburg, where he led a citywide beautification project and erected signs recognizing civic organizations. He has been honored by the chamber of commerce and is active in his church and Kiwanis. White (right) is seen here with Pat Thomas (left) and an unidentified person. (Courtesy of Eloise White.)

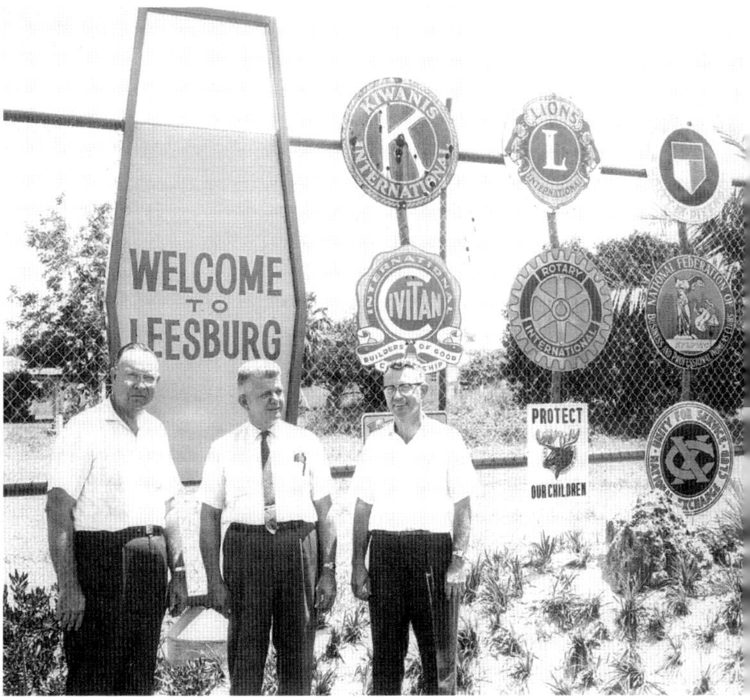

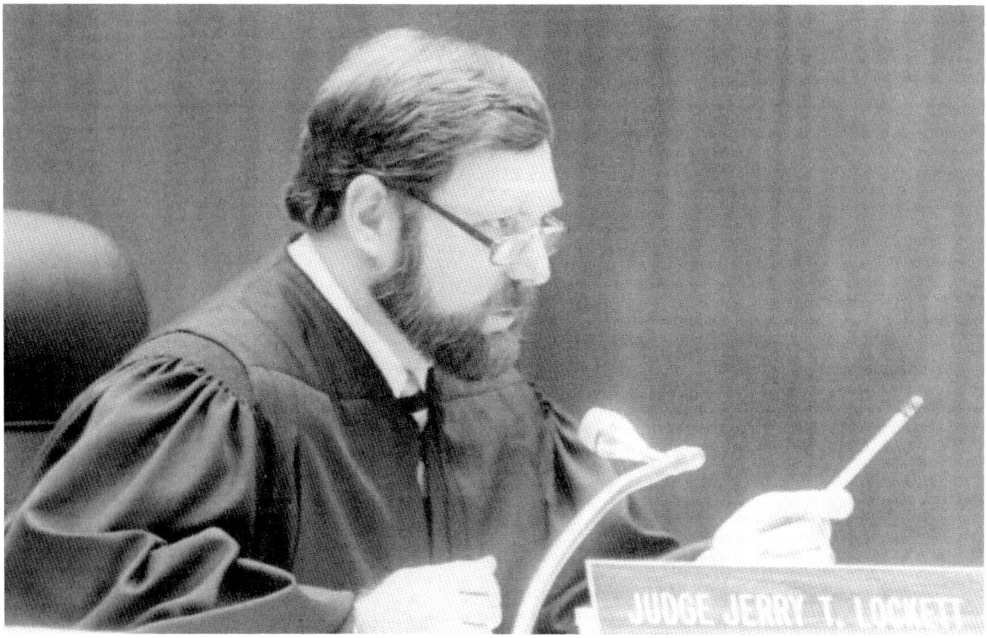

Judge Jerry Lockett
A no-nonsense courtroom demeanor earned Judge Jerry Lockett the nickname "Lock 'em up Lockett." During his 42 years with the Florida bar, he presided over numerous high-profile cases, including the infamous "Vampire Murders" trial. He is the only Florida circuit judge to be appointed by two governors. The former public defender and Navy officer is active in many organizations. (Courtesy of Ruth Lockett.)

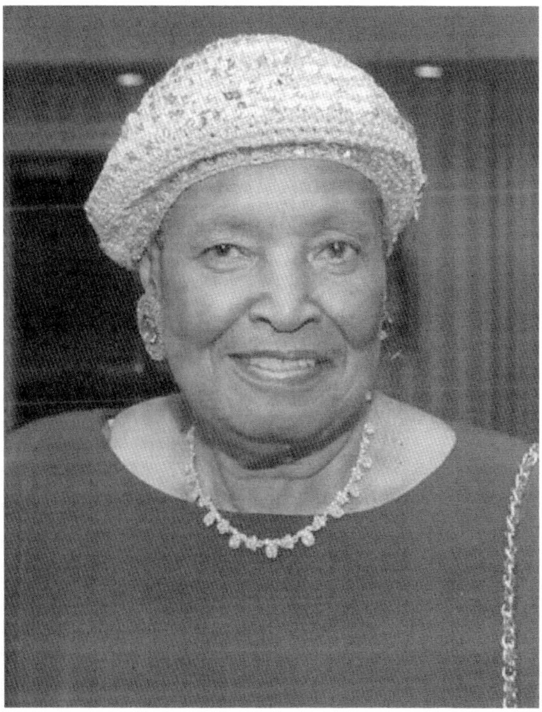

Margaret Cason Ward, Inspirational Teacher
Lifelong educator Margaret Cason Ward coached the Carver Heights High School girls' basketball team to two state championships. She was named to the 1995 Lake County Women's Hall of Fame and the governor's 2004 Wall of Fame as an Outstanding African American Educator. She founded the Ward Scholarship Fund and was a Bethune-Cookman University trustee. The Margaret Cason Ward Youth Opportunity Center was named to honor her lifetime dedication to helping young people. (Courtesy of the CDC of Leesburg and Vicinity.)

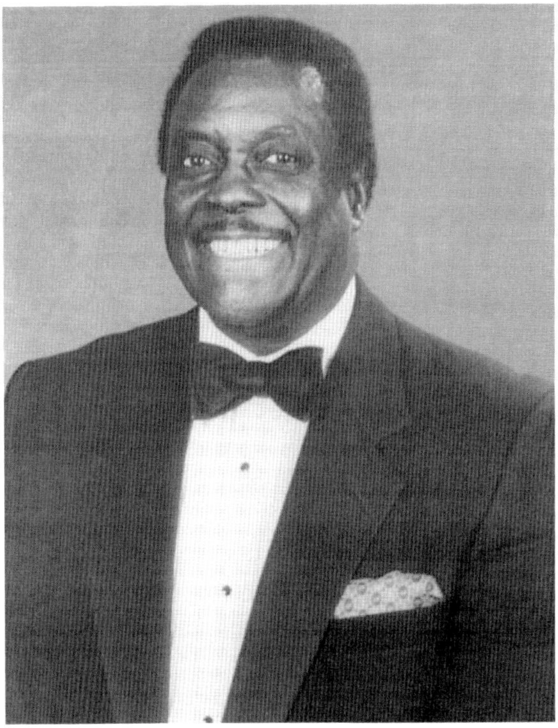

Johnny Thunder
Born Gil Hamilton, Leesburg native and singing sensation Johnny Thunder had a hit song and toured with top artists such as the Drifters, Dionne Warwick, and Jimi Hendrix. He performed at the Apollo Theater and on the popular television program *American Bandstand.* Bob Dylan said, "Johnny Thunder is the best live performer I've ever seen." Thunder continues to perform on cruise ships and in Las Vegas. (Courtesy of Johnny Thunder.)

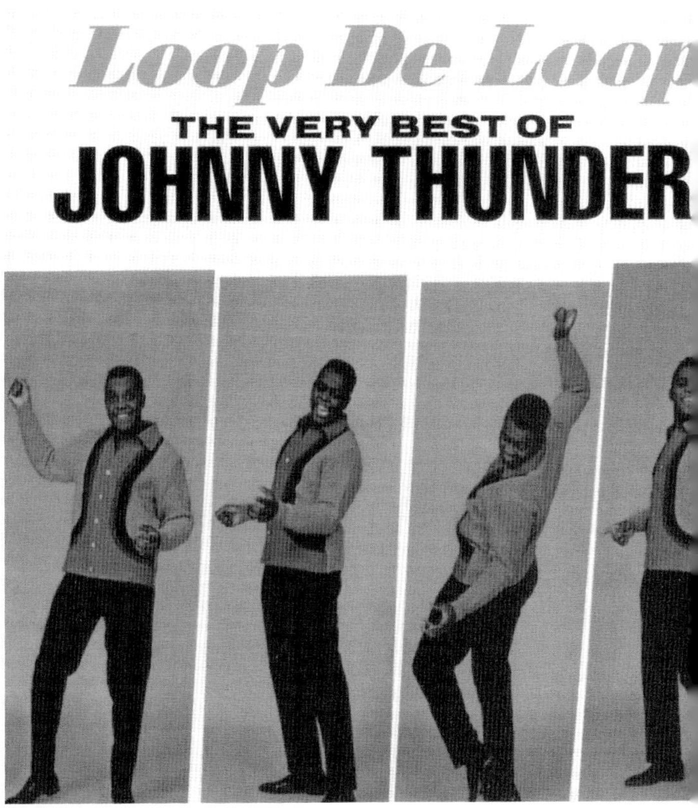

"Loop De Loop"
In 1963, Leesburg's Gil Hamilton linked up with record producer Teddy Vann to record an upbeat version of a children's nursery song, "Loop De Loop." He recorded the tune for the Diamond label under the name Johnny Thunder and performed the song on *American Bandstand.* The song rose to No. 4 on Billboard's top 100 chart and remains popular with his audiences. (Courtesy of Johnny Thunder.)

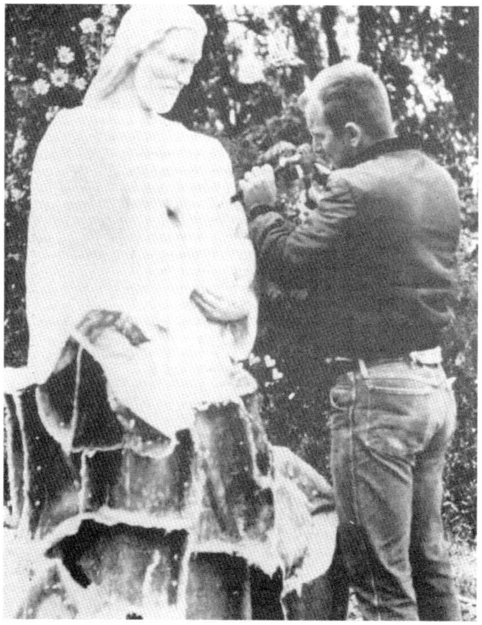

The Bosanquet Family
Gershon Bosanquet, shown working on a statue at Holy Trinity Episcopal Church in Fruitland Park, was a talented descendant of one of the city's pioneer families and church founders, Louis Bosanquet. Several members of the Bosanquet family were among the English colonists who arrived during the 1880s. Gershon's grandfather Louis Bosanquet and father, Alfred Bosanquet, were avid horticulturists who brought an extraordinary collection of plants to the area. (Courtesy of Holy Trinity Church.)

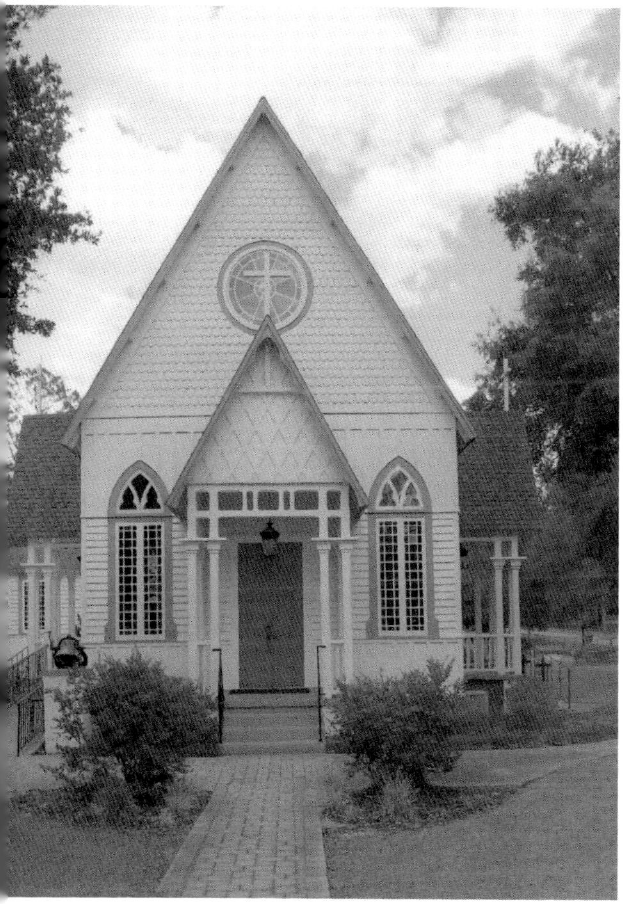

Holy Trinity Episcopal Church
The majestic, historic Holy Trinity Episcopal Church in Fruitland Park was built in 1888 for English colonists, including Louis Bosanquet. He was a senior warden for many years and would host "tea at the Bosanquets" following church services. It was a tradition that continued even after his death in 1960. The church includes an 1889 lych gate, thought to be the oldest in America. (Courtesy of the State Archives of Florida.)

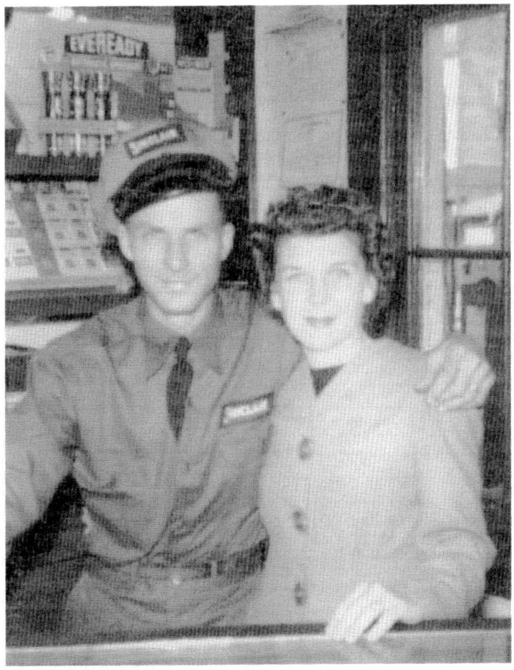

Ernest "Huxie" Hux, Firefighter

One of Fruitland Park's first volunteer firefighters, Ernest "Huxie" Hux (left) operated a Sinclair gas station before owning E.W. Hux Trucking Company. He and his wife, Edwina (right), had a daughter, Judy Hux Rainey, who was part of the "Camphor Tree Gang," a group of friends whose "clubhouse" was a giant camphor tree. Rainey is an active Lake County historian. (Courtesy of Judy Hux Rainey.)

Beverly Grizzard, Ad Man

Successful Fruitland Park business executive Beverly Grizzard (right) became director of the State Advertising Commission during the administration of Gov. Fuller Warren (left). Grizzard promoted Florida as a business and tourist destination. He also served as director of Lake County's chamber of commerce and was a Fruitland Park city council member. His family lived in the historic Palm Villa estate. (Courtesy of the State Archives of Florida.)

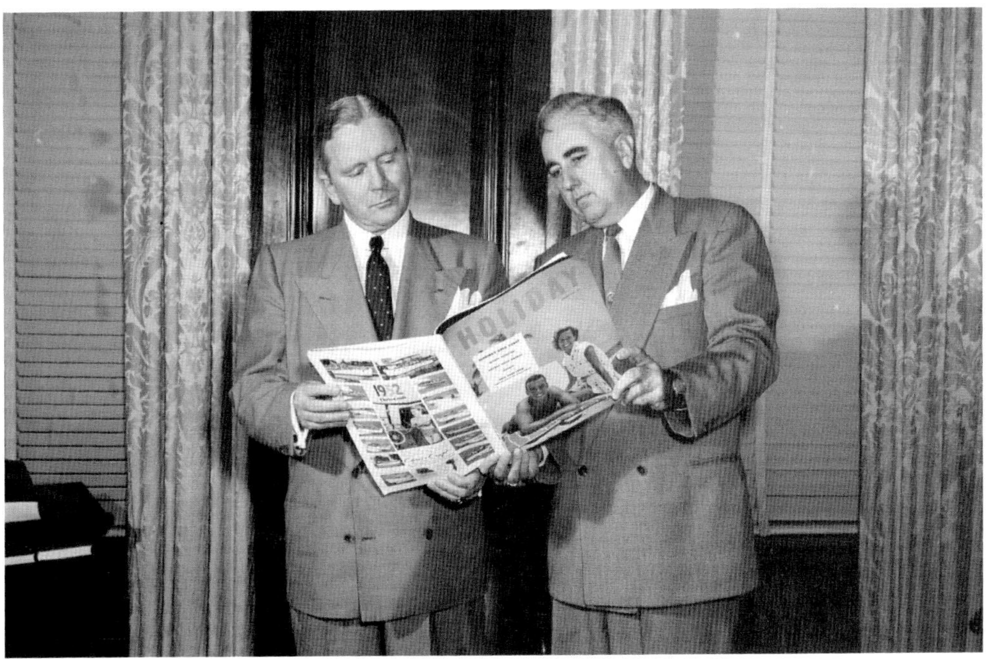

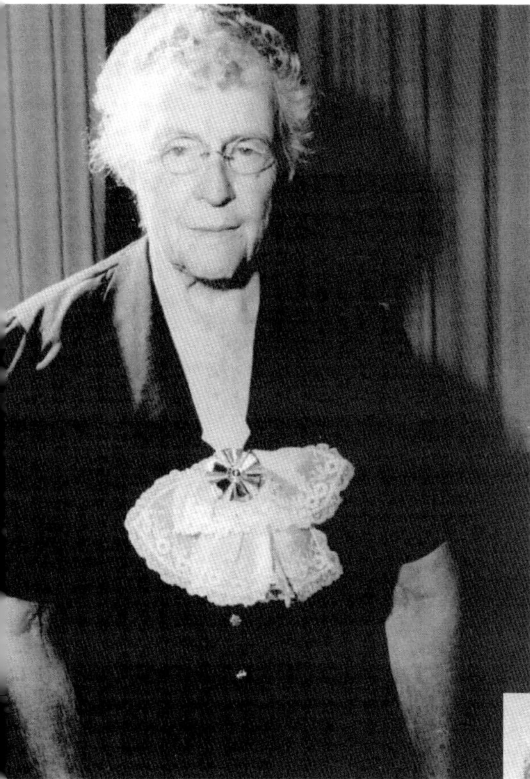

Minnie and William Dwight

Minnie Dwight (left) and her husband William Dwight (below) split their time between Holyoke, Massachusetts, and Fruitland Park, where, in 1915, they built a home they called Pine Eden. The Dwights gave memorable garden parties, often to benefit Holy Trinity Episcopal Church. They purchased a community center called The Casino, which they donated to the city and which is still in use. The Dwights ran their hometown newspaper, the *Holyoke Transcript and Telegram,* as a team. William Dwight became known as "the mayor-maker" because of the power of his endorsements. After her husband's unexpected death in Fruitland Park, Minnie Dwight became the newspaper's sole owner. She took strong stands on social issues affecting women and children. Her "Letters from Florida" column was eagerly anticipated. (Courtesy of Holyoke Public Library History Room and Archives.)

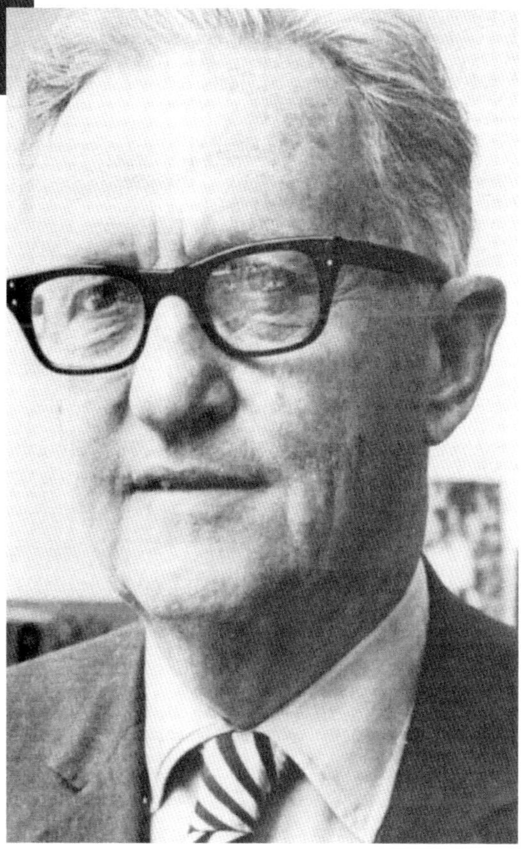

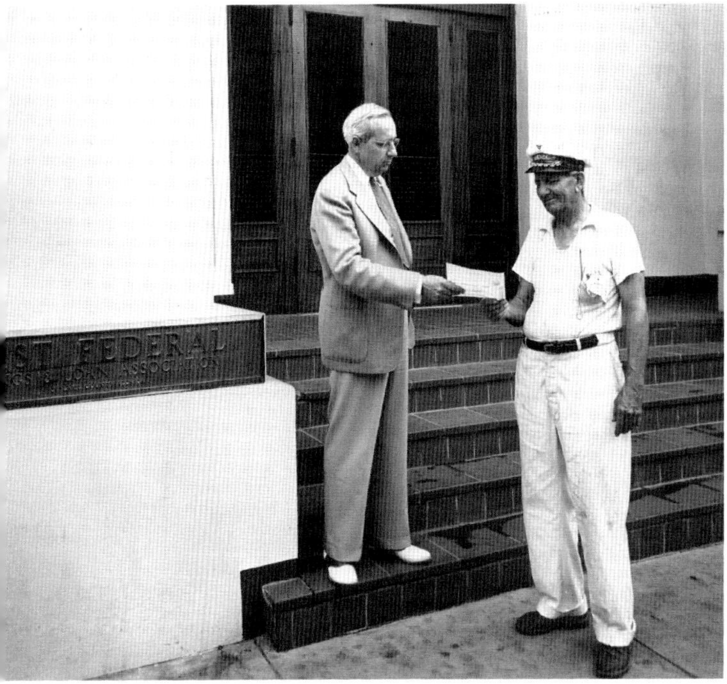

"Honest John" Yeftich

In 1882, Ivan "Honest John" Yeftich (right) was born into Yugoslavian royalty. He married Iowan Emma Young, and they lived the rest of their lives in Fruitland Park. He purchased the first war bond in Florida from banker Justin Langille (left). Yeftich always dressed in white and was known for his eccentricities. The unusual yellow "castle" he and his wife built still stands. (Courtesy of the State Archives of Florida.)

Mildred Clark

In this photograph, 14-year-old Mildred Kendrick Clark stands in front of Fruitland Park's first post office. In 1944, Clark, 53, was appointed postmaster and served until her retirement in 1964. Under her leadership, a new post office was erected and the volume of mail grew fivefold. She was named Outstanding Citizen in 1960 by the Fruitland Park Lion's Club and was a member of the historic Holy Trinity Episcopal Church. (Courtesy of the City of Fruitland Park.)

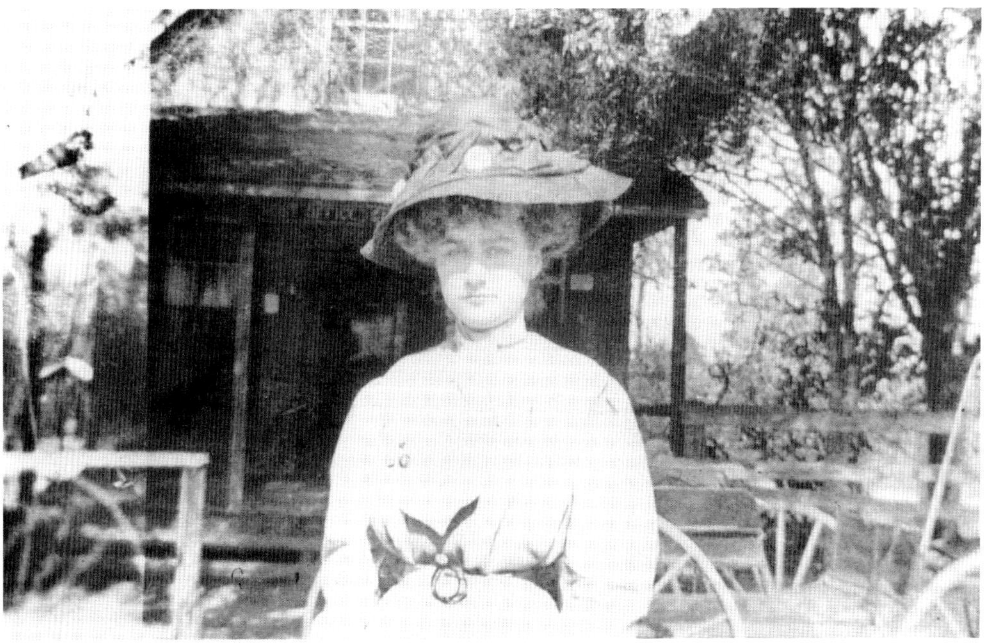

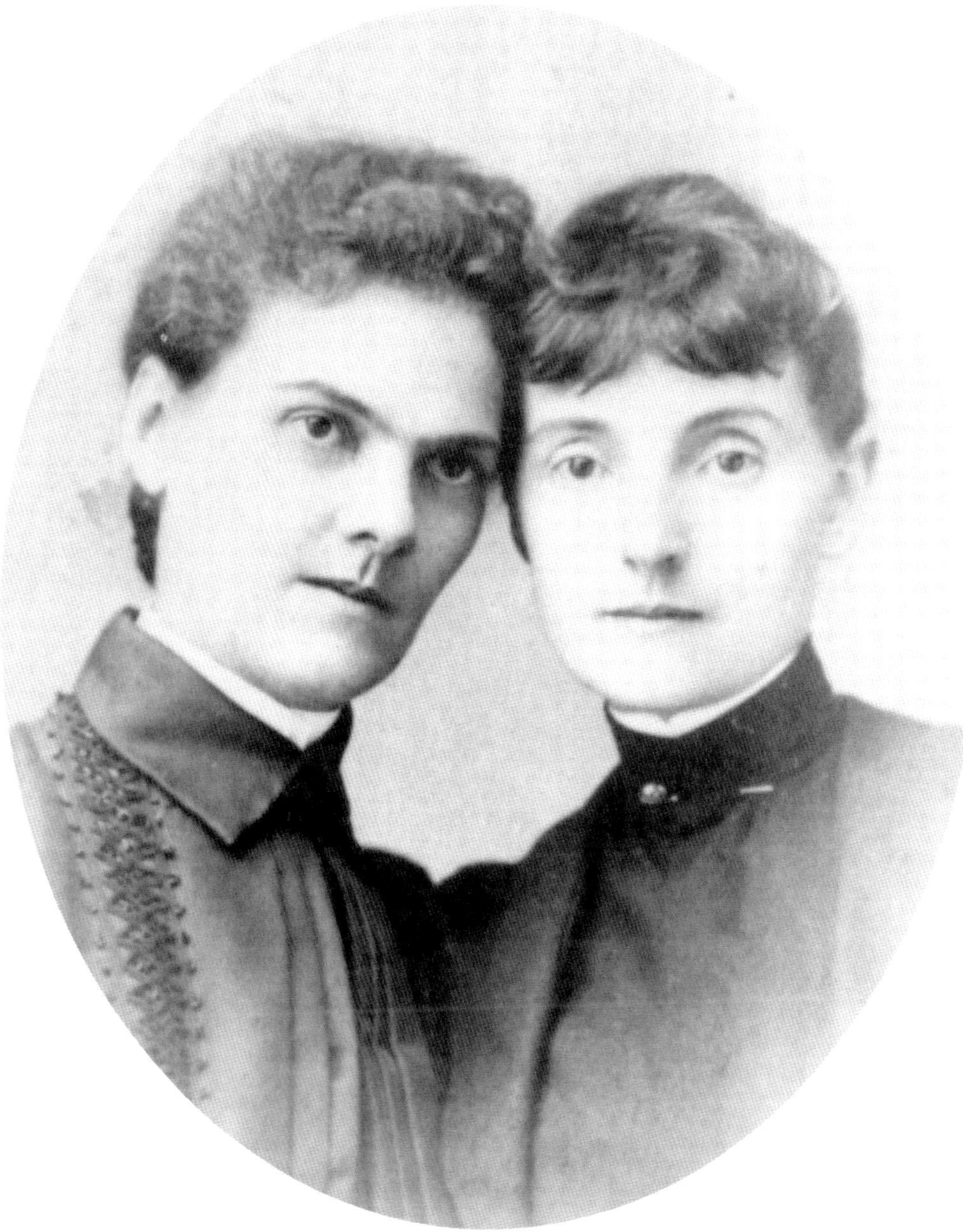

Dr. Olive Worcester Swan and Orpha Worcester
Known as "Miss Estelle," Olive Estelle Worcester (left) was born in Iowa in 1858. She received her medical degree from Northwestern University Women's Medical School in 1881. She and her younger sister, Orpha Worcester, moved with their family to Conant, known today as Lady Lake. The pioneer doctor married Chester Swan and got her Florida license to practice general medicine. For 40 years, the revered Dr. Olive Swan rode across the countryside in her buggy drawn by her horse, Cadmus, treating patients, no matter how far away or how inclement the weather. She was often accompanied by Orpha, who had studied at Oberlin College and the Arts Institute of Chicago. Orpha painted native birds for the Audubon Society and captured Florida's flora in watercolors. (Courtesy of the Lady Lake Historical Society.)

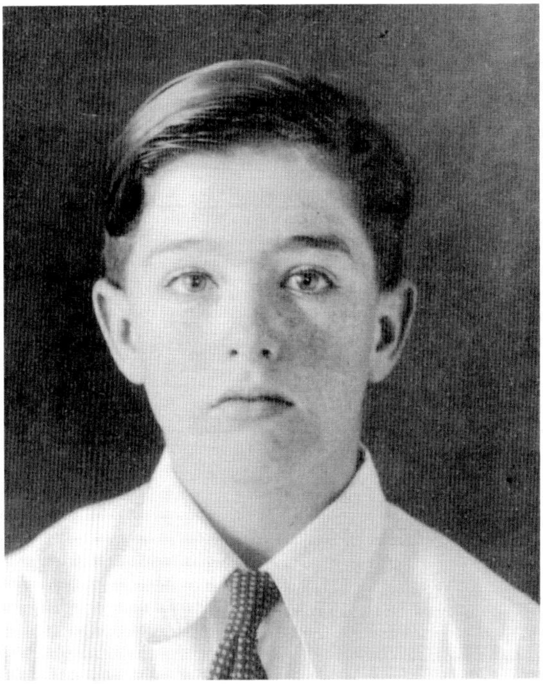

Atticus "Snooky" Blanton

As a youngster in Lady Lake, Atticus "Snooky" Blanton was known as a prankster. He joined the Navy in 1940 and, later, wrote home excited to be assigned to the USS *Arizona* battleship. On December 7, 1941, Blanton was one of 1,177 Americans who perished in the bombing of Pearl Harbor. The sunken battleship is a permanent memorial to their sacrifice. (Courtesy of the Lady Lake Historical Society.)

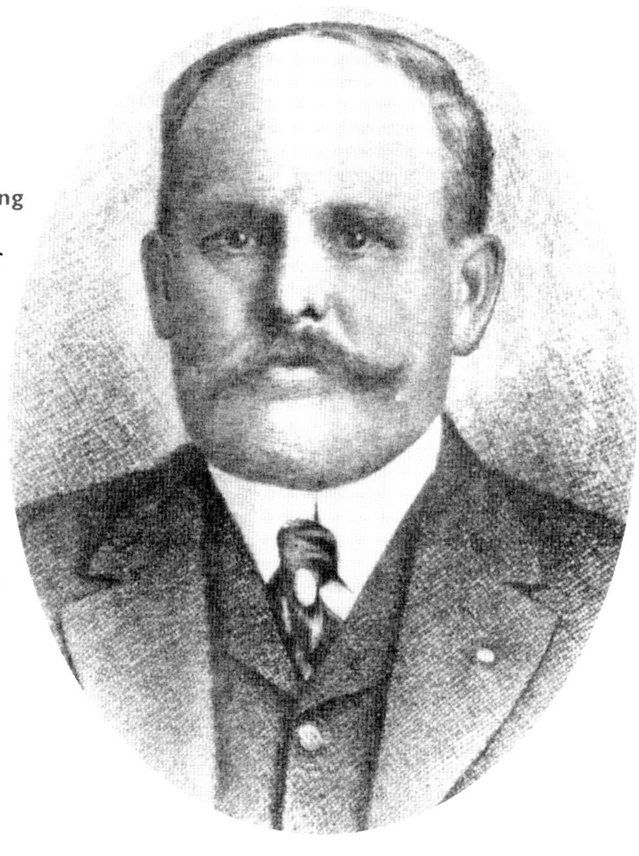

Daniel Seyler, Watermelon King of Lake County

German immigrant Daniel Seyler came to Lady Lake to grow citrus, but became so successful in another crop that he became known as the Watermelon King of Lake County. After the Great Freeze of 1894–1895 destroyed his crops, Seyler started over. He prospered and acquired considerable property. He was active in community affairs, including serving on the school board. (Courtesy of the Lady Lake Historical Society.)

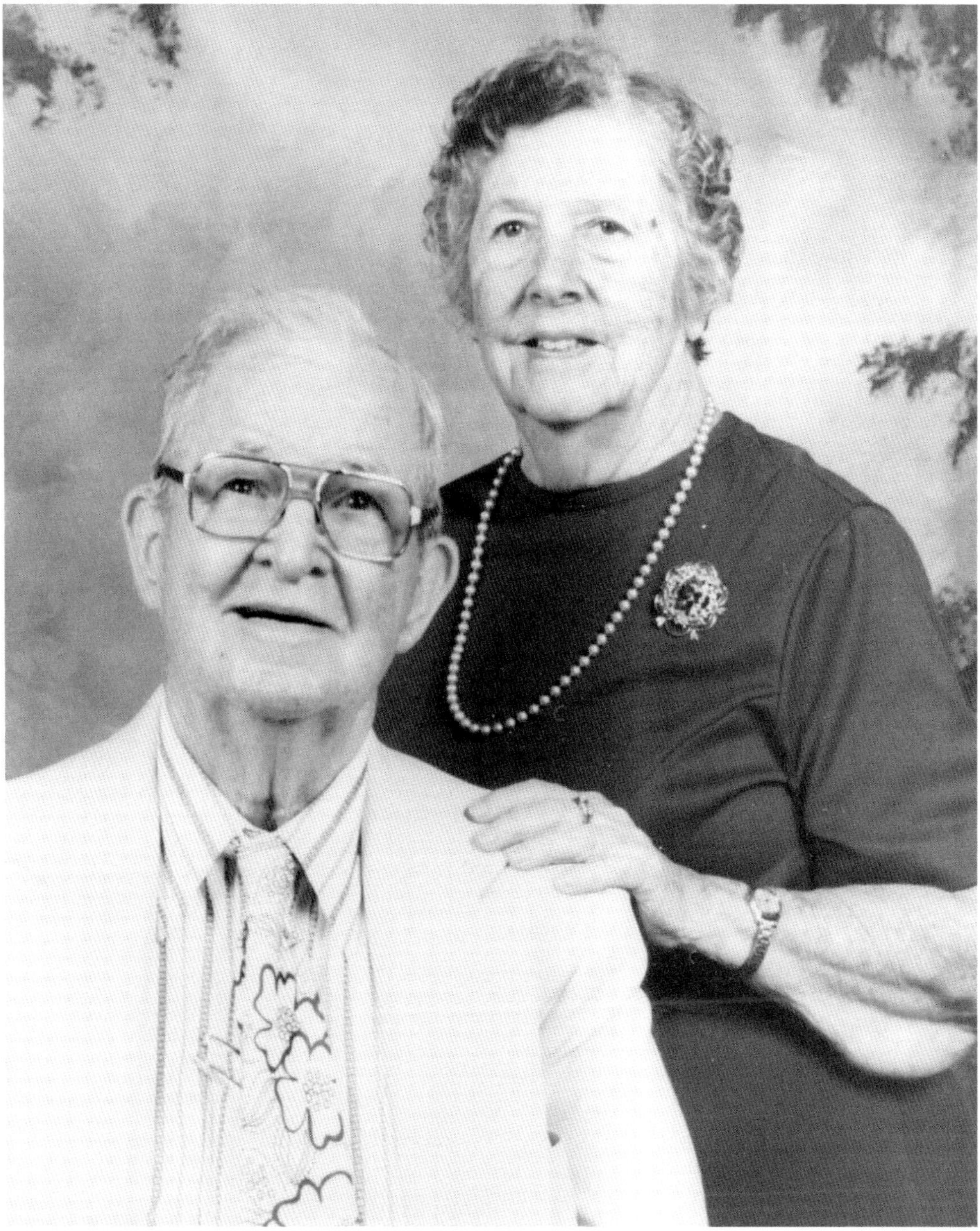

John and Carrie Griffin, Two Happy Railroaders
John Griffin (left) began his 46-year railroad career in 1926, working for the Atlantic Coast Line. His wife, Carrie Griffin, worked for the same railway line for 20 years. As station agent, he was an important figure in the Lady Lake community. The arrival of the train was cause for great excitement. More than a dozen children became regulars around the train depot. The patient station agent taught them Morse code and other basics, including passenger tickets, freight, and schedules. Many of the children followed in the Griffins' footsteps, becoming executives throughout the railroad industry. When the train depot later became the library, Carrie Griffin was the first patron through the door. The Griffins' tombstone in the Lady Lake Cemetery reads, "Two Happy Railroaders." (Courtesy of the Lady Lake Historical Society.)

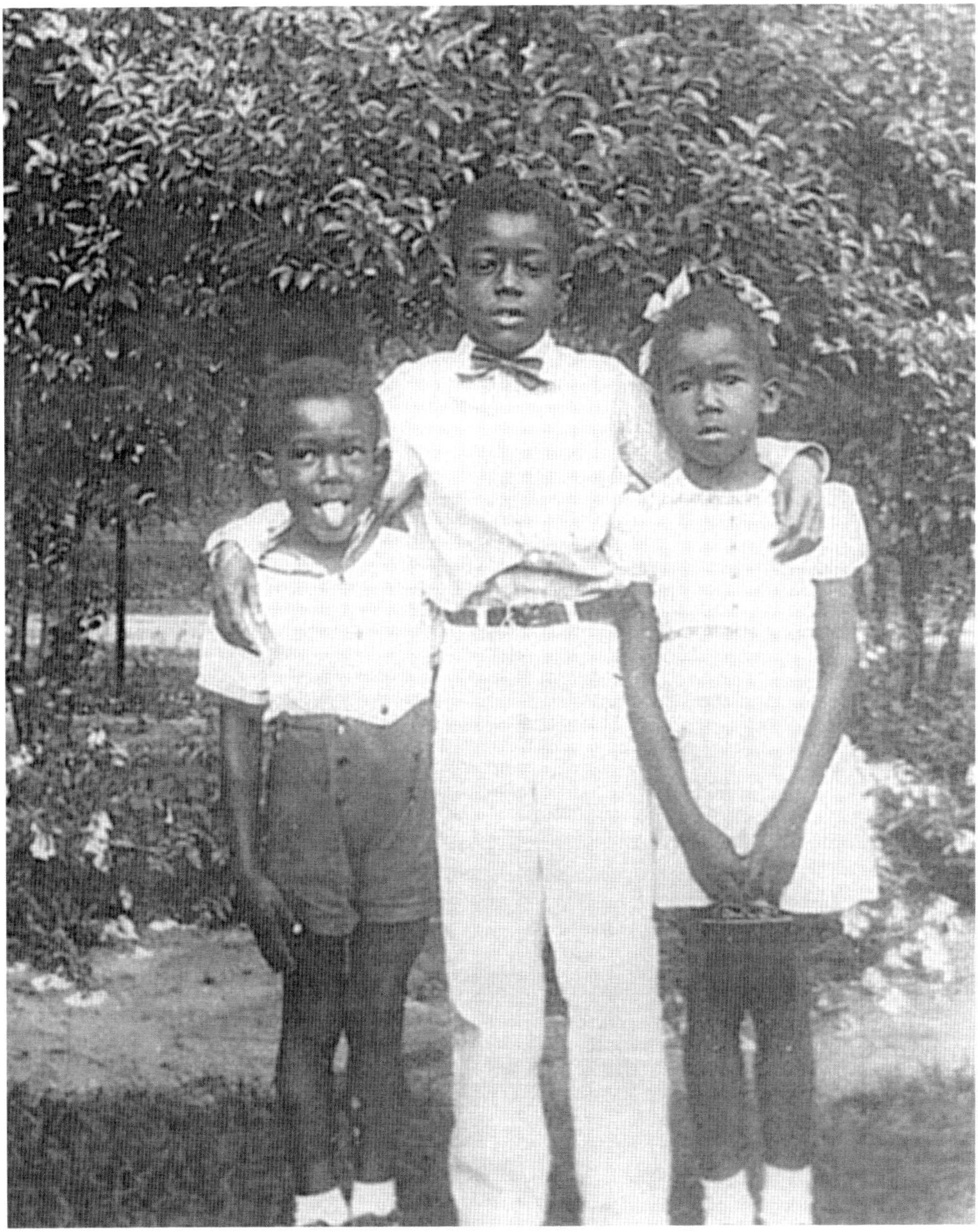

Brunzy Hardrick, Hometown Success Story

Clyde Hardrick left a Georgia plantation with high hopes, arriving in Lady Lake seeking work in the booming citrus industry of the late 1920s. He became a grove caretaker, and his employer, the Bonin family, took a special interest in his son Brunzy. The family offered to pay for Brunzy Hardrick's transportation and first month's living expenses at a college in nearby Daytona Beach. Inspired, the young Hardrick spent his summers working hard as a watermelon packer to earn the additional money. He graduated with honors in accounting and economics from Florida A&M University. He went on to enjoy a long, distinguished career with the Internal Revenue Service. In this photograph, Brunzy Hardrick is seen at left with two unidentified children. (Courtesy of the Lady Lake Historical Society.)

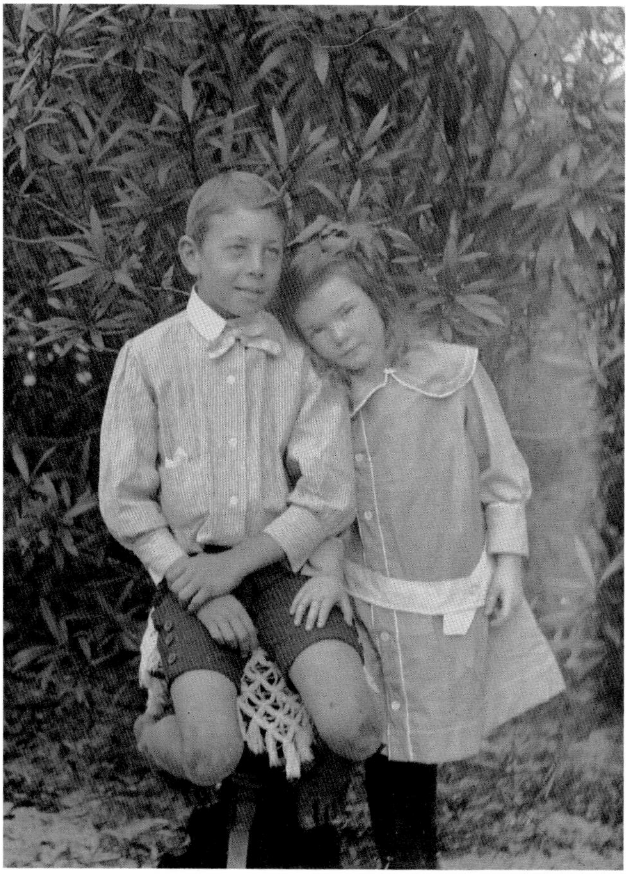

The Robbins Family

Burton Robbins moved from the Midwest to Florida after the Great Freeze of 1894–1895 and purchased one of Lady Lake's most beautiful, historic homes. Built in folk Victorian style, the home overlooked a beautiful lawn and lake. Below, Robbins (left) and his son, Lyle, stand in their yard overlooking the lake. Burton Robbins, a real-estate agent, and his wife, Bertha, had a daughter, Margaret (pictured at left with her brother Lyle around 1905), who loved the home and kept it in the Robbins family for nearly 80 years. Despite the Robbinses' seemingly idyllic lifestyle, tragedy struck in 1915 when Lyle drowned in Lake Hermosa, despite being a good swimmer. The town was in shock, and there was a great outpouring of sympathy for the Robbins family. (Courtesy of the Lady Lake Historical Society.)

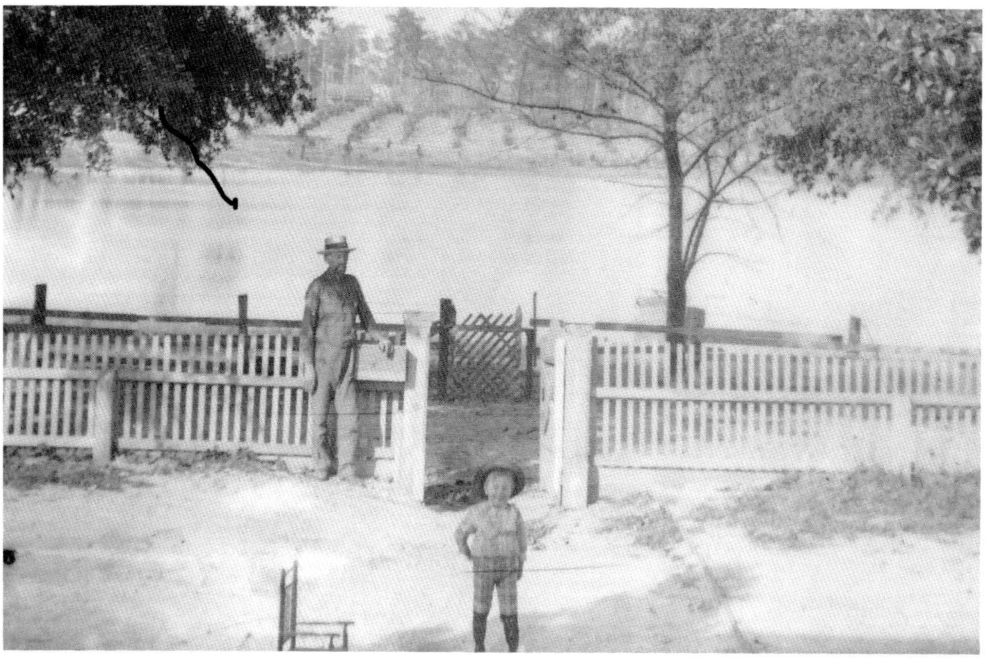

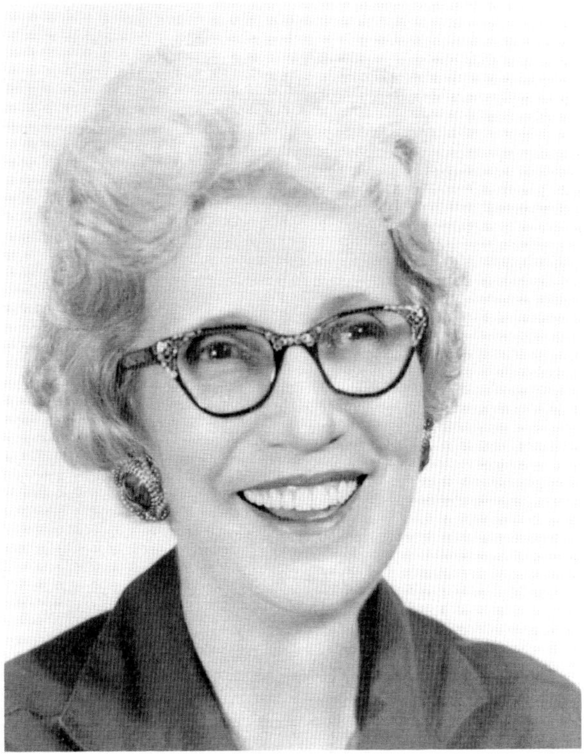

Sarah Teague-Reaves, Iron Lady
Sarah "Louise" Teague-Reaves was known affectionately as the "Iron Lady," a nickname she earned for her straightforward manner. She served as Lady Lake's mayor for six terms in addition to serving on the city council. Under her visionary leadership, side streets were paved. Every Christmas Eve, she played carols on her electric organ at Log Cabin Park. (Courtesy of the Lady Lake Historical Society.)

James Dudley, Hitchhiking Cop
In the 1950s, Lady Lake could not afford a patrol car for town marshal James Dudley. The resourceful cop had to shout at speeders, blow his whistle, or hitch a ride and try to catch up with lawbreakers. In 1962, he asked the town council for a car, to which one council member suggested the "hitchhiking cop" get a bigger whistle. (Courtesy of the Lady Lake Historical Society.)

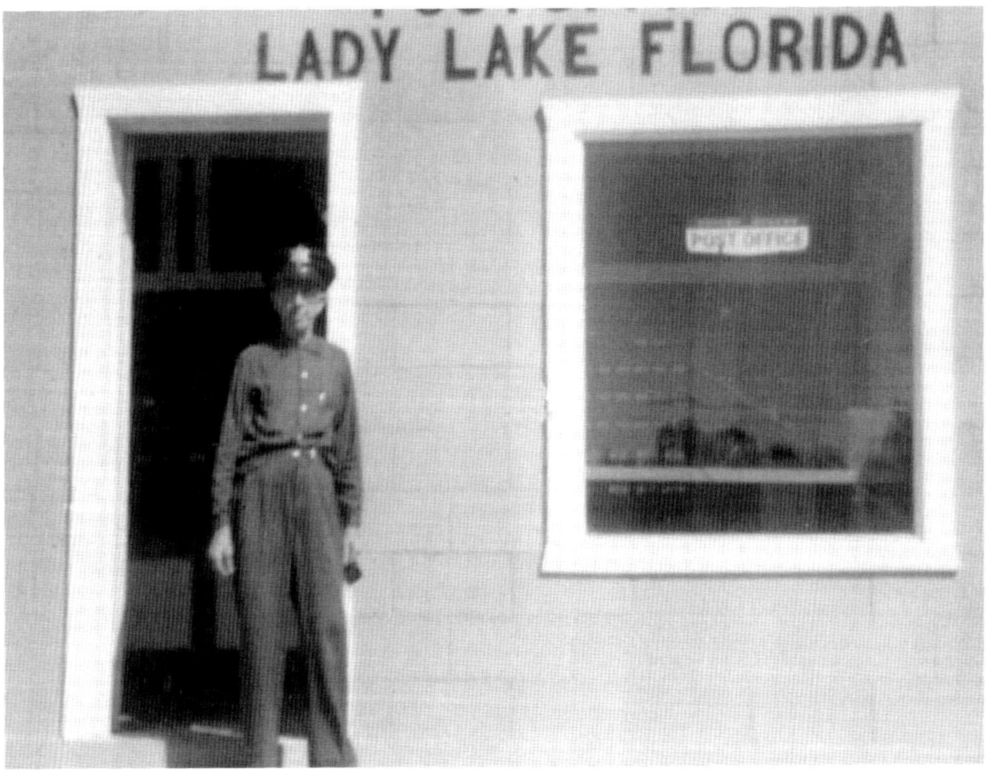

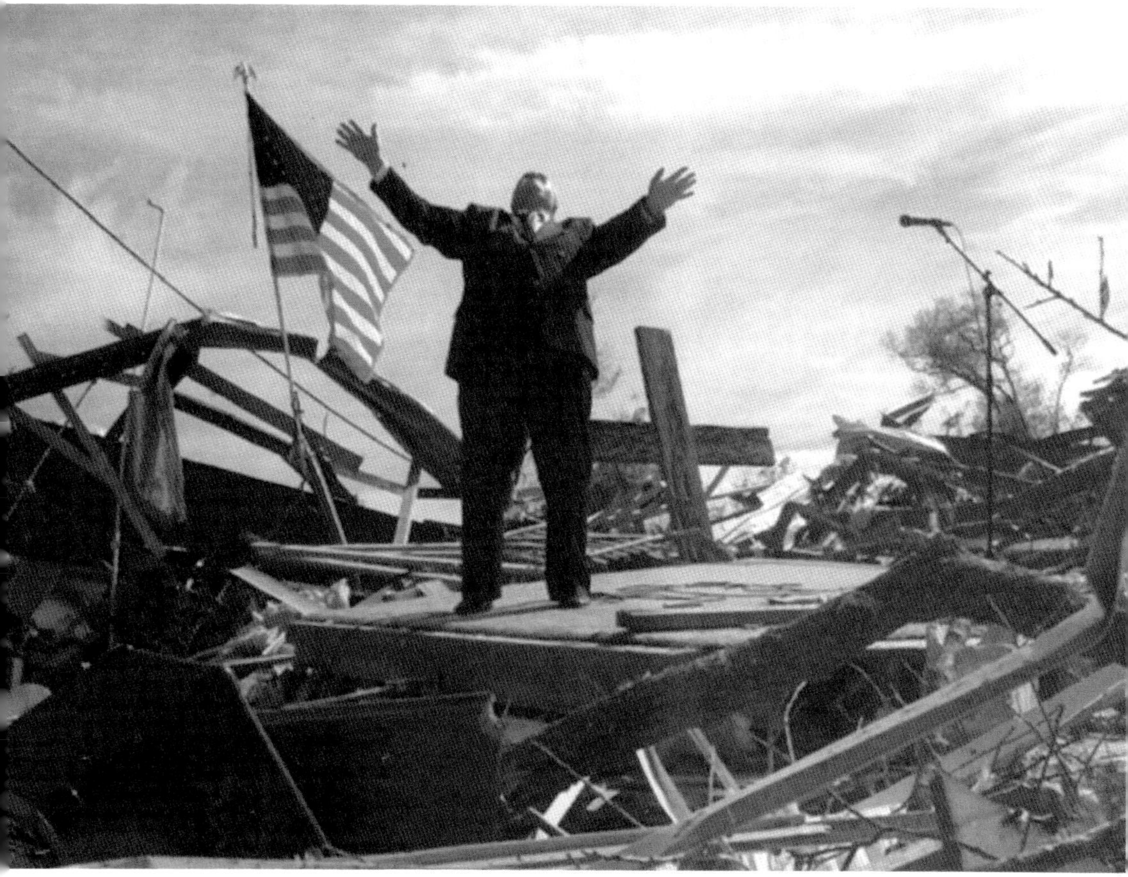

Reverend Larry Lynn

Two days after a 2007 Groundhog Day tornado ripped through the town of Lady Lake, killing 20 people, the Reverend Larry Lynn, pastor of the Lady Lake Church of God, gave the community hope. "Let everybody who has breath today, praise God," he said as he led Sunday services in the midst of the rubble where his church once stood. About 1,500 homes were destroyed by the pre-dawn storm that passed through four counties. Under Lynn's leadership, his congregation built a $2 million sanctuary that was twice the size of the original. (Courtesy of the *Daily Commercial* and Mark Diorio.)

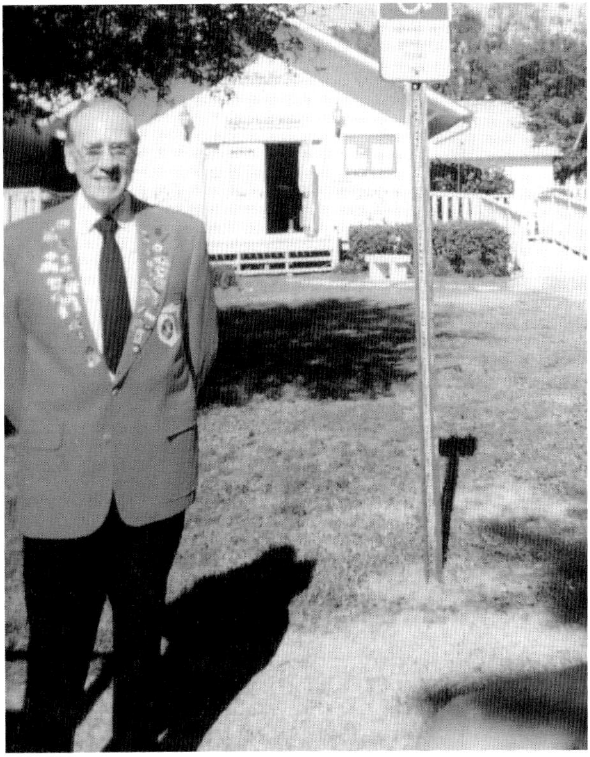

Earl Rowlette
A former auditor for General Motors, Earl Rowlette became the founding father of the Lady Lake Historical Society. He was the unofficial town historian, collecting records and seeking out artifacts and photographs from the community. He also recruited fellow citizens to be officers and helped fundraise. He is shown here as volunteer curator, with the museum in the background. (Courtesy of the Lady Lake Historical Society.)

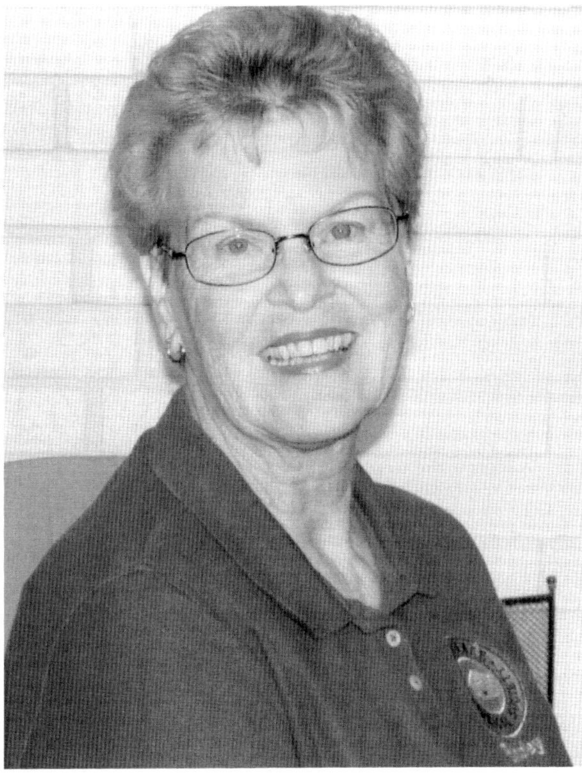

Shirley Kimmons
The Lady Lake Historical Society's first and only secretary is Shirley Kimmons, who has given tirelessly to the nonprofit organization. She has seen the historical museum grow from its early years in a log cabin to its current home in the former train depot. In appreciation of her service, the historical society named its reference library after her. (Courtesy of Shirley Kimmons.)

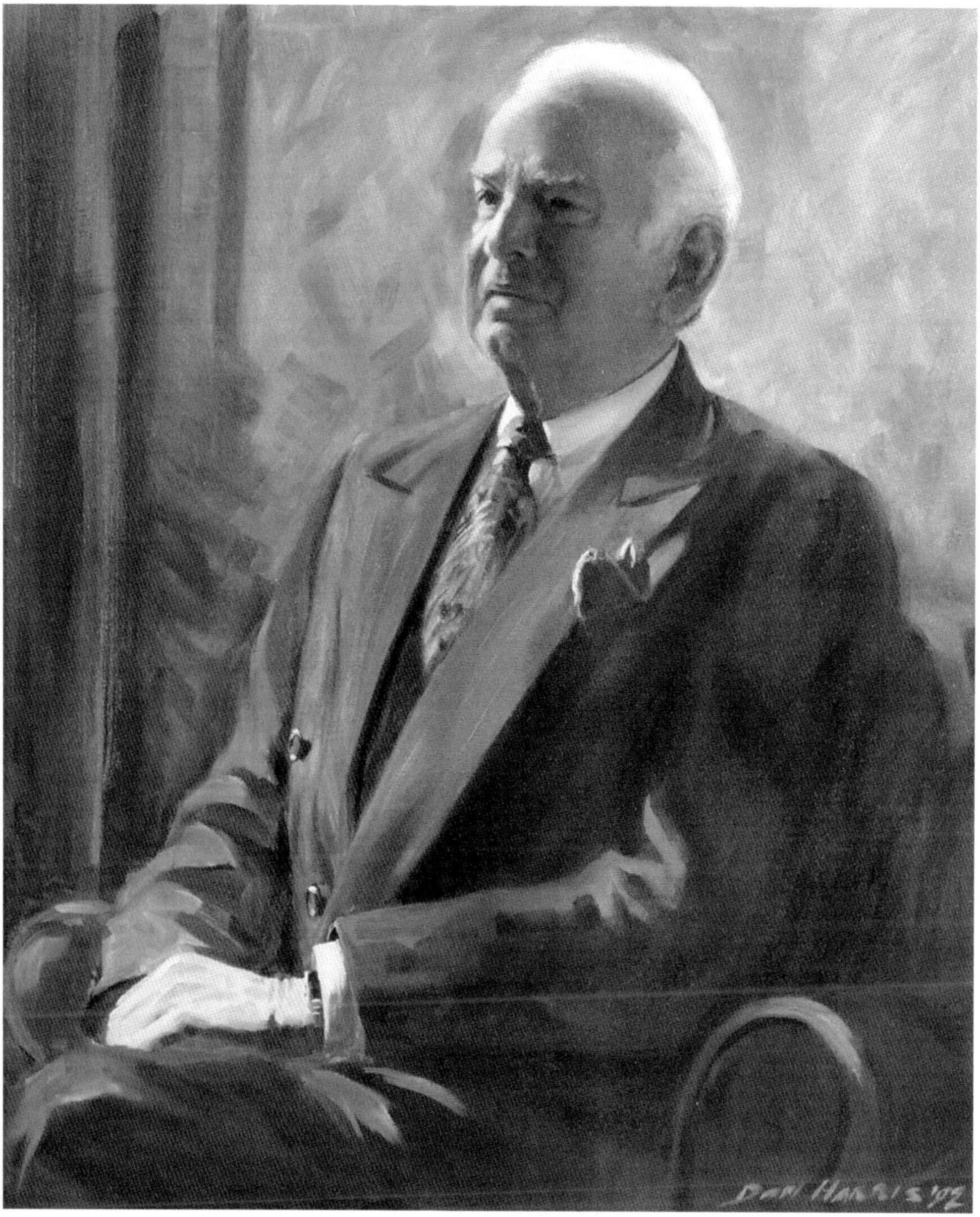

Harold Schwartz

A true visionary, Harold Schwartz turned a rural mobile home park into The Villages, an internationally renowned retirement community with more than 90,000 residents, spanning three counties. Schwartz, and his son, current president Gary Morse, redefined retirement, offering residents free lifetime golf on a total of 531 holes, including 11 championship courses. Two courses were designed by Nancy Lopez and Arnold Palmer. Residents enjoy free entertainment on the three town squares every night of the year. In addition to more than 1,800 clubs serving a wide range of interests, villagers have their own daily newspaper, radio station, and television network. Schwartz and Morse previously worked together in Chicago selling land in New Mexico and Florida. Schwartz also operated several radio stations, including one hosted by popular disc jockey Wolfman Jack. (Courtesy of The Villages.)

Harold Schwartz's Statue

In December 2003, Harold Schwartz, founder of The Villages, died at age 93. A bronze statue in "Florida's friendliest hometown" pays tribute to the man whose vision was of a community "where people's dreams can come true." His ashes were placed inside the statue, which stands in the Spanish Springs town square fountain. (Courtesy of Doris Bloodsworth.)

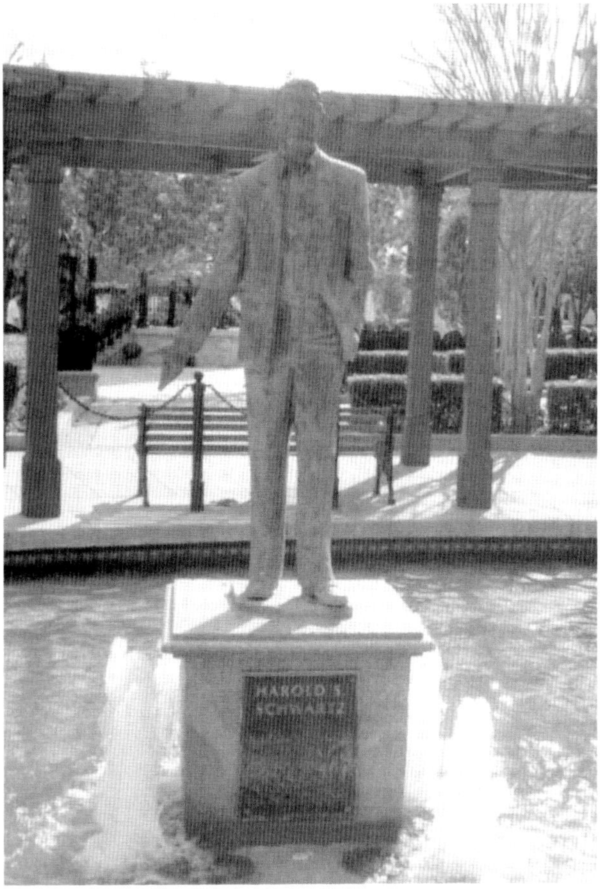

Downtown at The Villages

Harold Schwartz and his son, Gary Morse, redefined retirement by creating an active adult community that provided every amenity imaginable. Residents travel from their homes to shopping and golf in personalized golf carts. In addition to free golf for life, residents can join hundreds of activities, from musicals and cheerleading to a competitive polo club. (Courtesy of Doris Bloodsworth.)

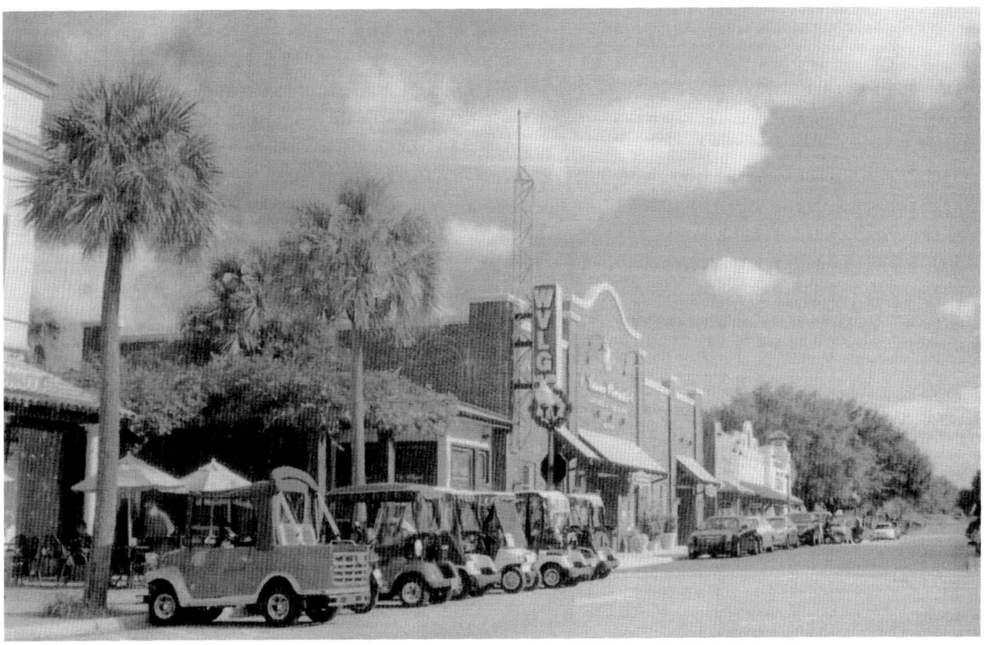

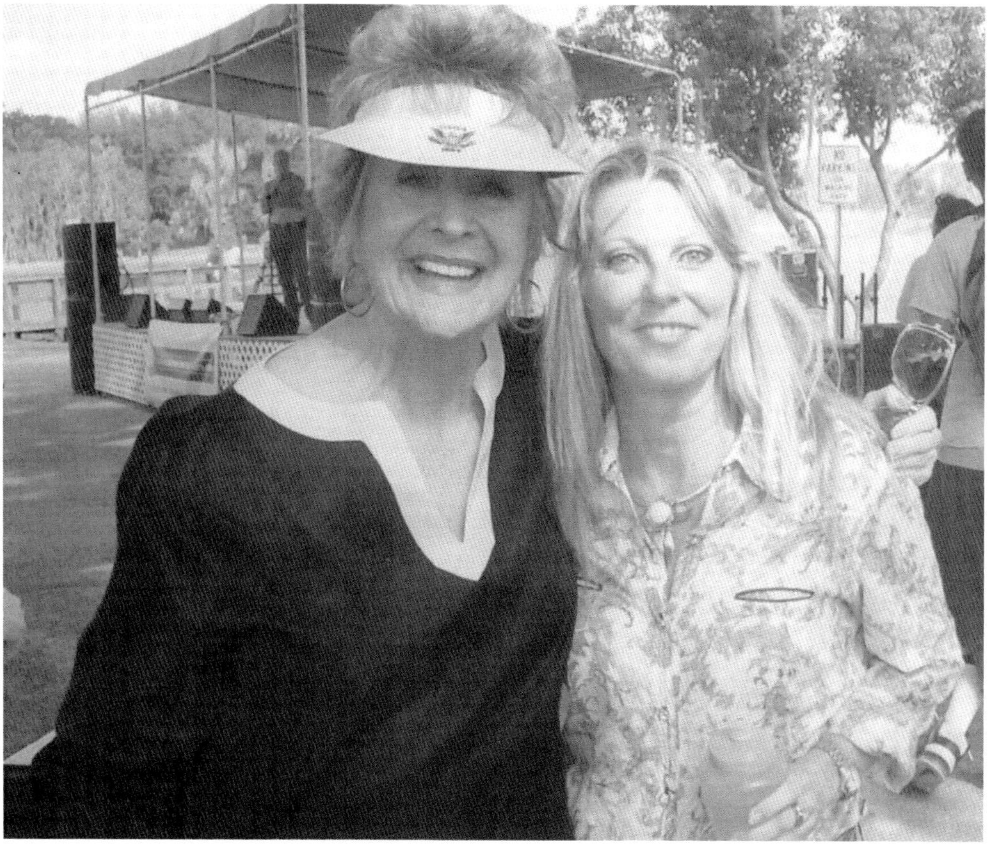

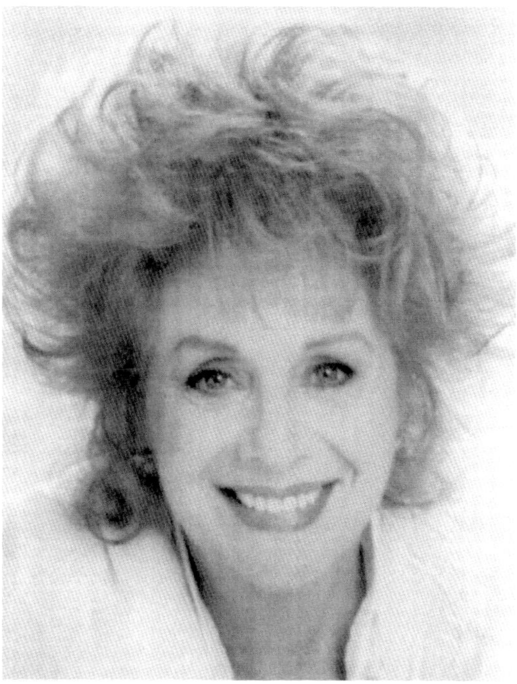

Kaye Stevens

The active lifestyle of The Villages drew actress and singer Kaye Stevens. Born Catherine Louise Stephens, she built a career singing to sold-out audiences in New York, Los Angeles, and Las Vegas with the Rat Pack. She also was a frequent guest on *The Tonight Show* and *Hollywood Squares*. Stevens went on a USO tour with Bob Hope and later showed some of those scenes at a charity fundraiser at The Villages. Before her death at The Villages Hospital in December 2011, she spent much of her time leading a Christian ministry and recording patriotic and spiritual songs. Stevens also became an active environmentalist. In the above photograph, Stevens (left) is shown at a water-preservation rally with country and western singer Carol Ann Allen. (Courtesy of Kaye Stevens.)

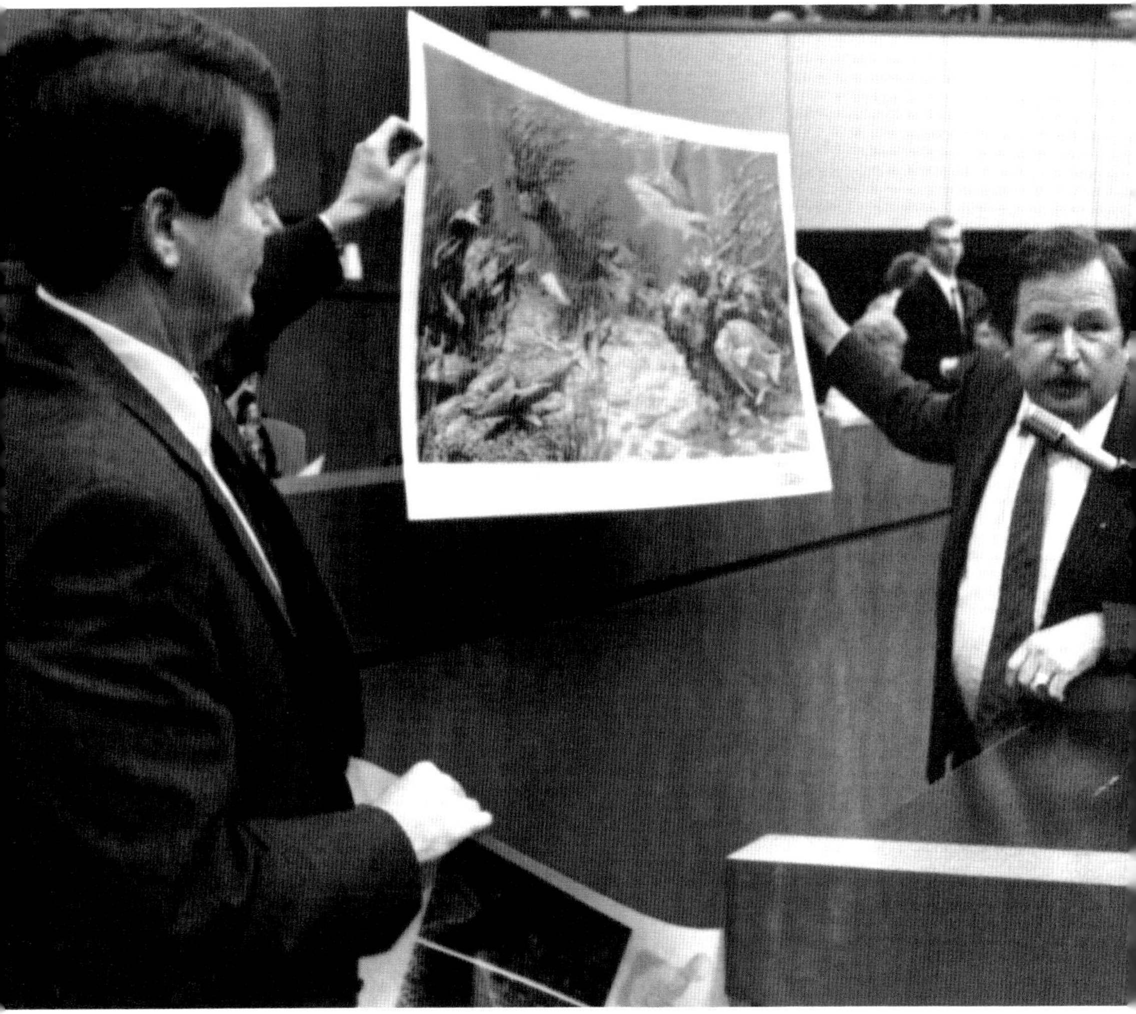

Everett Kelly

Former state representative Everett Kelly (right) has been a powerful friend of The Villages. Shown here when he was in the Florida legislature, he played a key role in helping The Villages when the developers sought to build a golf cart bridge over US Highway 27/441. The bridge is dubbed the "Everett Kelly Causeway." Today, the former pharmacist is the CEO of a medical center in The Villages area. As a legislator, he served as speaker pro-tem during his 22 years in the Florida House of Representatives. An avid outdoorsman, he wrote a column and hosted a television show about the outdoors. (Courtesy of the State Archives of Florida.)

CHAPTER TWO

East Lake County

Tavares, Eustis, Mount Dora, Umatilla, Sorrento, Astor, Mount Plymouth, and Altoona

The eastern cities of Lake County include the "Golden Triangle"—Tavares, Eustis, and Mount Dora—and its neighbors, Umatilla, Sorrento, Astor, Mount Plymouth, and Altoona. East Lake is bordered by two of Florida's most impressive natural resources, Ocala National Forest to the north and the mighty St. Johns River to the east.

Memorable characters played significant roles in east Lake County's past, such as the ambitious Alexander St. Clair Abrams, who aspired that Tavares be the county seat and the state capital. His first wish came true, in a tale that includes a secretive boat ride across Lake Harris and high drama. City leaders are still ambitious, having established an enviable park that combines its historic past with a vision as "America's Seaplane City."

Eustis residents enjoy tradition. Their Washington Birthday Celebration is the longest-running festival in the nation. Notable residents include archaeologist Edgar Banks, the original Indiana Jones; astronaut David Walker; and NAACP past president T.H. Poole.

Mount Dora's elegant Lakeside Inn and charming downtown district have made it popular for antique buffs, presidents, and unsung heroes, such as revered educator Ruthie Ann Watson and Coach Dan Spear.

East Lake County is also home to a string of small towns whose residents have a fierce sense of community pride. Umatilla, "the Sportsman's Paradise," is a gateway to the "Big Scrub," Ocala National Forest, the southernmost national forest in the United States. Descendants of founder Nathan Trowell maintain strong ties to the town's early roots. Sorrento, Mount Plymouth, and Astor have enjoyed eras of boom and bust. Settlers and tourists included wealthy families such as the Astors, and the famous and infamous, such as singer Kate Smith and the mobster Al Capone, an avid golfer.

Not to be overlooked, Altoona is the birthplace of Medal of Honor hero Robert McTureous, whose memory is kept alive by the Greater Altoona Society.

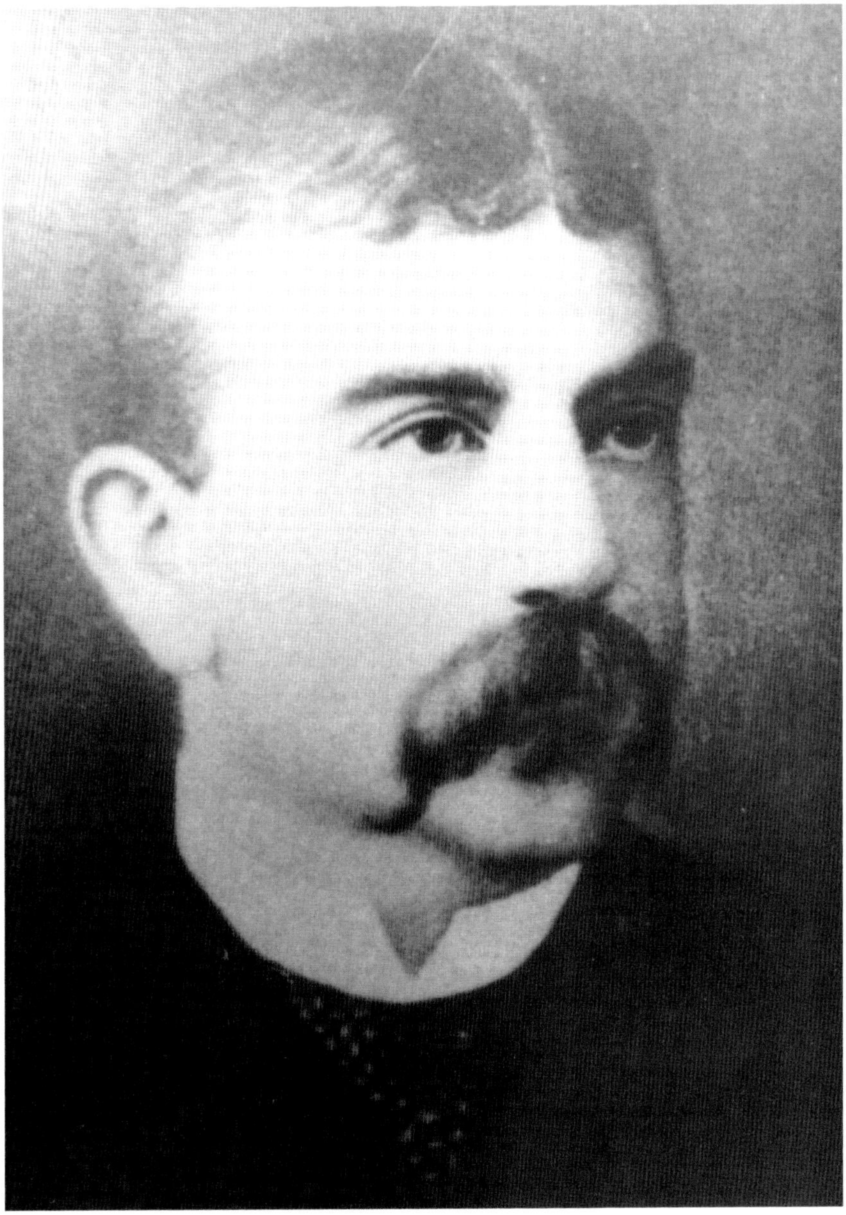

Alexander St. Clair Abrams

When Alexander St. Clair Abrams arrived in Florida in 1875, the 30-year-old was already an accomplished adventurer. He had served in the Civil War and been the *New York Herald's* foreign editor before starting an Atlanta newspaper. He became a prominent Orlando attorney. In 1880, he founded Tavares and worked with legislator Henry Duncan to form Lake County. St. Clair Abrams pushed for his town to become the county seat in a series of controversial moves. He spent a fortune building commerce and railways, dreaming that Tavares would become the state capital, before a fire destroyed much of the downtown. He was elected mayor and state legislator and got into a duel with the sheriff. In his sixties, he moved to Jacksonville, where he successfully defended a notorious murder suspect. (Courtesy of the Tavares Historical Society.)

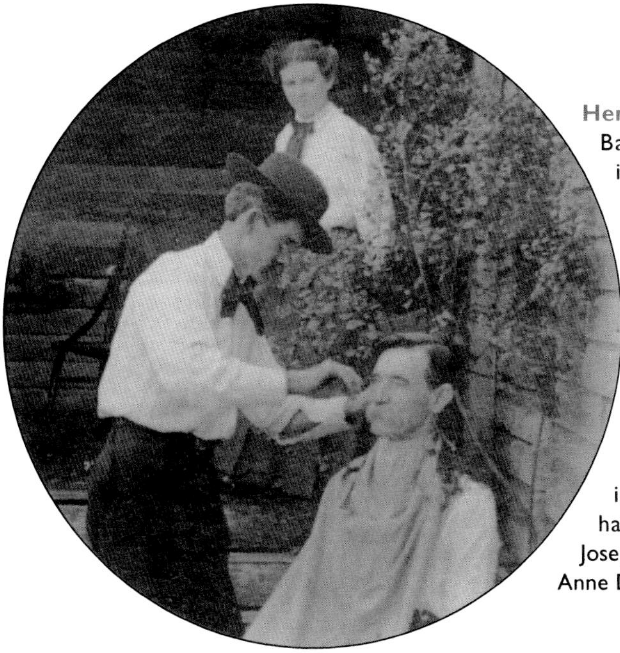

Henry H. Duncan

Barely surviving battle wounds and imprisonment, Confederate veteran and teacher Henry Duncan (seated) went on to become the state representative who, in 1887, along with state senator George Lee, helped form Lake County. He served as clerk of the court for 33 years and was instrumental in making Tavares the county seat. He and his wife, Marian Peet Duncan, had seven children who became legends in their own right. Duncan is pictured having his hair cut by his stepbrother Joseph Cottrell Jr. (Courtesy of Harryette-Anne Duncan.)

The Duncan Family

The history of Tavares is closely entwined with the Henry Duncan family. Shown here in 1904 at their home are, from left to right, (first row) Marian Peet Duncan (holding Carl Duncan), Henry Duncan, Wyeth Duncan, and Harriett Peet; (second row) Dolly Duncan, Cora Peet, Harry Duncan, Marian D. Duncan, and Leonard Duncan. Many descendants of Henry Duncan spent their lives in public service, education, and charitable works. (Courtesy of Harryette-Anne Duncan.)

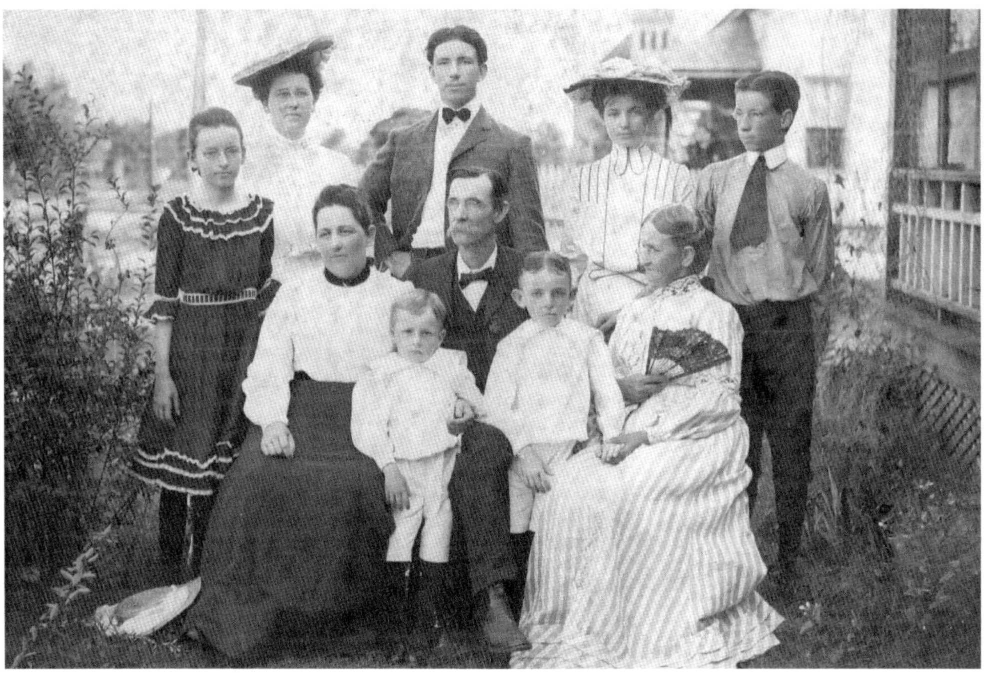

Capt. Melton Haynes
Almost forgotten to history, Capt. Melton Haynes has become known to Lake County residents thanks to Tavares historian Bob Grenier. Haynes, a Confederate soldier, served in the Florida House of Representatives and Senate. He brought the area's first sweet oranges to Lake County. His 1871 Woodlea cracker-style home was restored, destroyed by vandals, and then re-created at Tavares's downtown park. (Courtesy of Bob Grenier.)

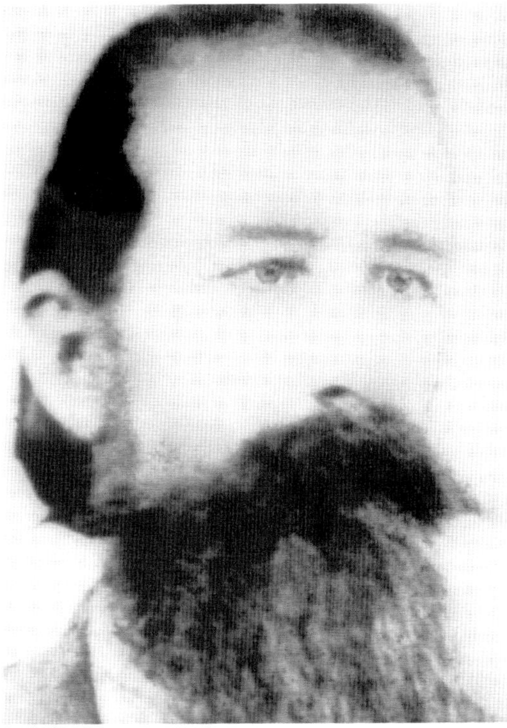

Jesse Walton Hunter, State Attorney
Though he displayed a down-home casualness in the courtroom, with his loosened tie and peanut munching, Jesse Hunter was a determined and successful attorney who rarely lost. He had little formal training, teaching himself the legal profession by reading law books. He passed the Florida bar exam and was state attorney from 1925 to 1953. (Courtesy of the Tavares Historical Society.)

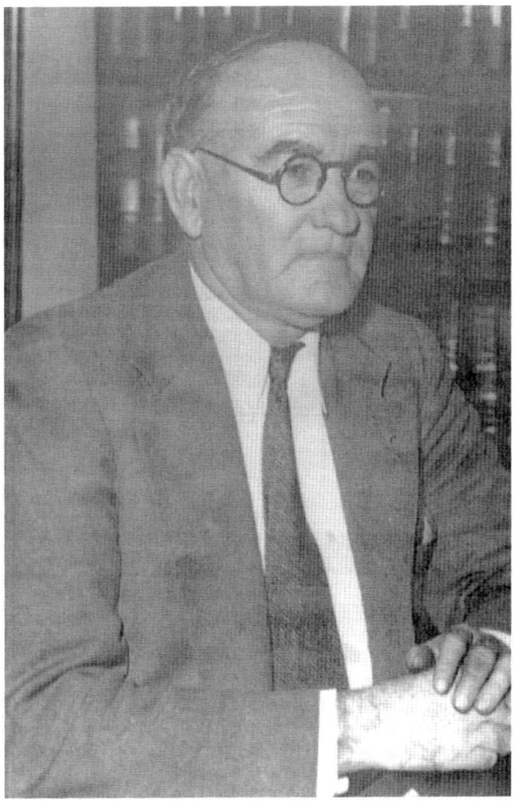

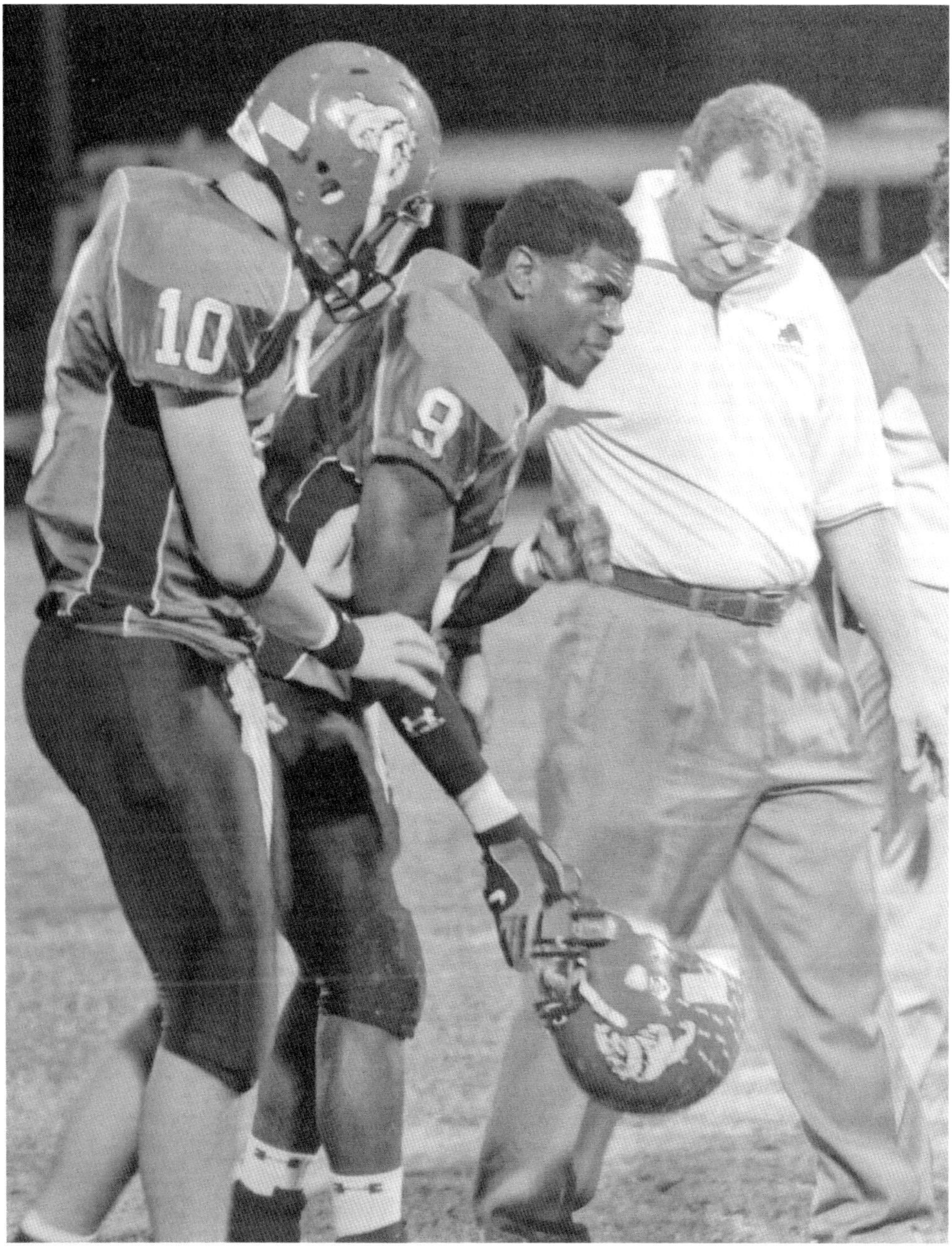

Drs. Argin and Dan Boggus

Father-and-son physicians Argin and Dan Boggus have been family physicians to many Tavares residents for generations as well as fixtures on the sidelines of Tavares High School football games. In appreciation of Dr. Argin Boggus's 40-year service as team physician for the Bulldogs, the football stadium was named in his honor in 1998. As a child, Dan Boggus would be at his father's side during the games. He served as team physician with his father for the last nine years of Argin's career. The Tavares physicians performed team physicals as well, and sometimes patched up players after the games in the Boggus home. Dan Boggus (right) is shown here helping an unidentified player off the field. (Courtesy of *Lake* magazine.)

Bernice Odums, Lane Park Historian

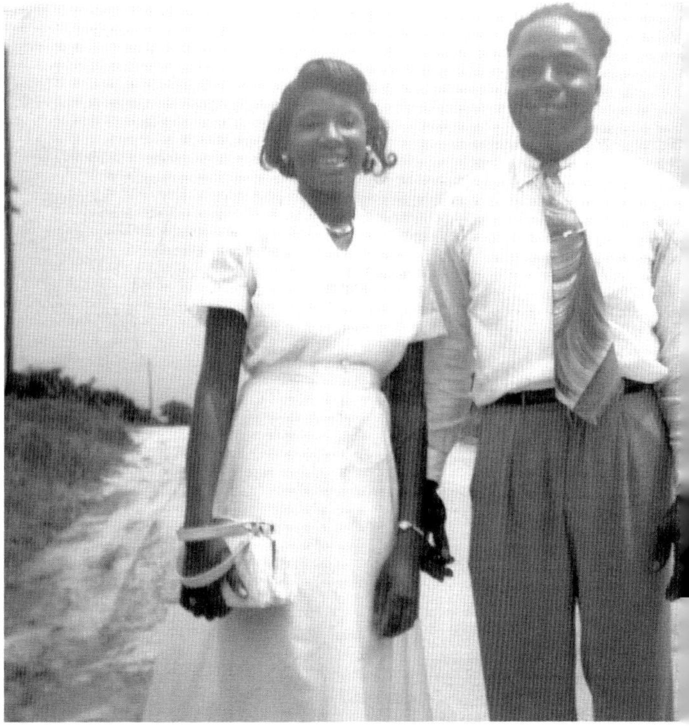

One of Tavares's most respected hometown heroes is Bernice Shorts Odums, shown here with her cousin Samuel Parker. Odums was born and raised in Lane Park. She attended National Business College and Boston College for Business. She worked for the Lake County School System as a teacher's aide and assistant purchasing agent. She is the vice president of the Tavares Historical Society. (Courtesy of Bernice Odums.)

Rupert Deleveaux, Artist

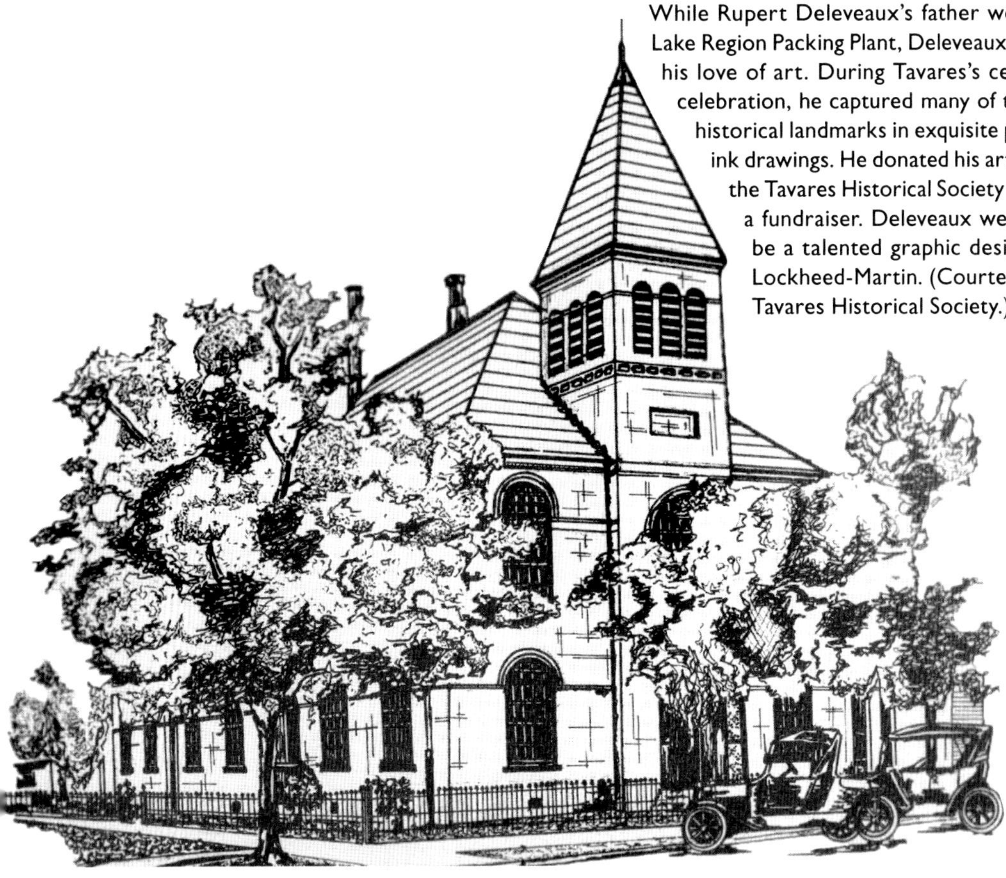

While Rupert Deleveaux's father worked at Lake Region Packing Plant, Deleveaux pursued his love of art. During Tavares's centennial celebration, he captured many of the city's historical landmarks in exquisite pen-and-ink drawings. He donated his artwork to the Tavares Historical Society to sell as a fundraiser. Deleveaux went on to be a talented graphic designer for Lockheed-Martin. (Courtesy of the Tavares Historical Society.)

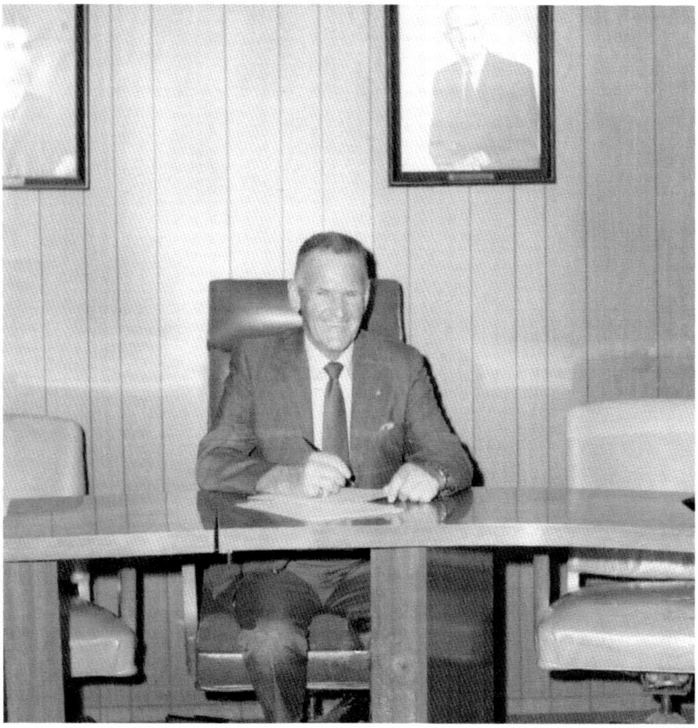

Fred Stover, Mayor
An interest in providing modern sports equipment to area students led Tavares mayor Fred Stover to play a leading role in building new athletic fields. Stover served as city councilman and died in 1973 while serving as mayor. The Fred Stover Sports Complex, which includes four ball fields, located on Clifford Street, is named in his honor. (Courtesy of the Tavares Historical Society.)

Emogene Stegall, Supervisor of Elections
Inducted into the Lake County Women's Hall of Fame in 2005, Emogene Stegall has served as supervisor of elections since 1972. She has held a variety of positions in the Florida State Association of Supervisors of Elections and is active in the community as a volunteer with the League of Women Voters, the Tavares Women's Club, and the Pilot Club. (Courtesy of *The Daily Commercial.*)

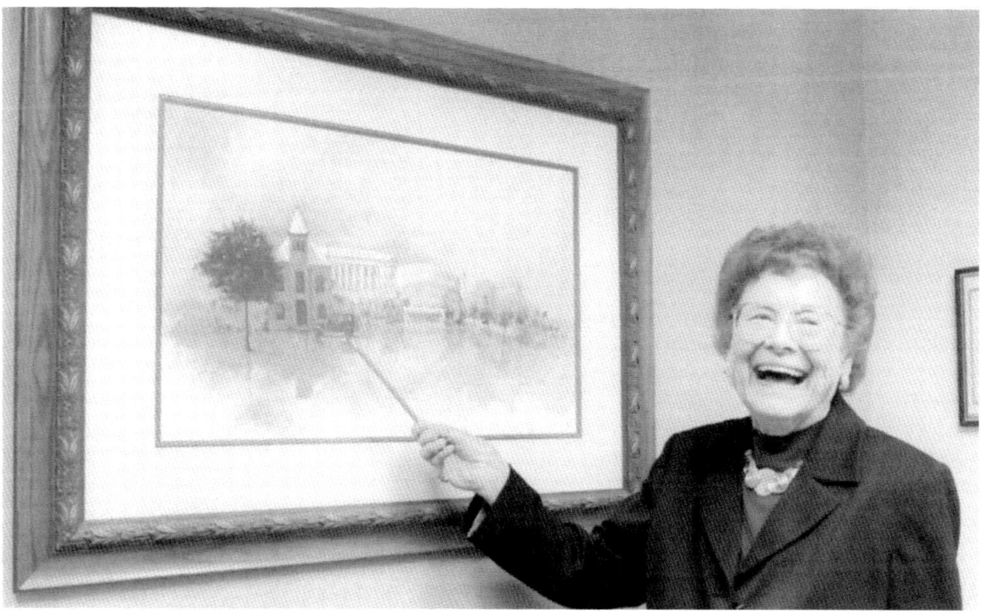

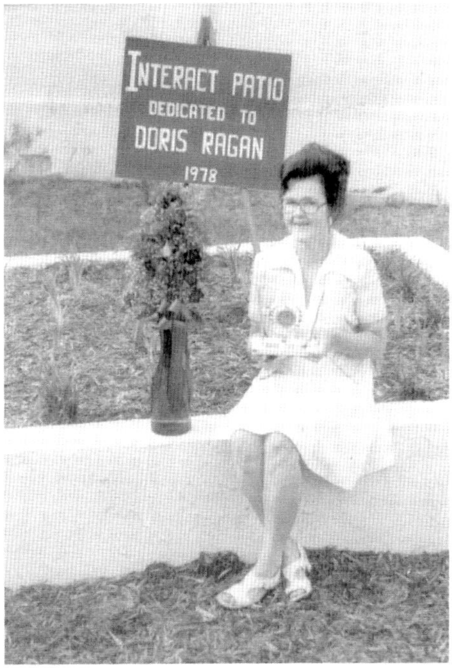

Doris Ragan, Teacher and Gardener
Friends say Doris Ragan is good at nurturing, whether it's the students she taught during her 37-year career, or the 200 flower arrangements she creates yearly for shut-ins and civic events. Ragan, a master gardener, was inducted into the Lake County Women's Hall of Fame. She has played piano at First Baptist Church of Tavares for 60 years. (Courtesy of Tavares Historical Society.)

Ken LaRoe, Visionary Banker
Tavares High School alumnus and second-generation Eustis resident Ken LaRoe already enjoyed a successful banking career when he sold Florida Choice Bank and hit the roads in an RV with his wife, Cindy. A year later, he began realizing a vision that combined environmental concern with smart banking. First Green Banks are built with strict environmental standards, and the employees receive incentives to drive hybrid cars. (Courtesy of Ken LaRoe.)

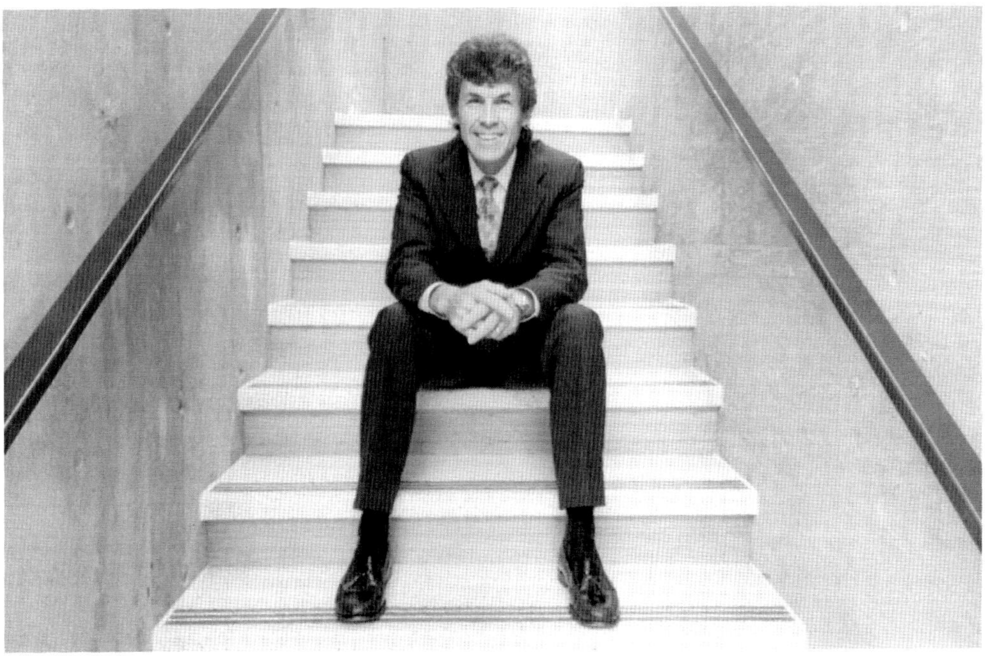

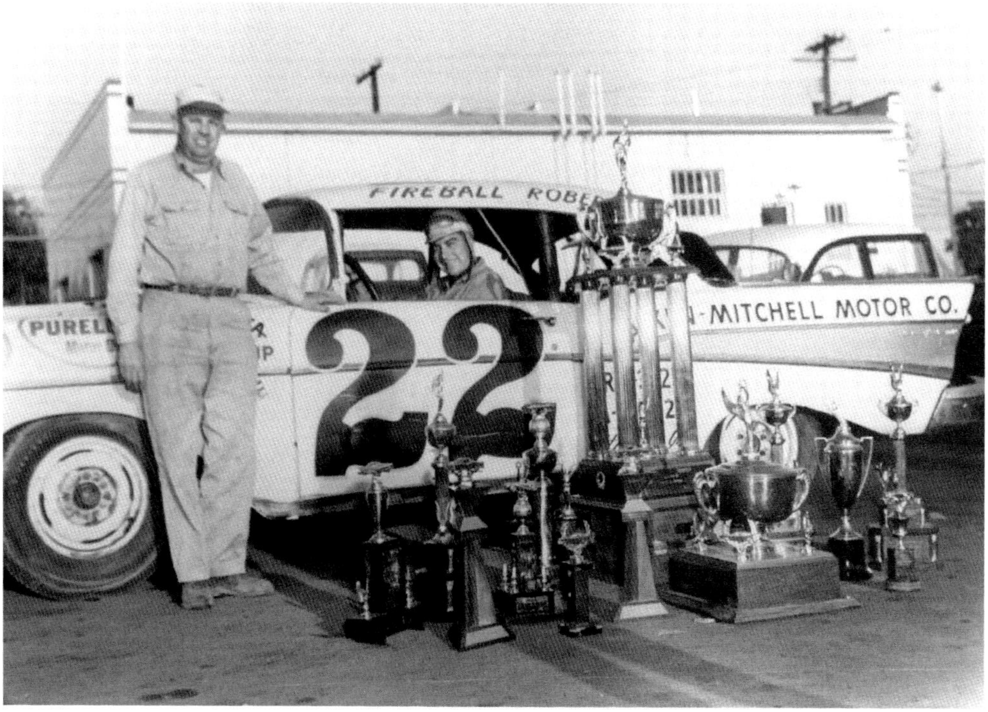

Edward Glenn Roberts, Racing Legend
Edward Glenn "Fireball" Roberts, born in Tavares, always loved auto racing and baseball. His nickname came from his fastball. At 19, he won a 150-mile race, and he went on to win 33 Grand National races. In 1964, Roberts crashed during the World 600 in Charlotte and died a few weeks later. He was named one of NASCAR's 50 greatest drivers. He is shown here with NASCAR Chevrolet team owner Frank Strickland in 1958. (Courtesy of the State Archives of Florida.)

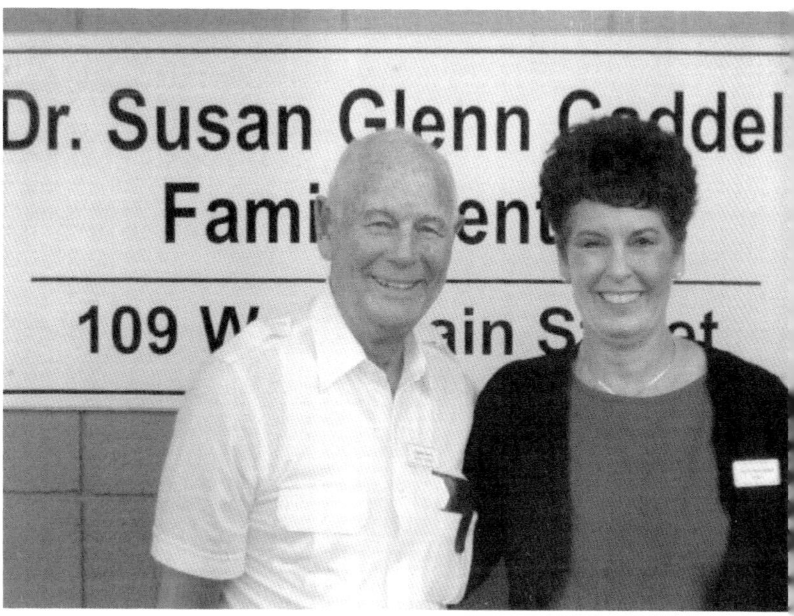

Dr. Eugene Glenn and Dr. Susan Glenn Caddell
For more than 50 years, father-and-daughter dentists Dr. Eugene Glenn and Dr. Susan Glenn Caddell have treated Tavares families at their downtown office. Theirs is the oldest business on Main Street. Eugene Glenn also served the city as mayor for 20 years before retiring to Colorado. In 2012, the two held an open house to thank the community. (Courtesy of Dr. Susan Glenn Caddell.)

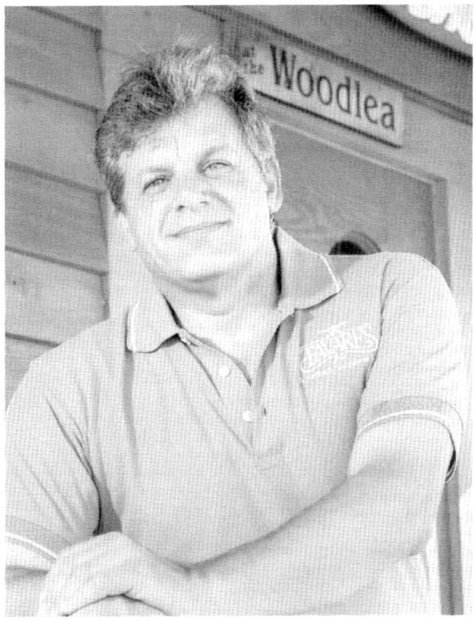

Bob Grenier, Historian Extraordinaire
A love of history and public service keep Tavares vice mayor Bob Grenier busy. His leadership in restoring the historic Woodlea House led to a revival of the city's downtown. Grenier is an award-winning author and is president of the Tavares and Lake County historical societies. The Chicago native initiated the Black Heritage/Senior Luncheon, participates in Civil War reenactments, and is a successful business owner. (Courtesy of Bill Casey.)

Woodlea House
After arsonists destroyed the historic Woodlea House, Tavares residents rallied and reconstructed the wood-frame home at Wooton Park. Attending the 2010 ribbon-cutting ceremony are, from left to right, John Drury, Kirby Smith, Mayor Lori Pfister, Mayor Robert Wolfe, Gov. Charlie Crist, Sen. Alan Hayes, Bob Grenier, Sandy Gamble, Nancy Clutts and Brenda Smith. Tavares embraces its historic past and is designated "America's Seaplane City." (Courtesy of Bob Grenier.)

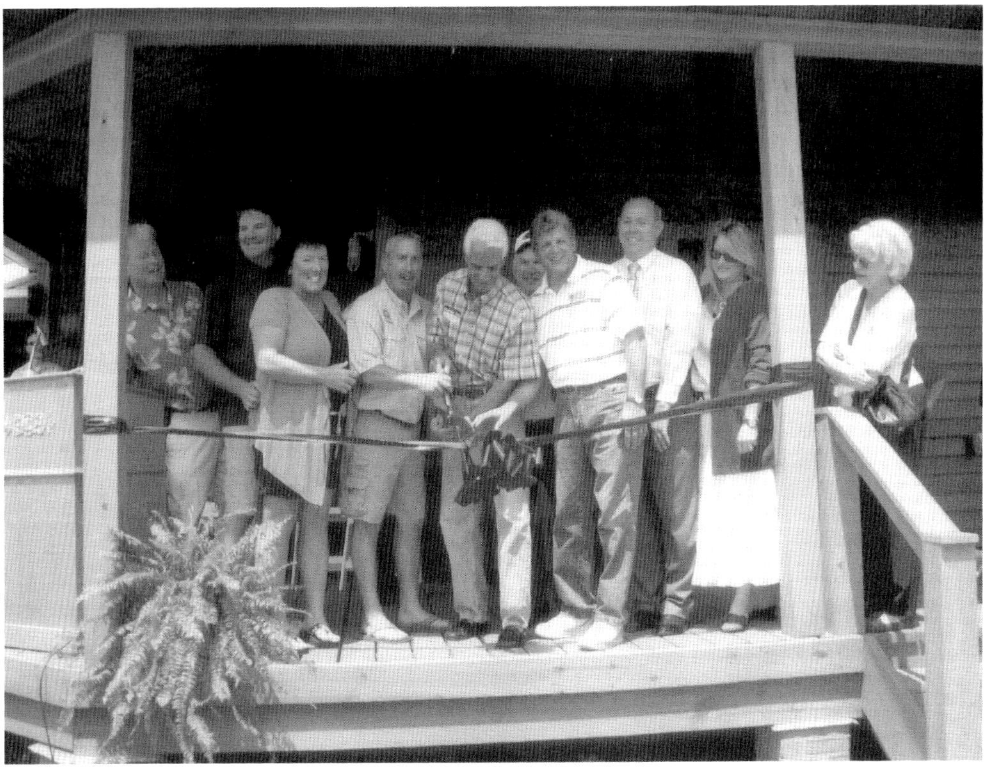

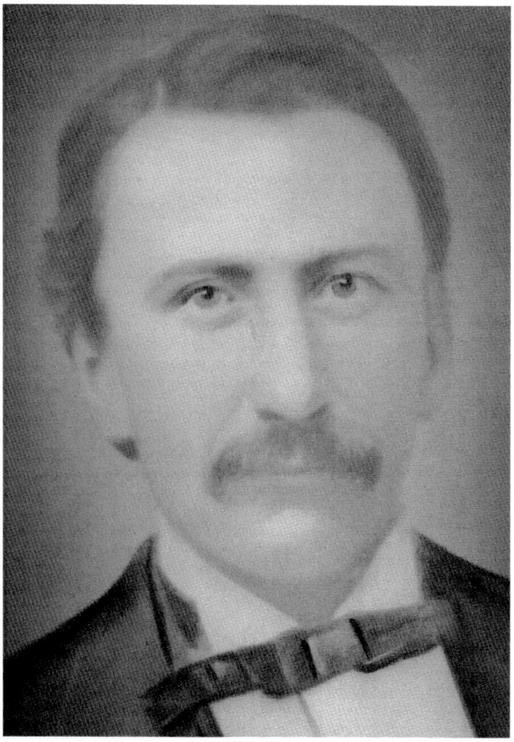

Guilford David Clifford

Pioneer entrepreneur Guilford Clifford was one of Eustis's first settlers. He moved to the area in 1875 and built a home and general store and founded the first mail service. Above the general store was a meeting hall that served as an opera house and was home to several churches. Clifford is remembered for laying the groundwork for Eustis. (Courtesy of the Eustis Historical Museum and Preservation Society.)

Eustis Historical Museum

Located on Lake Eustis, the Clifford House was completed in 1911 and in 1983 became home to the Eustis Historical Museum and Preservation Society. In 1975, Guilford Clifford's oldest daughter, Lottie Clifford Taylor, helped list the home in the National Register of Historic Places shortly before her death at age 103. Beside the Clifford House is the only independently housed citrus museum in Florida. Eustis was once known as the "Orange Capital of the World." (Courtesy of Connie Fleetwood.)

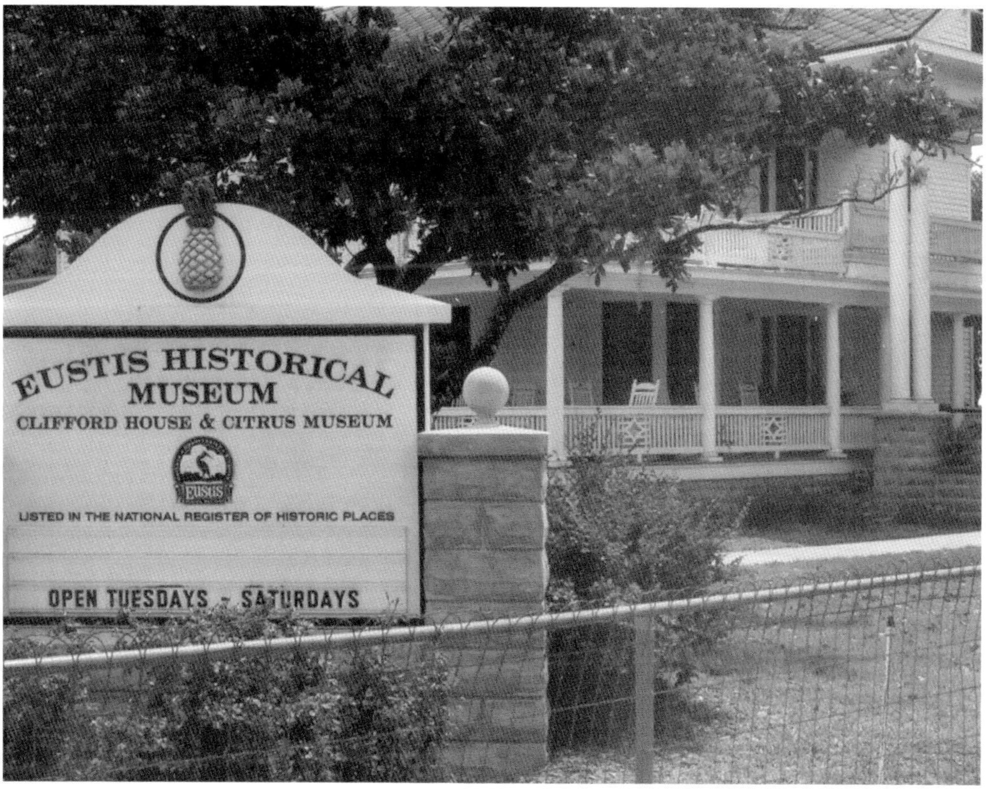

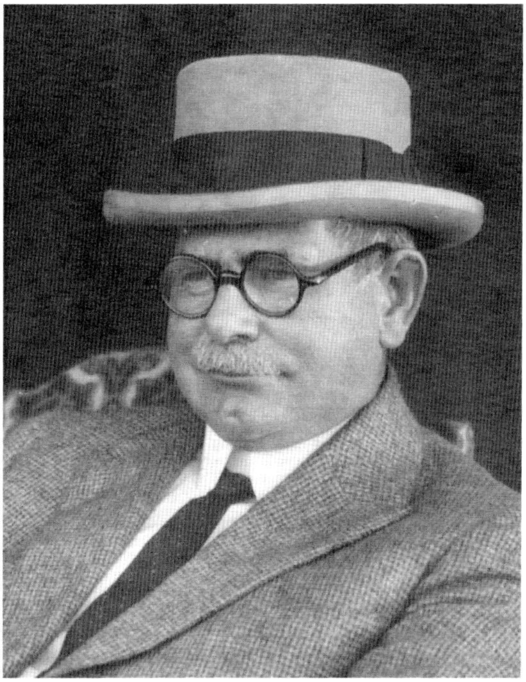

Edgar J. Banks, Archeologist, Diplomat, and Explorer
Often referred to as the original Indiana Jones, archaeologist Edgar J. Banks was born in 1866 and began coming to Eustis in 1916. He is most noted for excavating Bismya in Iraq; in 1912, he was the first American to climb Mount Ararat. Some of his artifacts and furniture are on display at the Eustis Historical Museum. (Courtesy of the Eustis Historical Museum and Preservation Society.)

Clayton Bishop
A third-generation Lake County native and former florist, Clayton Bishop is shown looking through some of the 9,000 postcards he has collected during the past 40 years. An avid deltiologist, he has 5,000 postcards of Lake County cities. Bishop also has an extensive Rotary memorabilia collection and has been a member of the Eustis Rotary Club for 55 years. (Courtesy of Connie Fleetwood.)

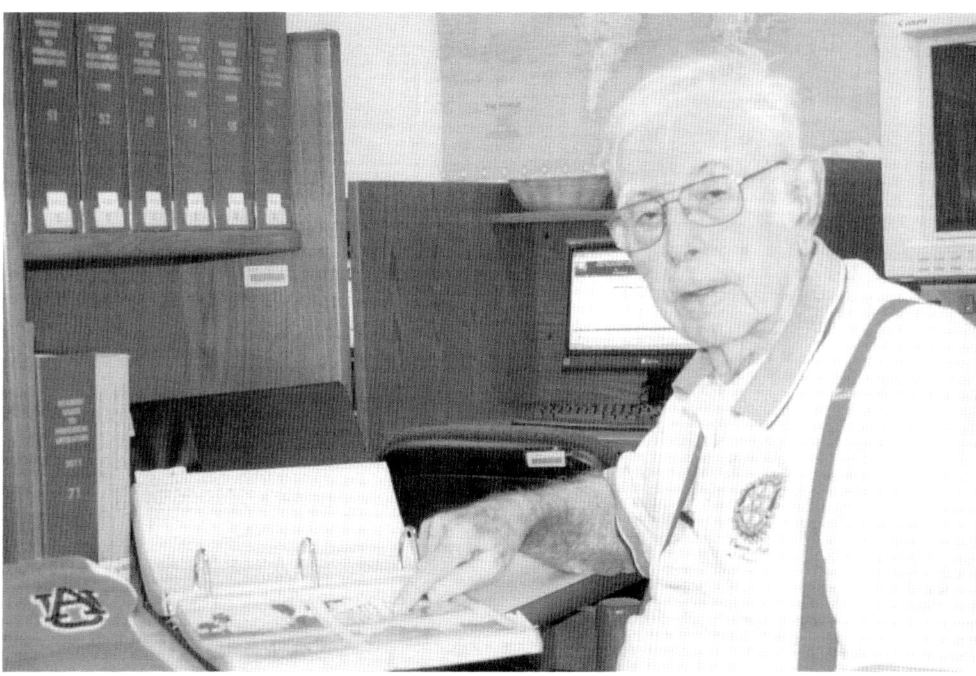

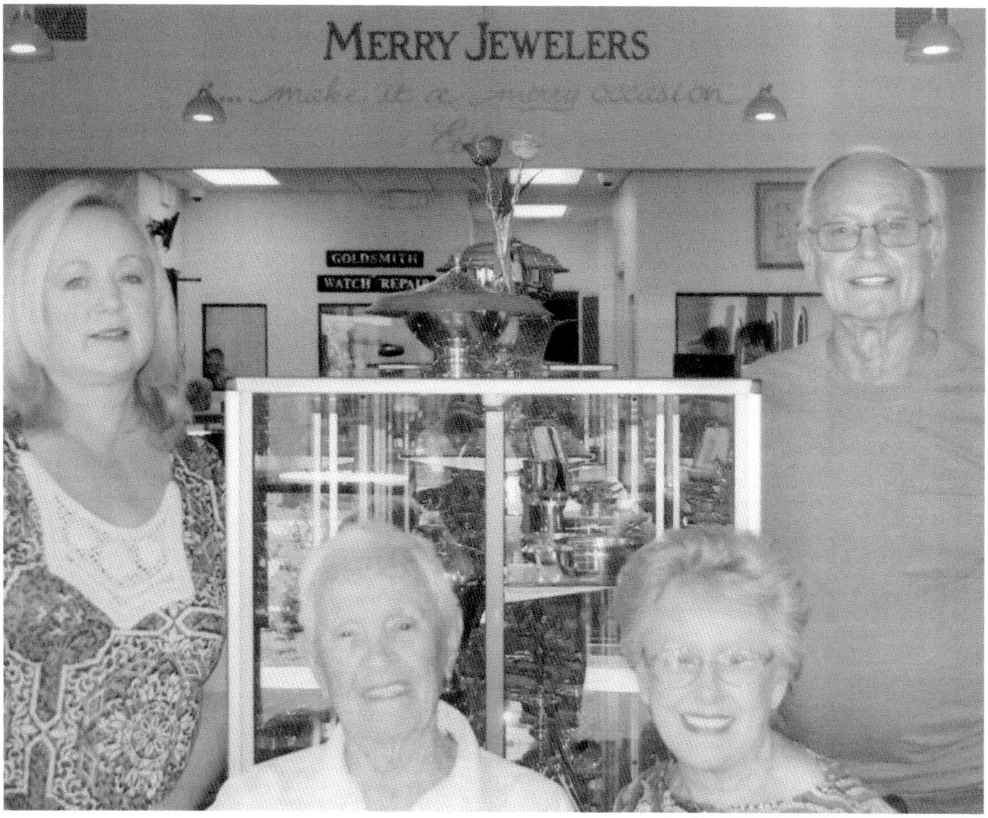

The Merry Family

Guy "Smiley" Merry is the founder of Merry Jewelers, a family-run business in downtown Eustis. Merry opened the store in 1946 after serving in the Navy Seabees during World War II. He was instrumental in getting Eustis approved as a Main Street City. Shown here are, from left to right, Merri Sichko (Guy's granddaughter), Guy Merry, Judy Merry (Guy's daughter), and Jim Merry (Guy's son). (Courtesy of Connie Fleetwood.)

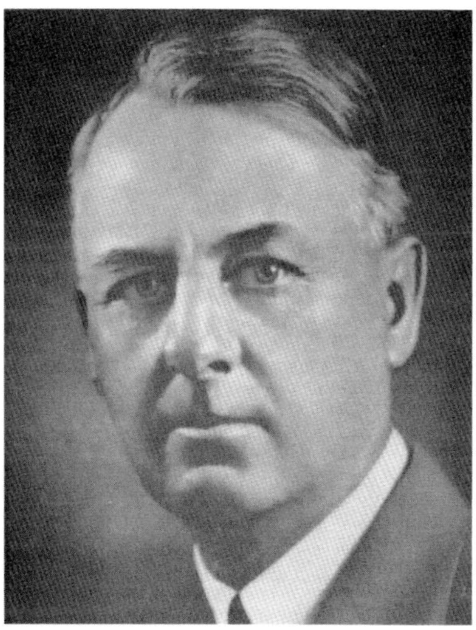

Sen. William Monroe Igou

A citrus grower until the Great Freeze of 1894–1895, William Igou opened mule lots in Eustis and throughout the South until heavy machinery came along. He opened W.M. Igou Inc., a livestock and livery business, which was considered to be the largest of its type in Florida. Igou was a county commissioner, state legislator, and secretary of state. (Courtesy of the Eustis Historical Museum and Preservation Society.)

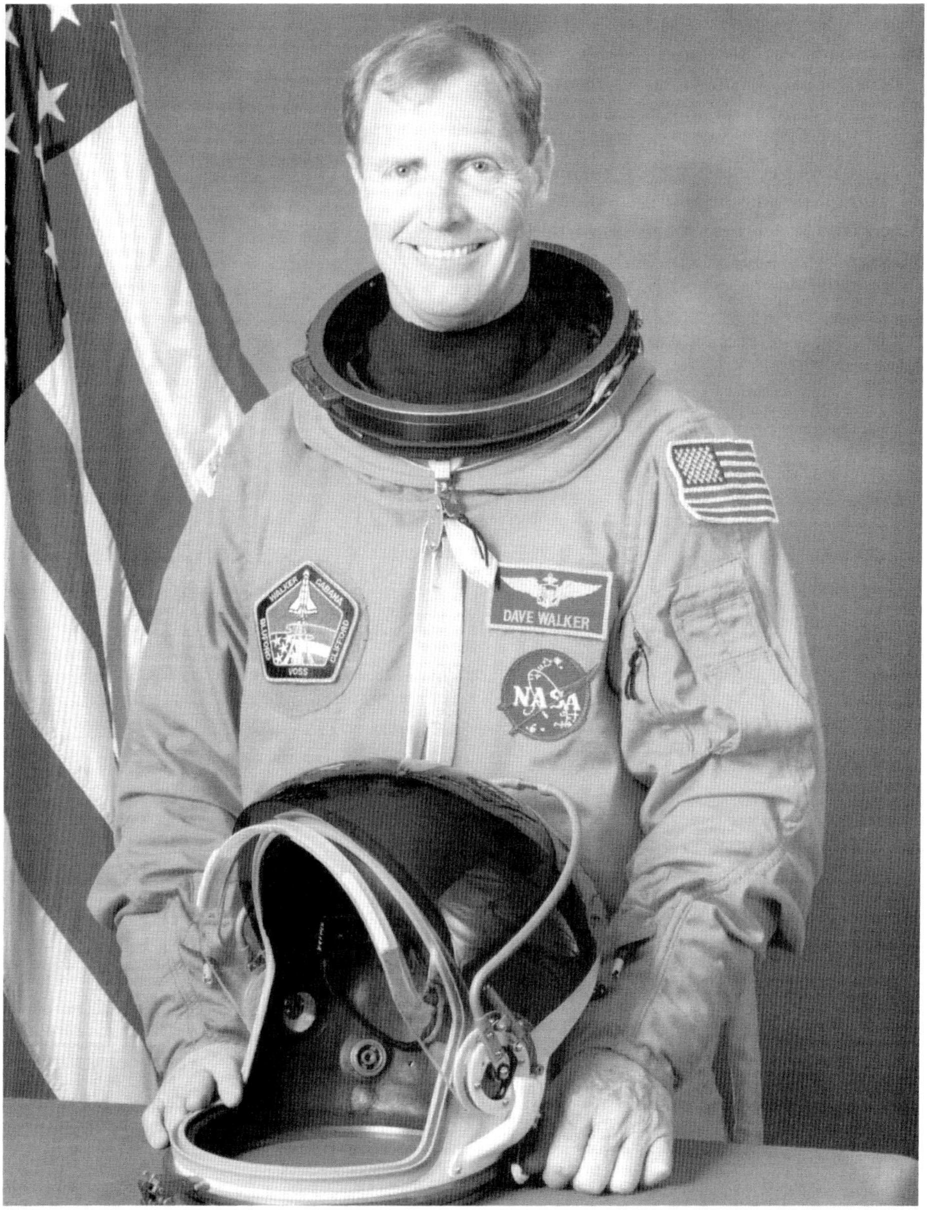

Capt. David Mathieson Walker

William Igou's great-grandson, David Walker, was a 1962 honor graduate of Eustis High School and a graduate of the US Naval Academy. He flew F-4 Phantom fighters during the Vietnam War before becoming an astronaut. Walker was commander on three of the four shuttle missions he flew. He was awarded numerous medals, including the Defense Superior Medal, Distinguished Flying Cross, National Medal of Achievement, Legion of Merit, two Defense Meritorious Service Medals, six Navy Air Medals, Battle Efficiency Ribbon, Armed Forces Expeditionary Medal, National Defense Service Medal, two NASA Distinguished Service Medals, NASA Outstanding Leadership Medal, and four NASA Space Flight Medals. He worked in the aerospace industry after leaving NASA and was a consultant on the film *Deep Impact*. After his 2001 death, he received a hero's burial in Arlington National Cemetery. (Courtesy of NASA.)

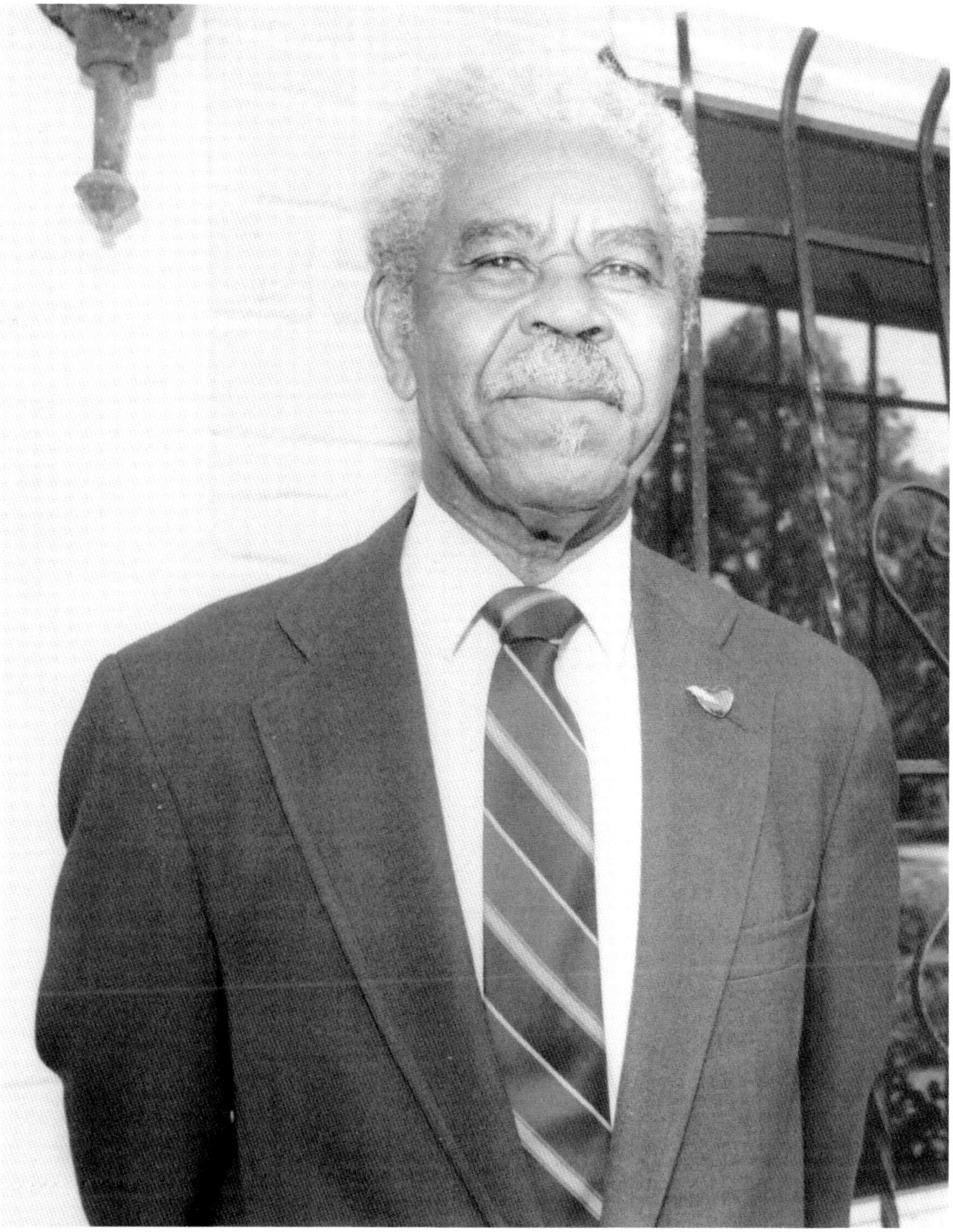

Thomas H. Poole Sr.

A tireless civil-rights activist, teacher, and football coach at Curtwright High School, Eustis resident T.H. Poole Sr. was president of the Tri-City NAACP for 26 years. He also served as Florida's chapter president for 10 years, was a member of the National NAACP board of directors, and was a Lake-Sumter Community College trustee. In 1994, Lake County commissioners voted to make December 31 "T.H. Poole Day" to honor his efforts ensuring that all people were treated equally. Poole also led an effort to build a new sanctuary for St. James African-Methodist Episcopal Church in Eustis. A bronze bust of Poole is on display at the Lake County Historical Museum. (Courtesy of the Mount Dora Historical Society.)

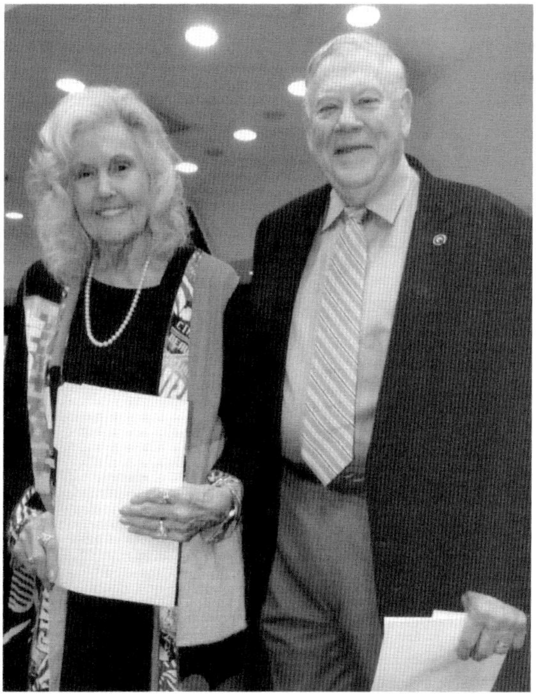

Evelyn and John Smith
Married 50 years, Evelyn and John Smith are one of Lake County's power couples. He is the second-generation head of Lake Mechanical Contractors and was named National Contractor of the Year in 2009. She is a four-time Eustis mayor and served on the city council for 20 years. She was recently named to the Lake County Women's Hall of Fame. (Courtesy of Evelyn Smith.)

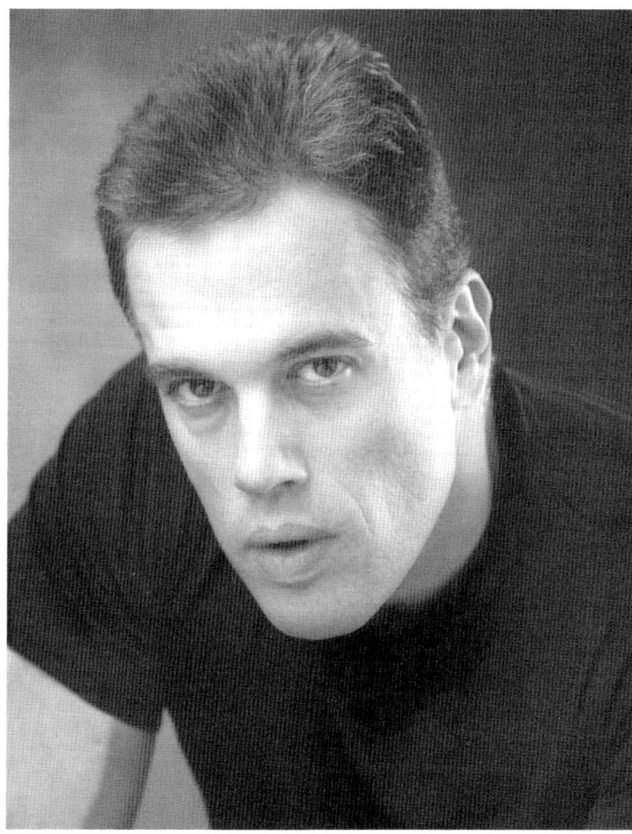

Tzimon Barto
Internationally renowned classical pianist Tzimon Barto, a Eustis native and son of John and Evelyn Smith, began piano studies at the age of five, wrote an opera at age nine, and studied at the Julliard School of Music. Barto, a bodybuilder who speaks seven languages, helped found an enrichment program at Round Lake Elementary that teaches children music, art, and ancient Greek. (Courtesy of Malcolm Yawn Photography.)

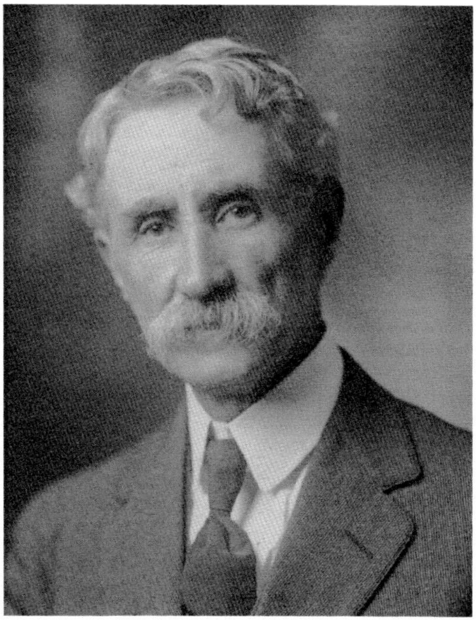

Edgar L. Ferran
Known as the "Grand Old Man of Eustis," Edgar "E.L." Ferran was entranced with the city's beauty and warm climate. He moved his family to Eustis in 1884 and founded E.L. Ferran Company Department Store. Ferran was an active member of his community and church. Ferran Park along Lake Eustis is named after him. (Courtesy of the Eustis Historical Museum and Preservation Society.)

Ferran Park
The 14-foot-tall sculpture of a heron in cattails erected within the fountain at Ferran Park honors one of the city's earliest business and community leaders, Edgar L. Ferran. Ferran Park is the city's first public park and sits on land purchased in 1913. The park's signature landmark is the Alice McClelland band shell, which is listed in the National Register of Historic Places. (Courtesy of Connie Fleetwood.)

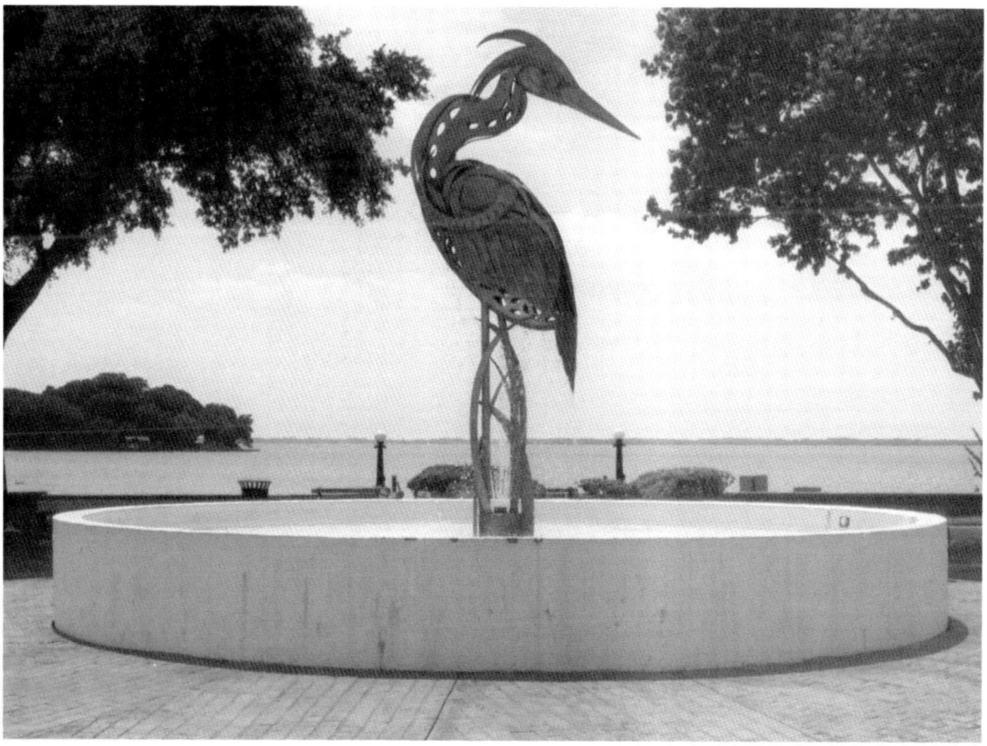

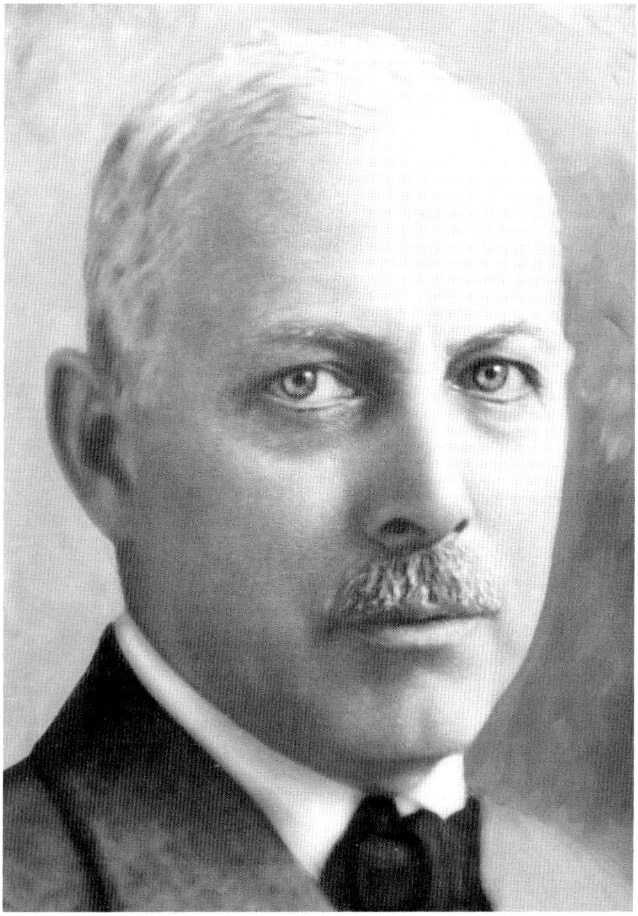

Frank Dan Waterman
After helping his uncle successfully market the Ideal Fountain Pen from their New York City headquarters, Waterman came to Eustis in 1901 in search of a winter residence. He lived at Blue Lake, and, with the urging of the town's residents, he decided to build the Fountain Inn to help establish Eustis as a major tourist destination. The hotel closed in 1936 because of the Great Depression. The next year, Waterman gave his hotel to a group of doctors, who turned it into Lake County Medical Center, depicted in the postcard below. The hospital, later named Waterman Memorial Hospital in honor of its benefactor, operated for 65 years in downtown Eustis. In 1992, Florida Hospital took over Waterman and relocated it to Tavares. (Right, courtesy of the Eustis Historical Museum and Preservation Society; below, courtesy of Clayton Bishop.)

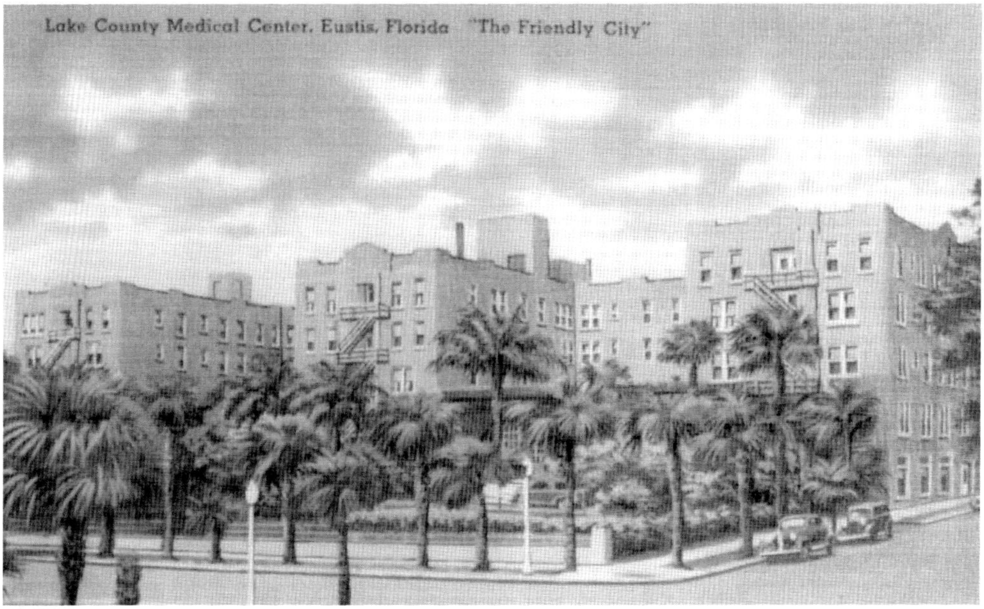

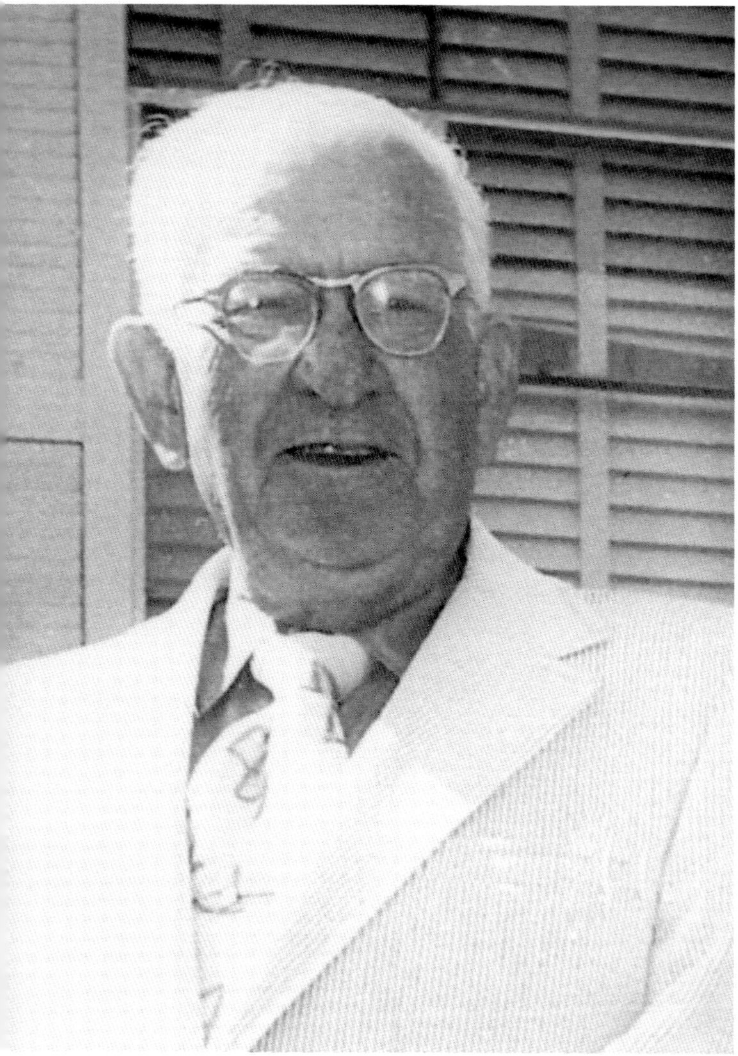

Dr. C.M. Tyre

Beloved physician Dr. C.M. Tyre, shown here, and his brother James Tyre, a citrus grower, moved to Eustis in 1925. C.M. Tyre and colleagues Dr. Louis Bowen and Dr. Rabun Williams practiced family medicine ranging from general medical care to delivering babies to performing surgery—often in the patient's home during the early days. Tyre was the personal physician of Frank D. Waterman, owner of the Fountain Inn Hotel. When the hotel failed during the Great Depression, Waterman turned over the top two floors to the doctors, to be used as a hospital. Later, the entire hotel was converted into a modern medical center, named Waterman Memorial Hospital. (Courtesy of the Eustis Historical Museum and Preservation Society.)

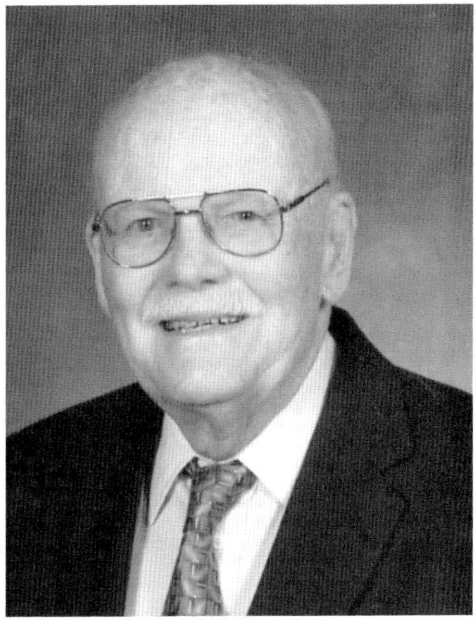

R. Eugene Isted

Second-generation banker R. Eugene Isted moved to Eustis in 1925 after his father took a position at First State Bank & Trust Company, the oldest bank in Lake County. Isted graduated from the University of Florida and served in World War II. He became executive vice president of the bank, retiring in 1984 as president and chief executive officer. (Courtesy of R. Eugene Isted.)

Judge William Andrew Milton III

Born in 1934 at his Grand Island home, W.A. "Bill" Milton Jr. was elected county and juvenile court judge in 1960 and served until his retirement in 1985. He continued to practice law until 1995. Well respected for his civic and benevolent contributions, Milton resides with his wife of 56 years, Mary Ellen, on the 100-year-old family farm. (Courtesy of Bill Milton.)

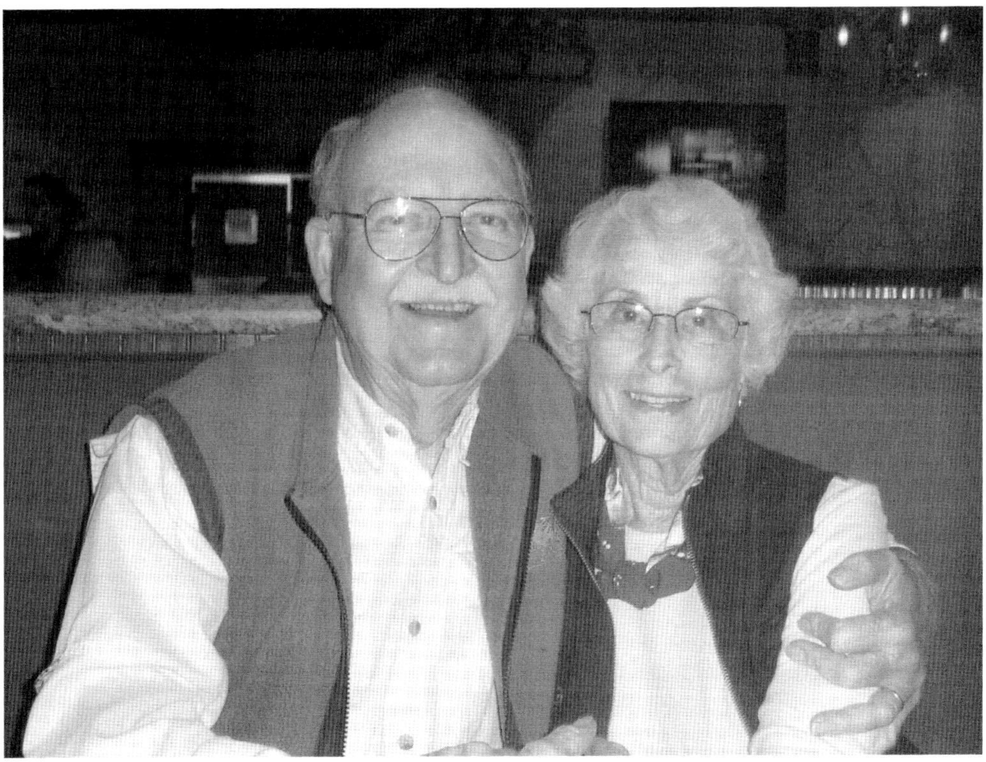

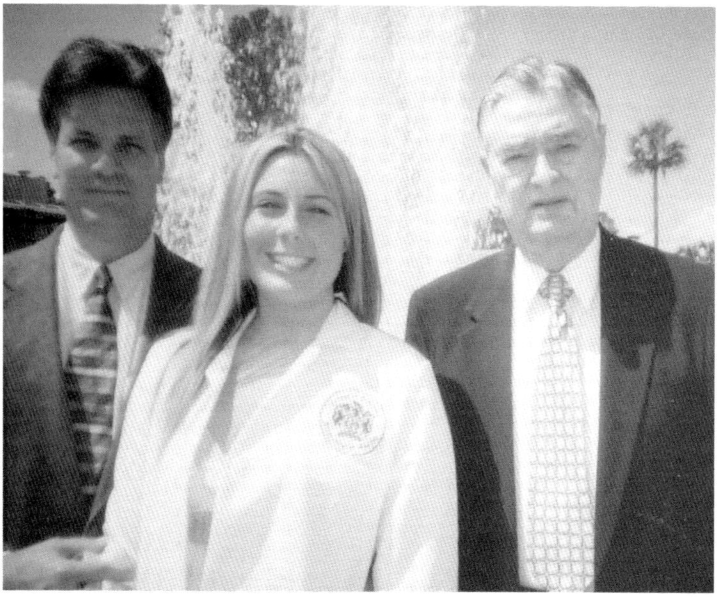

Legendary Pharmacists

Bay Pharmacy has been a fixture of downtown Eustis since 1955. George Warren Sr. began his career at Laws Pharmacy before purchasing Bay Pharmacy in 1962. George Warren Jr. purchased Lake Pharmacy nearby in 1983. The Warrens began major renovations in 2006 to the 100-year-old building that is home to Bay Pharmacy, pictured below, at the corner of Bay Street and Magnolia Avenue. Founder George Warren Sr. died in June 2007 before renovations were completed. Granddaughter Kristin graduated that year and continued the family tradition. Today, the two family-run pharmacies employ more than 35 "local legends in their own rights," including two of the founder's grandchildren, Ryan Warren and Ana Semento, and his daughter-in-law, Doris Warren. Shown in the above photograph are George Warren Jr. (left), Kristin Warren (center), and George Warren Sr. (Courtesy of George Warren Jr.)

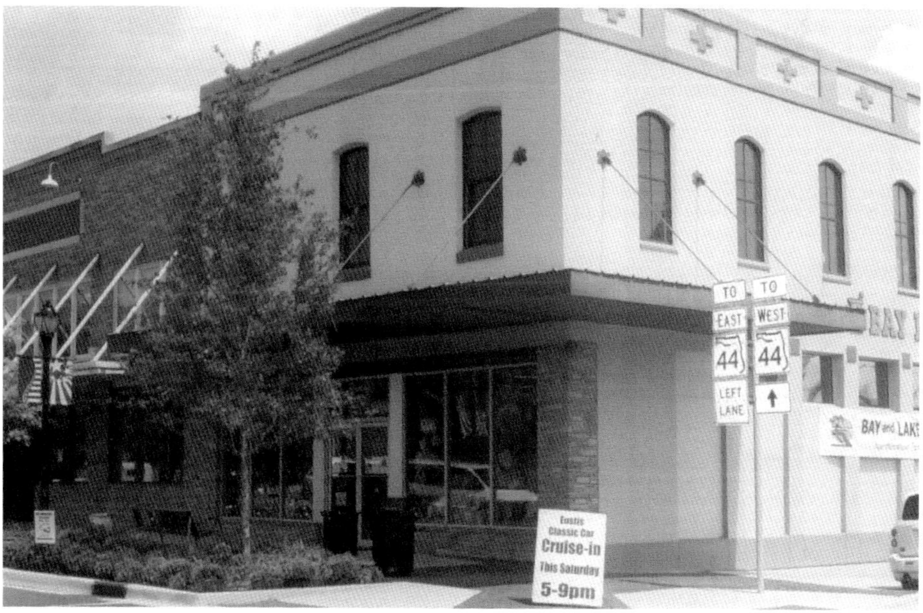

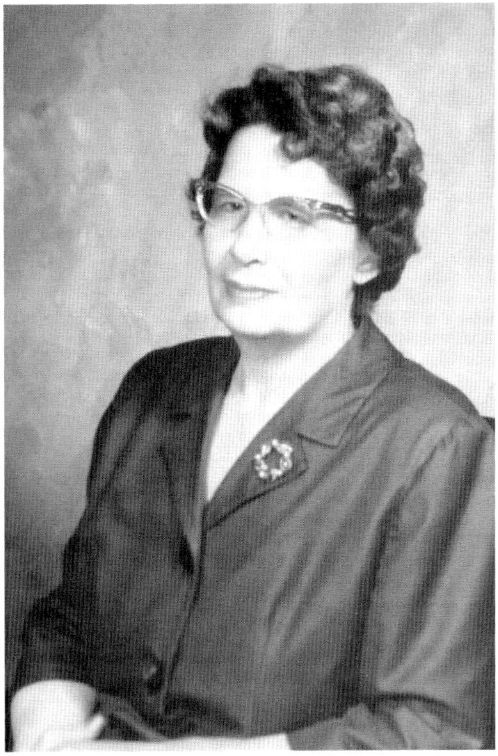

B.E. and Pauline Thompson

Married in 1935, B.E. Thompson (below) and his wife, Pauline (above), moved to Eustis in 1936 to open the B.E. Thompson Furniture Company. They eventually opened stores in Clermont, Mount Dora, and Winter Garden. The Thompsons were active business and civic leaders, especially when it came to economic development. They were members of the Downtown Village Merchant Association, Ferran Park Beautification Project, Eustis Little League, and First Baptist Church of Eustis. The B.E. Thompson float could always be seen in the Washington Day Festival Parade, celebrated annually since 1902. Pauline Thompson was respected for her experience and insights when it came to business. She served on the board of directors of First National Bank and Barnett Bank of Lake County, and was the Orange Queen in 1982. (Courtesy of the Thompson family.)

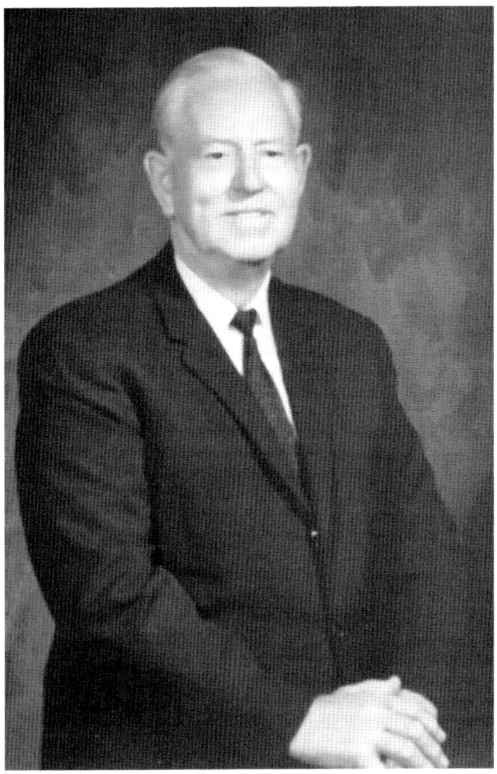

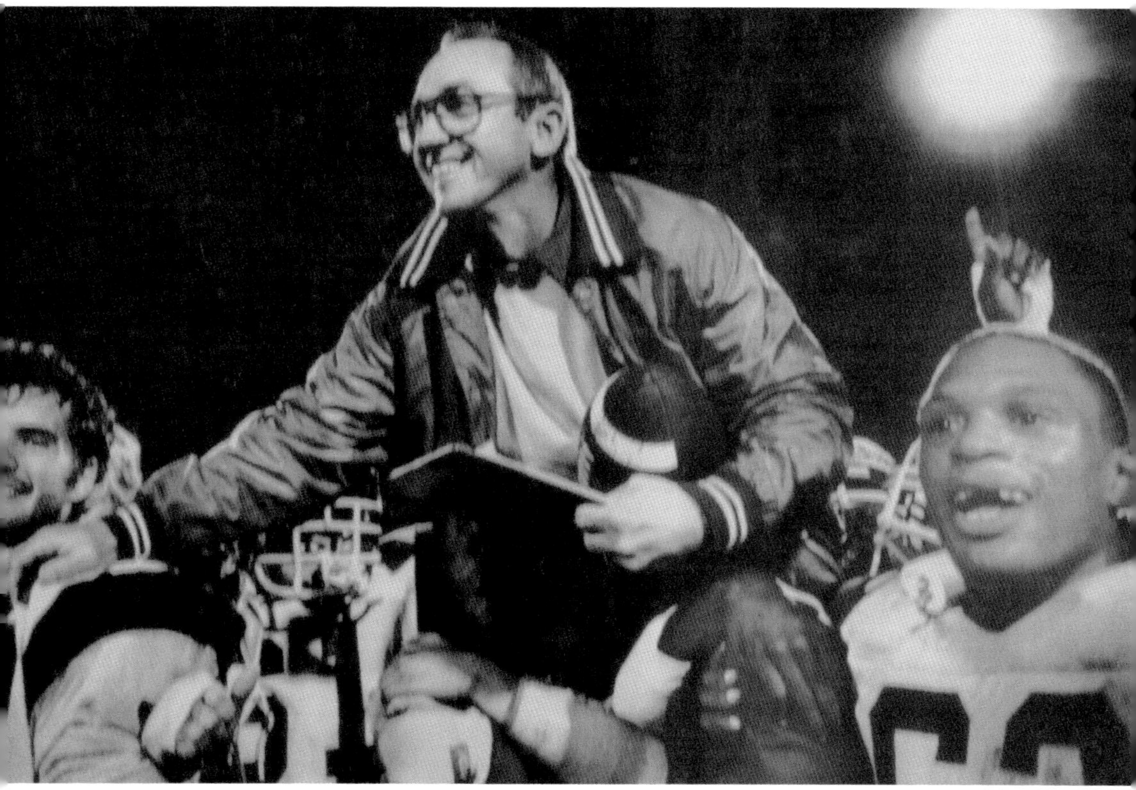

Coach Clark Blake

Renowned football coach Clark Blake led the 1983 Eustis High School Panthers to the 2-A State High School Football Championship. Blake began teaching and coaching in 1971. Well respected for being a positive role model, he coached football for 15 years, coached soccer for 5 years, and taught at Eustis High School for 32 years. Students recall fondly how Blake dressed in costumes on Fridays and simulated game shows to review students for tests. In 1990, he collaborated with Jack Prickett on a five-year project in which students bought, renovated, and sold houses. He was awarded Best Economics and Private Enterprise in Education, voted Coach of the Year in 1983, and named Kiwanis Citizen of the Year in 1992. Shown here are, from left to right, Bill Bailey, Coach Clark Blake, and Wayne Perry. (Courtesy of Clark Blake.)

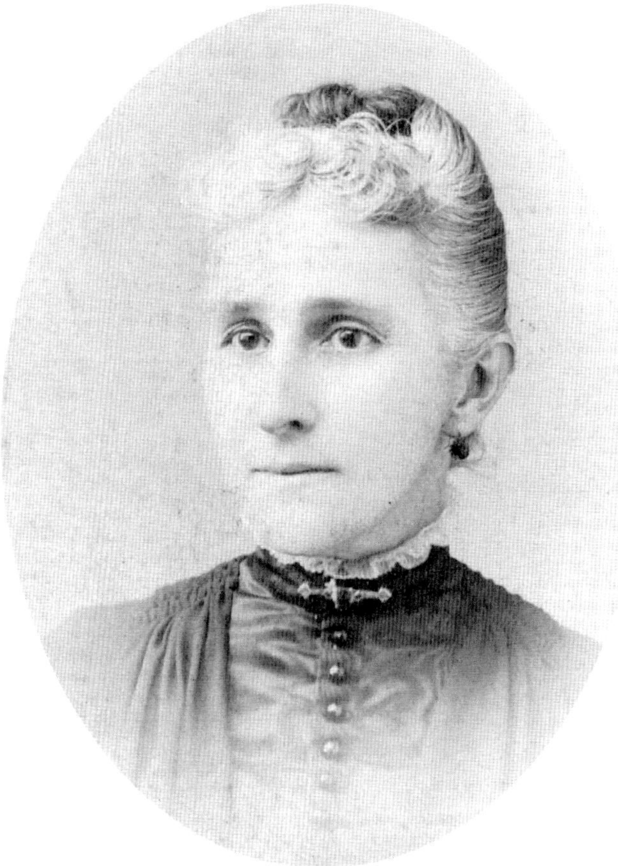

Georgia Risley Tremain
Georgia Tremain and her husband, Ross Clark "R.C." Tremain, moved to near Lake Dora from Blue Earth, Minnesota, where he had been a pharmacist. He became the community's postmaster, and the town was named Royellou after their three children: Roy, Ella, and Louis. In 1883, the town changed its name to Mount Dora. (Courtesy of Roy Tremain.)

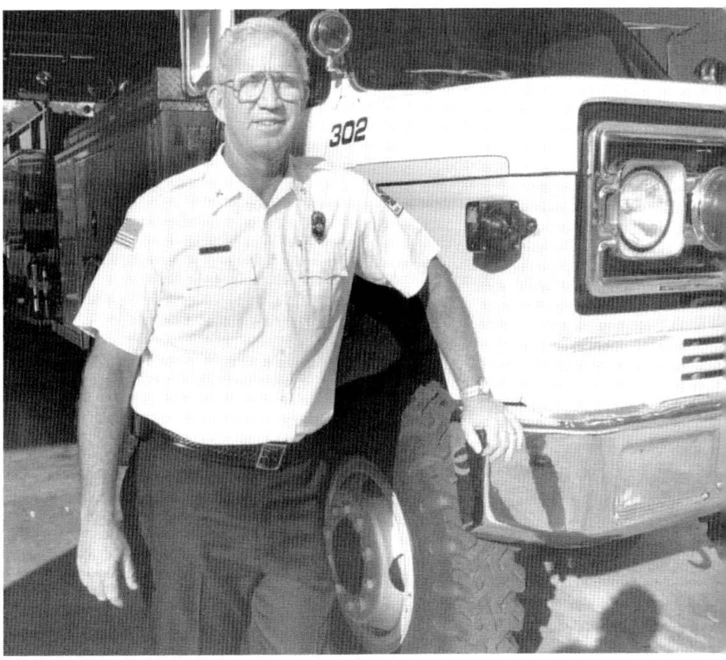

Roy Tremain
Great-grandson of early Mount Dora settler R.C. Tremain, Roy Tremain is a 1964 graduate of Mount Dora High School and a Marine veteran who served in Vietnam. He was the first firefighter/EMT the city hired. After serving 24 years, he became captain of the Eustis Fire Department. He served for 13 years and retired as fire chief in 2009. (Courtesy of the Mount Dora Historical Society.)

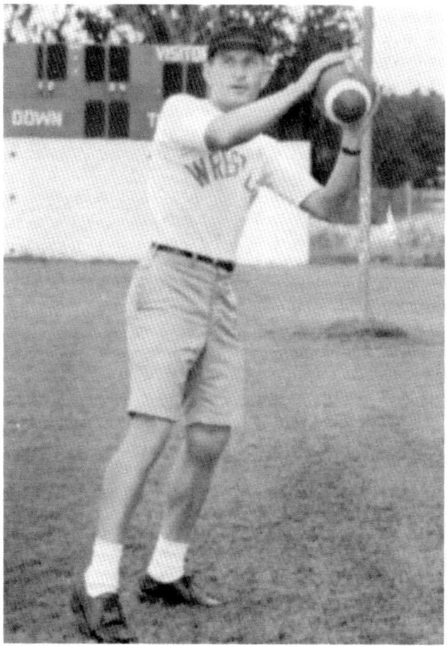

Coach Dan Spear
Legendary Mount Dora High School football coach Dan Spear came to the city in 1948 to coach football and teach math. He compiled an enviable record of 131-54-9 that included an undefeated season in 1951 and three straight conference titles. His career was featured in the book *A Roast for Coach Dan Spear: Small Town Football Dreams from Florida's '50s*. (Courtesy of the Mount Dora High School Yearbook.)

Daniel Douglas Roseborough
Born in 1897, Daniel Douglas Roseborough earned his bachelor's, master's, and law degrees at Stetson University. "Prof," as the Mount Dora principal was respectfully known, oversaw the growth of the town's schools from four buildings to a campus with dozens of classrooms, a gymnasium, cafetorium, and athletic field. Roseborough Elementary School, now called Montessori at Roseborough, was named in his honor. (Courtesy of Connie Fleetwood.)

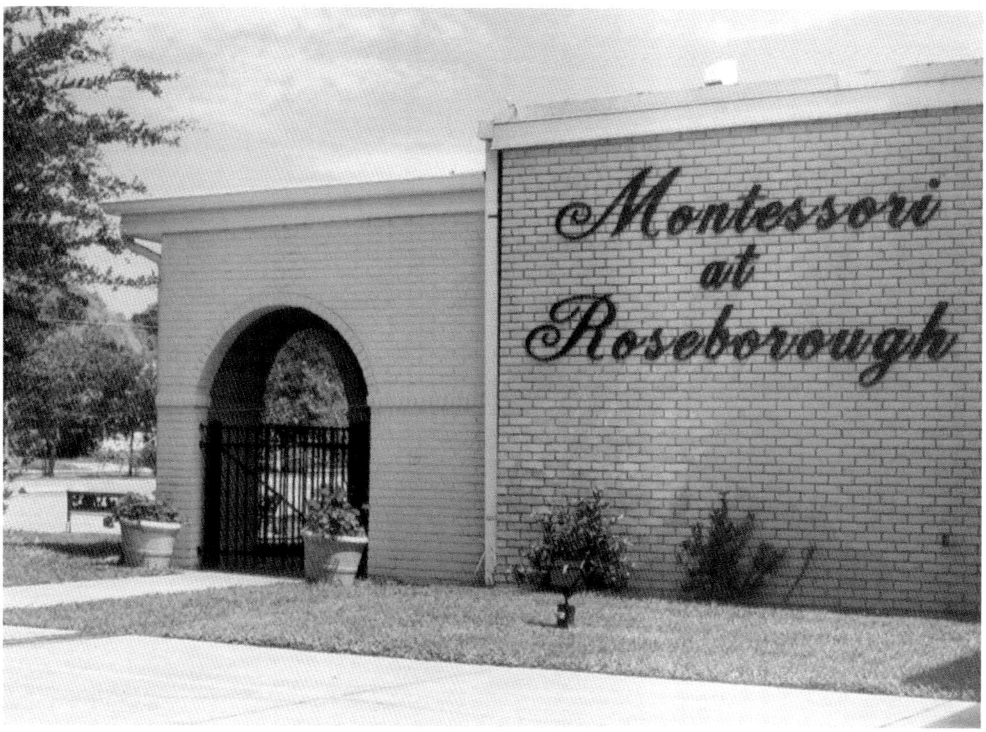

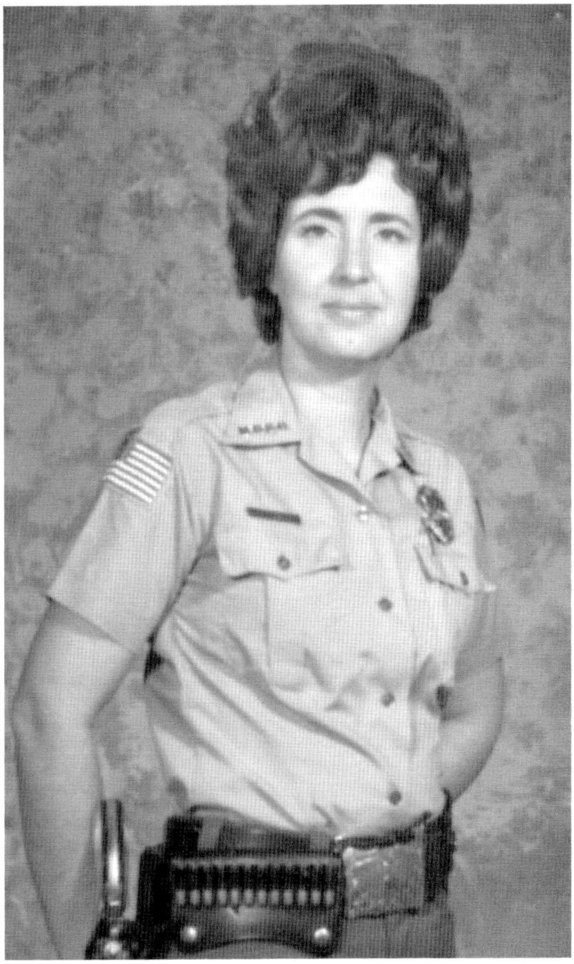

Jo Tucker
Lake County's first female detective, and 1997 Women's Hall of Fame inductee, Jo Tucker moved to Mount Dora from Kentucky after her husband accepted a position with the city's police department. In 1971, Tucker attended the Lake Tech police academy and was hired after graduation by the Mount Dora Police Department. She rose to the rank of lieutenant during her eight-year career. (Courtesy of Jo Tucker.)

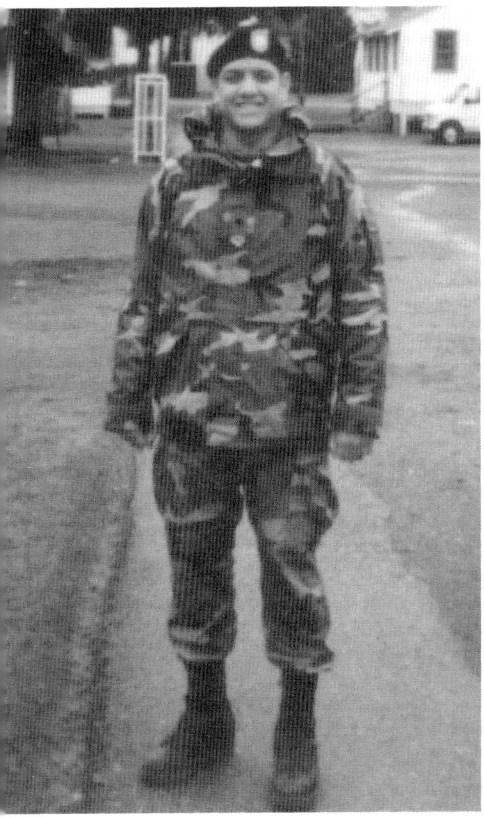

Eric Ulysses Ramirez
Sgt. Eric Ramirez, assigned to the 670th Military Police Company in the Army National Guard, died on February 12, 2004, after his unit was attacked while on patrol near Abu Ghraib prison in Iraq. Ramirez was a 1991 Mount Dora High School graduate who was married and a father to two children. A highway and post office were named in his honor. (Courtesy of the Ramirez family.)

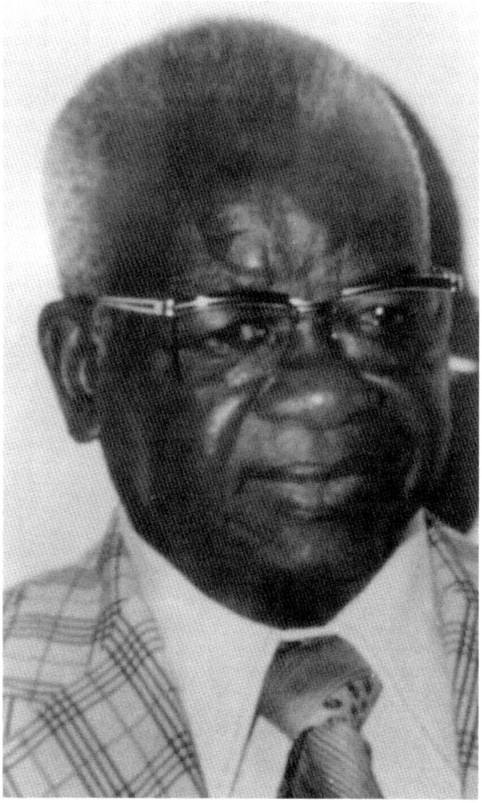

Cauley Lott
Attending school during the day and working at night, Cauley Lott earned his bachelor's degree at Florida A&M University in Tallahassee and his master's degree from the University of Pittsburgh. In 1936, he became a math teacher and principal at Milner-Rosenwald Academy in Mount Dora, where he remained for 34 years. He served 10 years on the city council. (Courtesy of Mount Dora Historical Society.)

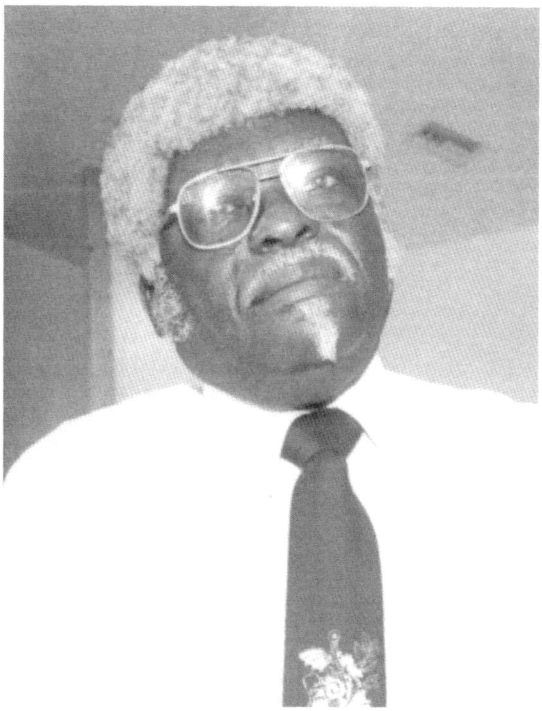

Rev. Dr. R. Eugene Burley
Born and raised in Mount Dora, the Reverend Dr. R. Eugene Burley served in the Army Air Force and pastored churches in Atlanta and New York. He earned three master's degrees and a doctorate. Burley returned to Mount Dora, where he served as the first African American president of the chamber of commerce and chairman of the Northeast Community Redevelopment Board. (Courtesy of the Mount Dora Historical Society.)

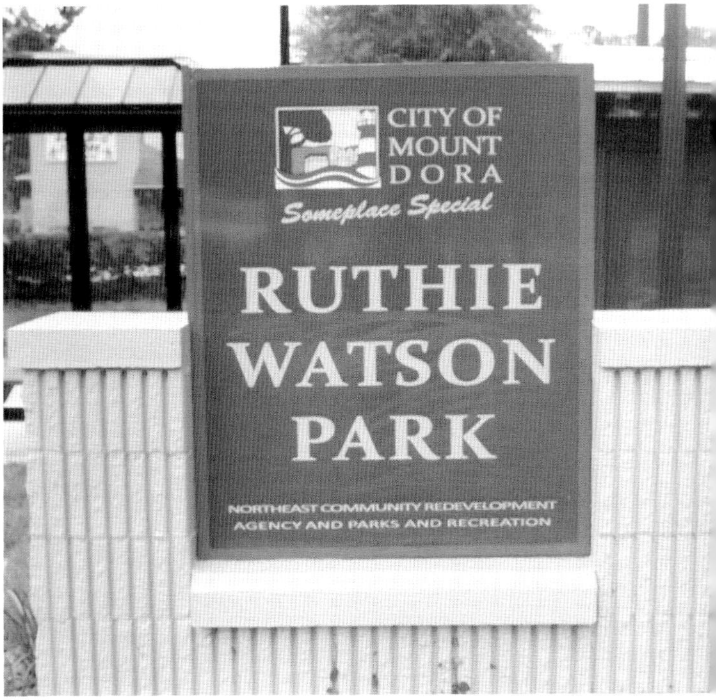

Ruthie Watson, Educator
Beloved Mount Dora teacher and community leader Ruthie Ann Watson graduated from Bethune-Cookman College and New York University. During the 1950s, Watson came to Mount Dora to teach at Milner-Rosenwald Academy and was one of the first black educators to teach at Roseborough Elementary School. Watson devoted her life to community service. Ruthie Watson Park is named in her honor. (Courtesy of Connie Fleetwood.)

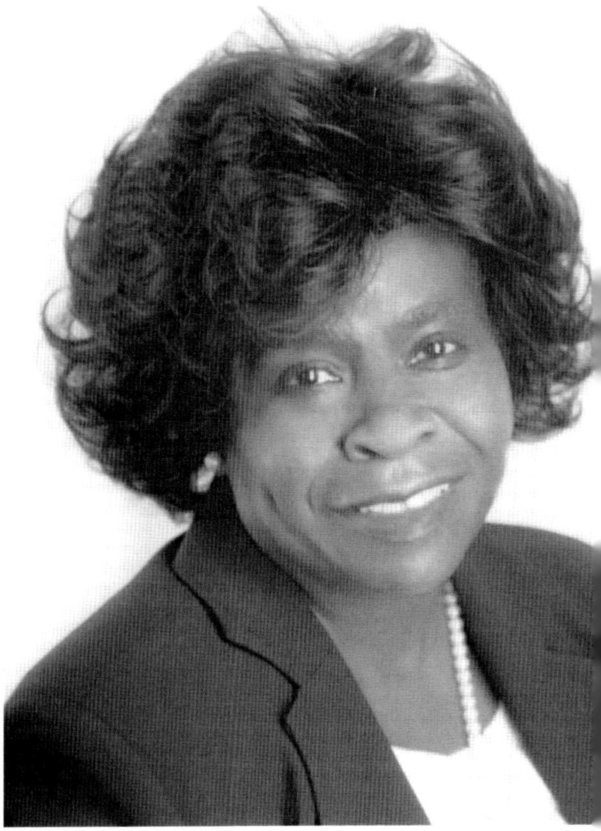

Vivian Owens, Author
The daughter of the Reverend Charles and Essie Mae Williams, Vivian Owens is the author of nine books, including *The Mount Dorans: African American History Notes of a Florida Town*. One of her books won a Writer's Digest Best Children's Book Award, and she wrote a newspaper column titled "Parenting for Education." She is a graduate of Tuskegee University and James Madison University. (Courtesy of Vivian Owens.)

John Philip Donnelly, First Mayor
Arriving from Pittsburgh in 1879, John Philip "J.P." Donnelly (right) lived briefly in Eustis before moving to the Lake Dora area, where he started acquiring real estate. In 1891, he married Annie McDonald. The couple joined properties that developed into Mount Dora's downtown and waterfront district. In 1883, the couple partnered with John Alexander and Col. John McDonald to build the Alexander House, which was the predecessor of Lakeside Inn. In 1910, Mount Dora was incorporated and Donnelly was elected the town's first mayor. The Donnellys are tied to another landmark. In 1893, J.P. Donnelly built the Queen Anne–style house shown below for his wife. After his death, the local Masonic lodge purchased the home, which is listed in the National Register of Historic Places. (Right, courtesy of the Mount Dora Historical Society; below, courtesy of Connie Fleetwood.)

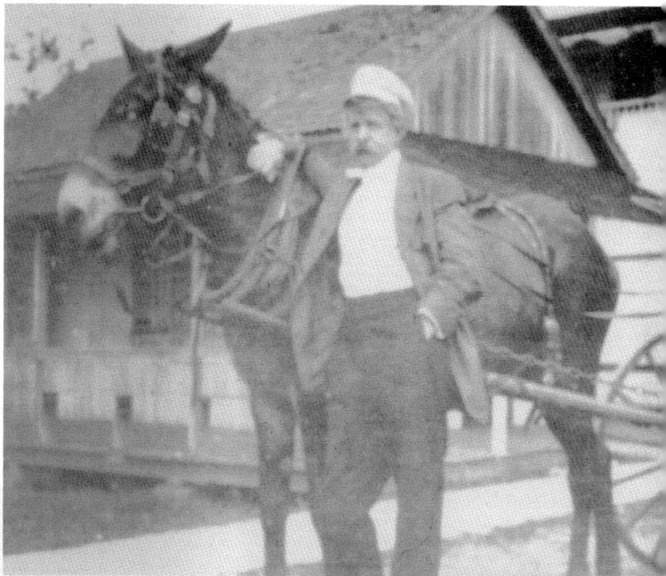

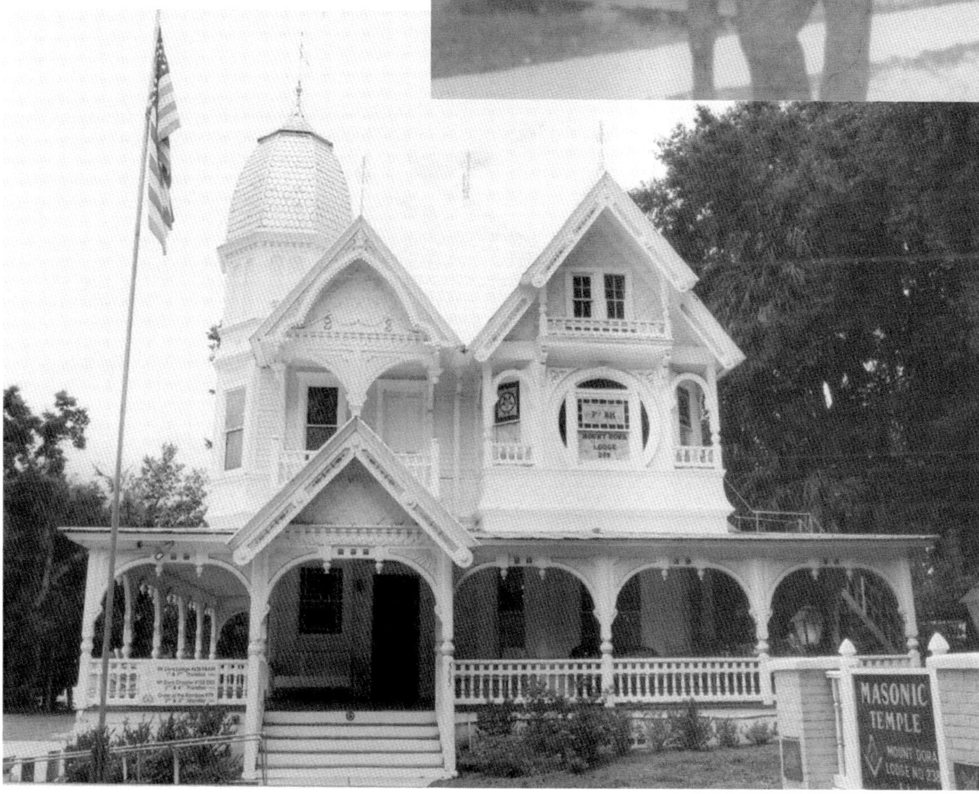

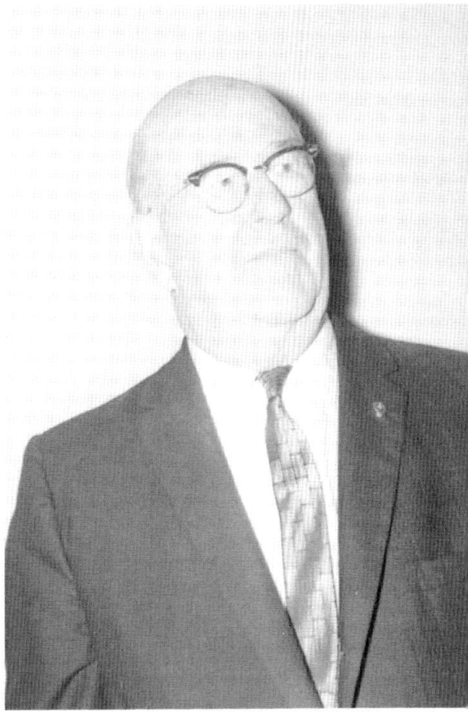

George White Sr.

Born in 1896 in Jacksonville, Florida, George White left his position at the Federal Reserve Bank in 1927 to become executive vice president of the First National Bank of Mount Dora. He was later promoted to president and served for 30 years until he became chairman of the board in 1966. White also helped found Peoples State Bank in Groveland, where he served as chairman of the board. He was active in numerous civic organizations, including the Mount Dora Chamber of Commerce, where he served as president for 26 years; Kiwanis, where he had perfect attendance for 48 years; and the American Legion, where he served as commander. Pictured below is First National Bank of Mount Dora as it appears today. (Right, courtesy of John D. Pease III; below, courtesy of Connie Fleetwood.)

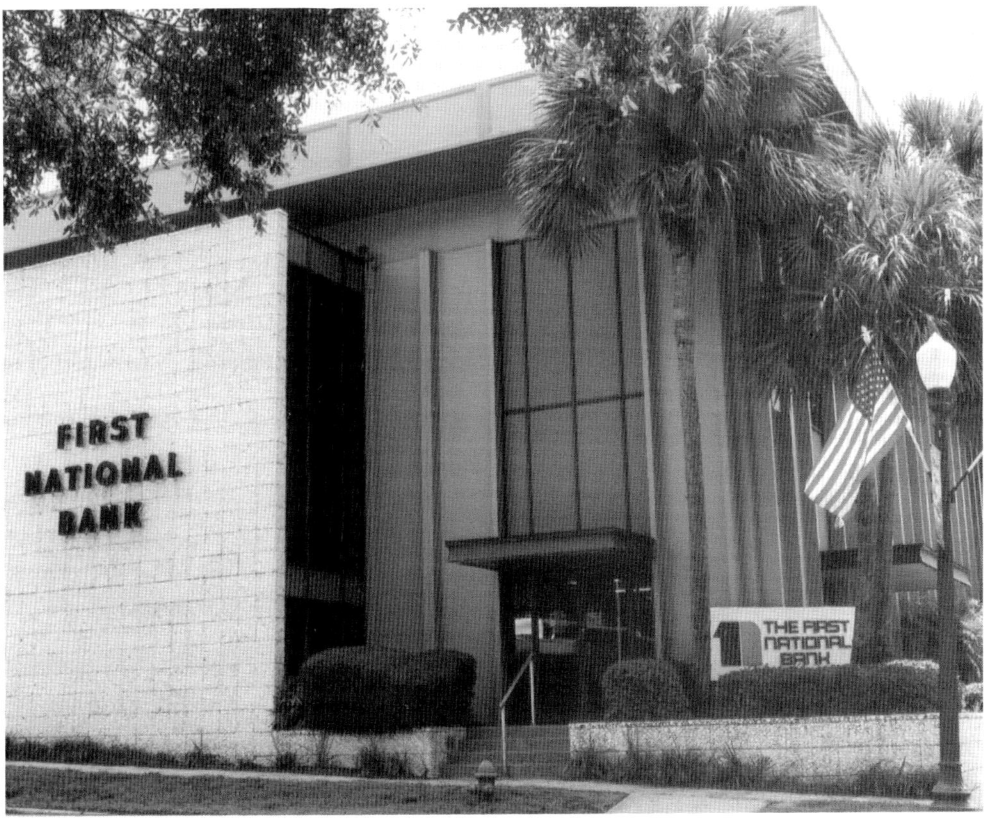

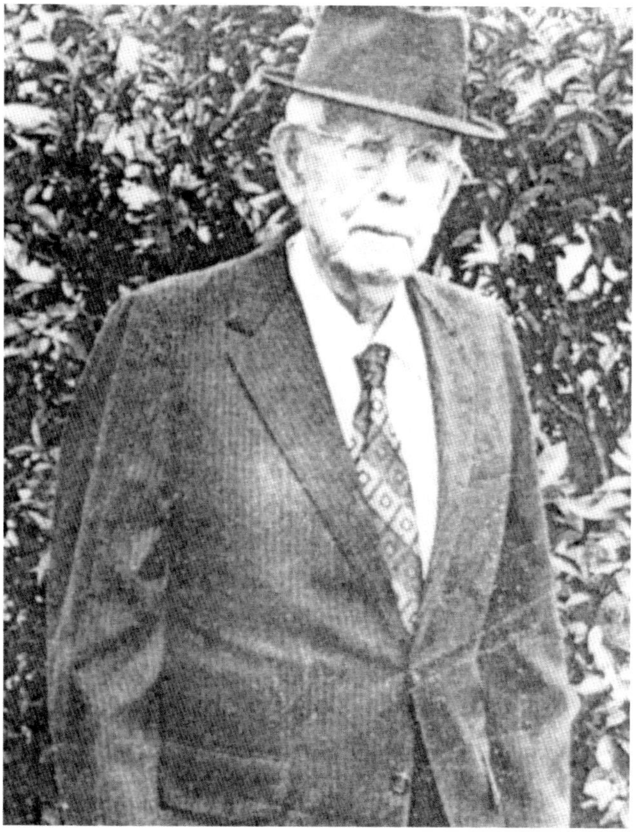

James Simpson
Born in 1878 to David and Mary Simpson, the first homesteaders in Mount Dora, James Simpson spent most of his life in the citrus industry. He was a grower, built a packinghouse, and founded the Mount Dora Citrus Association. He was the first president of the Mount Dora Bank and Trust Company and served on the city council. He built an ice plant and other significant buildings. (Courtesy of *The Daily Commercial.*)

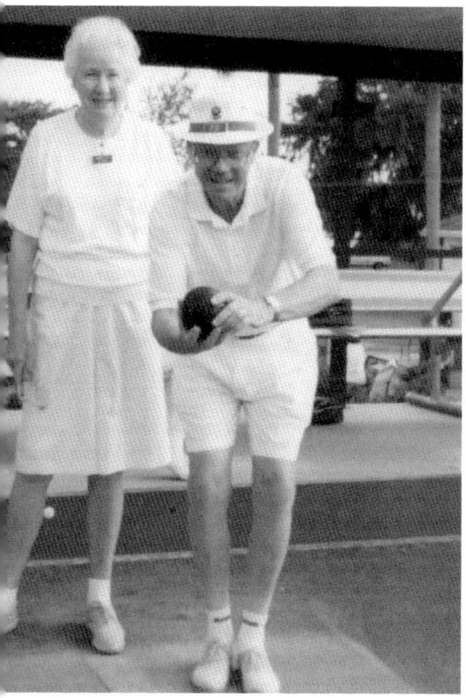

James Laux, Historian, Author, and Lawn Bowler
Local historian and author James Laux (right), and his wife, Barbara, are active members of the Mount Dora Lawn Bowling Club, which was founded in 1928. Laux is a retired professor of history from the University of Cincinnati. His published works include *Mount Dora, Florida: A Short History* and *A History of the Mount Dora Lawn Bowling Club.* (Courtesy of the Mount Dora Historical Society.)

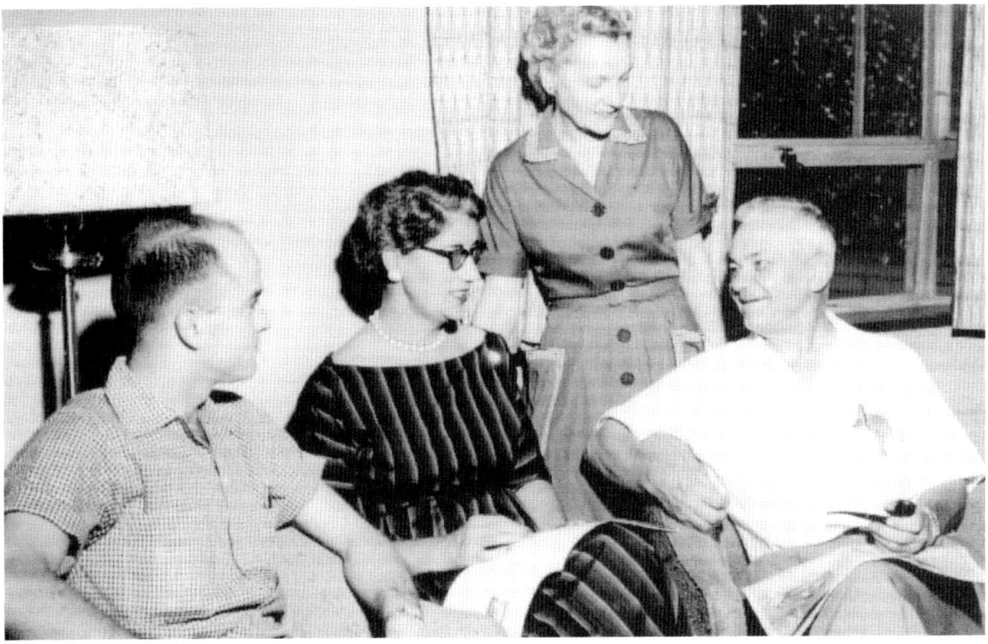

Mabel Reese, Fearless Journalist

Mabel Norris Reese (center) talks to fellow journalists at the 1956 conference of the International Society of Weekly Newspaper Editors. Reese and her husband, Paul, purchased the Mount Dora *Topic* in 1947 and published the weekly newspaper until 1960. She was honored by fellow journalists for taking on controversial, social-justice issues facing Lake County. (Courtesy of the International Society of Weekly Newspaper Editors.)

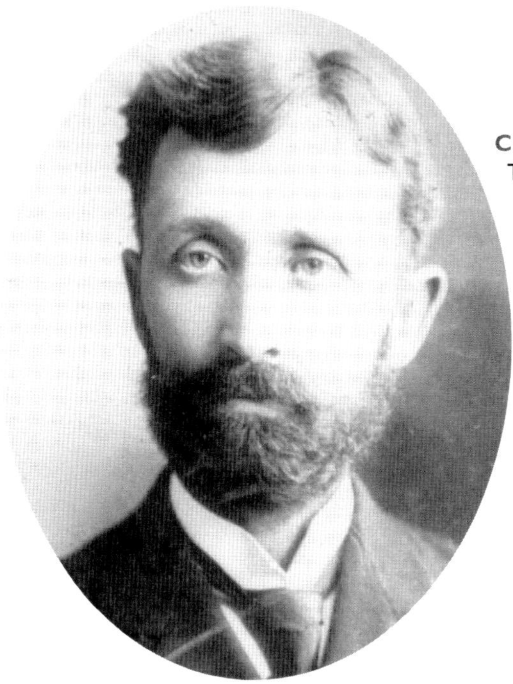

Charles Edgerton

Traveling to Mount Dora from Philadelphia for the first time in 1895, Charles Edgerton stayed at the Lake House, which became the Lakeside Inn. In 1924, he and a group of investors purchased the popular inn. He was an inventor and engineer who built power plants throughout the eastern United States. His son, Richard, became manager of Lakeside Inn. His other son, David, wrote *Memories of Mount Dora and Lake County* and helped lead fundraising for the current library. (Courtesy of the Mount Dora Historical Society.)

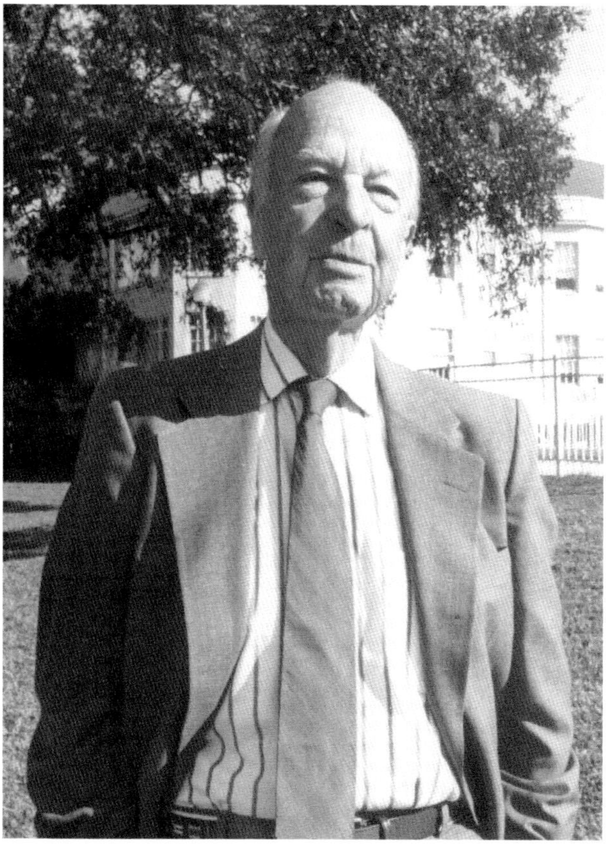

Richard "Dick" Edgerton
Standing in front of the elegant Lakeside Inn is longtime president and general manager Dick Edgerton. Early inn visitors were mostly sports enthusiasts who enjoyed fishing and snake hunts. During the Roaring Twenties, a trap door in the lobby stirred speculation that the inn (below) was a speakeasy. Edgerton built an Olympic-sized pool and guesthouses that were dedicated by Pres. Calvin Coolidge. Other visitors included Thomas Edison and Henry Ford. The inn was painted pink for the filming of *Honky Tonk Freeway*. Edgerton managed the inn for more than 40 years. He served four terms as the national director of the American Hotel and Motel Association. Lakeside Inn is the oldest continuously operated hotel in Florida and is listed in the National Register of Historic Places. (Right, courtesy of Mount Dora Historical Society; below, courtesy of Clayton Bishop.)

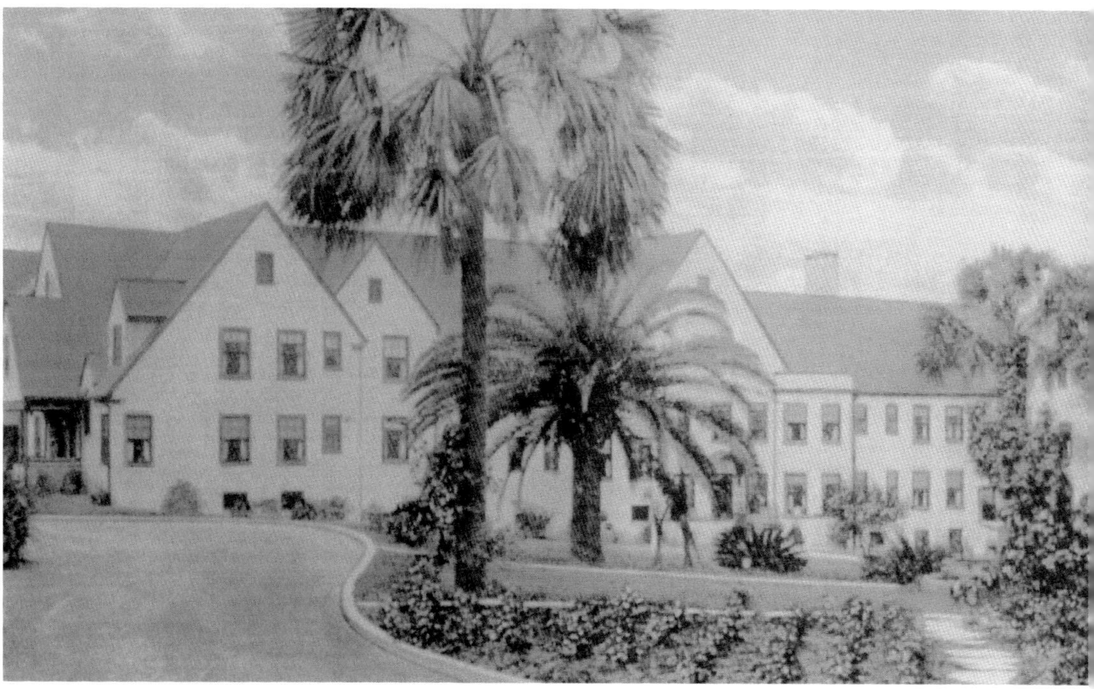

Nathan Trowell

In 1856, Nathan Trowell founded Umatilla on the edge of the "Big Scrub," Ocala National Forest. He was a merchant and the town's first postmaster. He also built a gristmill and cotton gin. He and his first wife, Rebecca, had four sons. After her death, he had nine more children with his second wife, Sevenah. Great-granddaughter Evelyn Sebree was the Umatilla Historical Society's first president. (Courtesy of Evelyn "Sis" Sebree.)

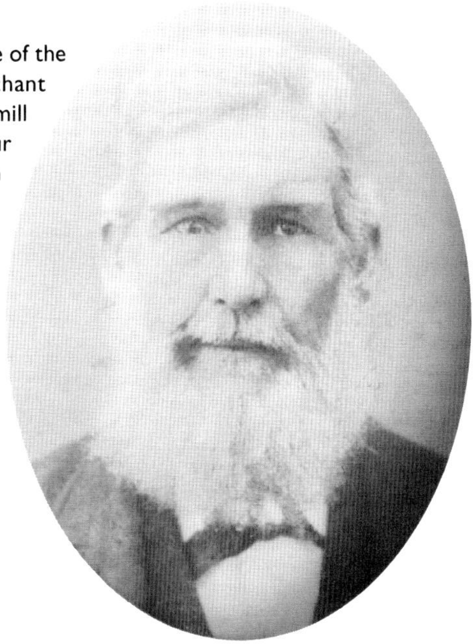

Robert Collins, Citrus King

Robert Lee Collins came to Umatilla in 1884 with a suit of clothes, $10, and a strong work ethic. By the 1920s, his citrus empire made him one of the area's wealthiest men. Pictured here are, from left to right, (first row) William Devault, Robert Trowell, and Evelyn Louise; (second row) Robert Lee, Catherine Drucilla Trowell, Harry Lee, Bena Bertha, and Paul Eugene. (Courtesy of Evelyn "Sis" Sebree.)

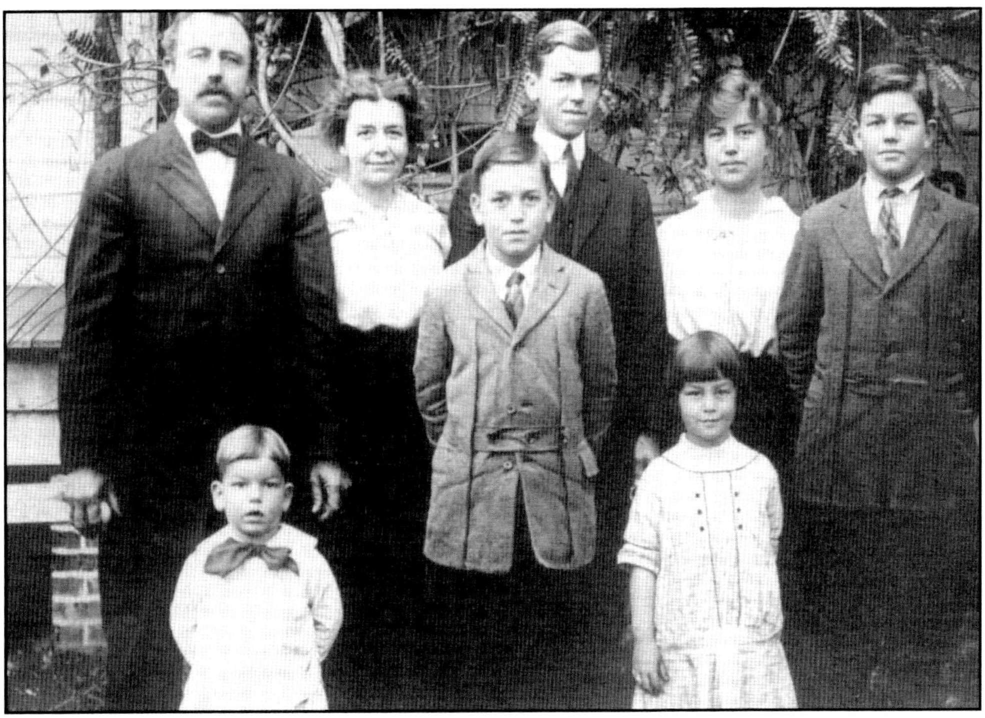

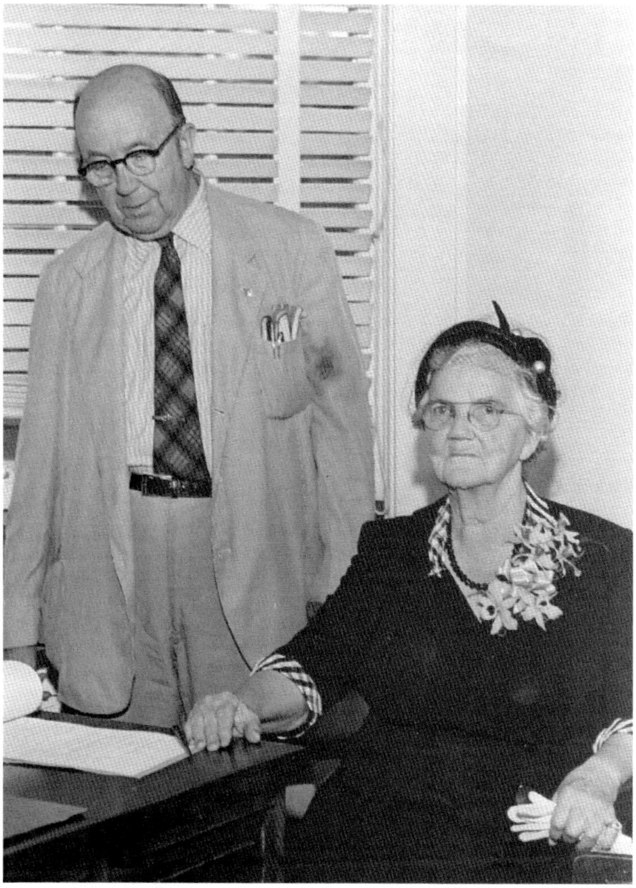

Harry-Anna Crippled Children's Home

Eustis financier Harry Miller and his wife, Anna, (left) owned a large, three-story hotel in Umatilla called the Rowebuilt Hotel. David Sholtz, a friend of the Millers, talked them into donating the hotel to the Florida Elks so that the building could be turned into a much-needed hospital where disabled children could get help for free. The Harry-Anna Home for Crippled Children in Umatilla was dedicated on November 1, 1931. Decades later, the home became a pediatric orthopedic hospital. Throughout the institution's lifespan, the Elks ensured that children were admitted for free. Below, an Elks chaplain paying tribute to the many donors described the outpouring of help as "such a rallying as this part of the country has never seen in intensity, in earnestness, and in love." (Courtesy of the Lake County Historical Society.)

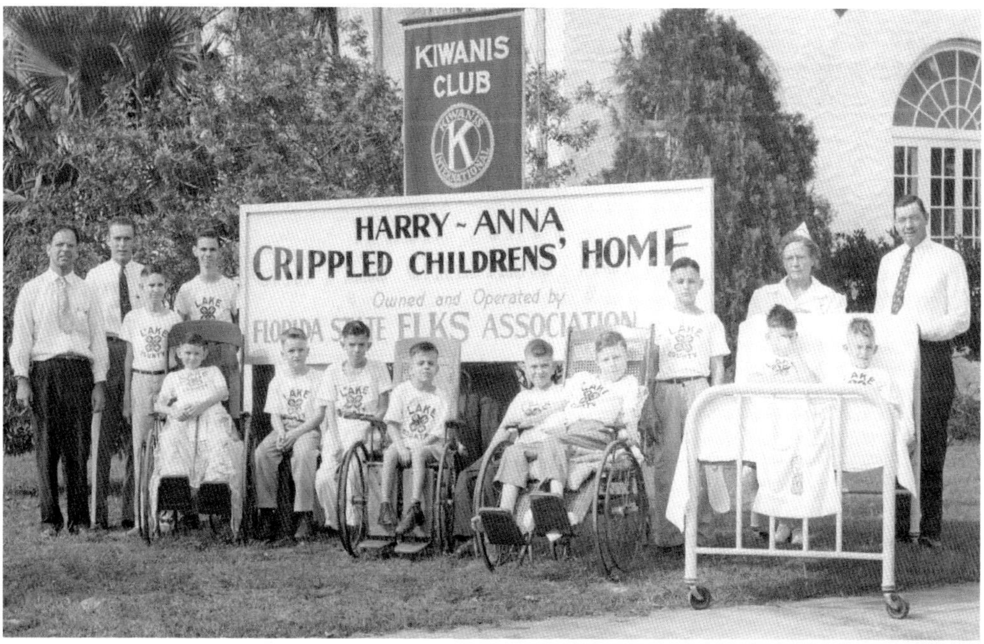

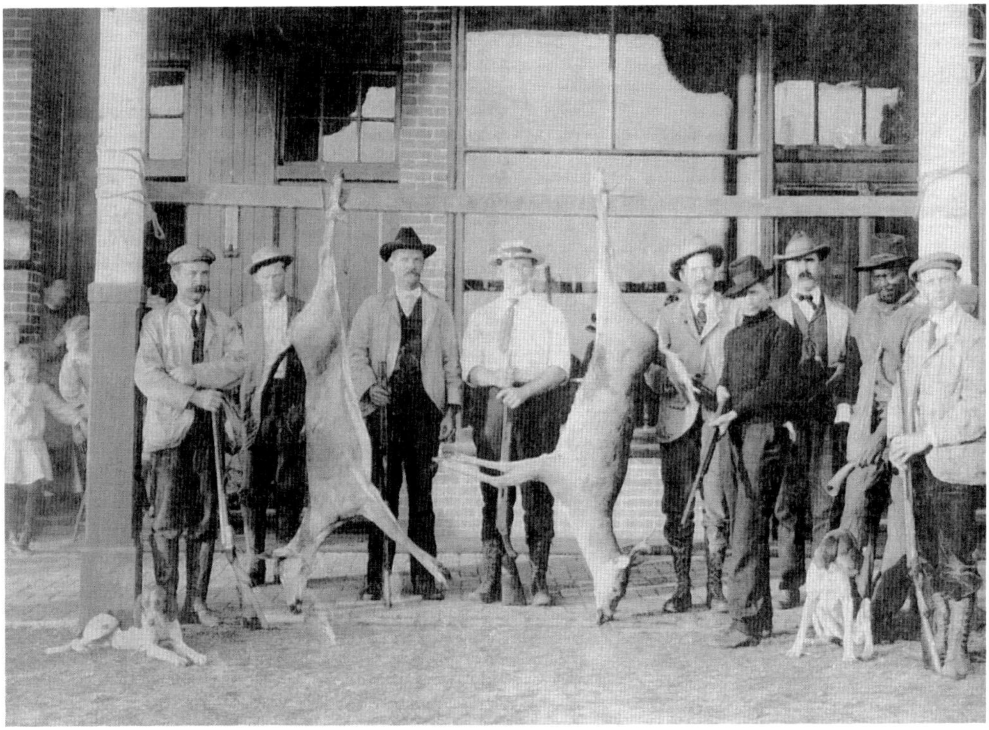

Carlie Avant "C.A." Vaughn Sr.
Folklore has it that C.A. Vaughn came to Umatilla in 1900 with a change of clothes, a bottle of liquor, and a .45 pistol. In a scant 15 years, he was mayor of the town known as a "Sportsman's Paradise" and the gateway to Ocala National Forest. Vaughn is pictured above second from left with close hunting friend Harry C. Duncan (third from left). (Courtesy of Harryette-Anne Duncan.)

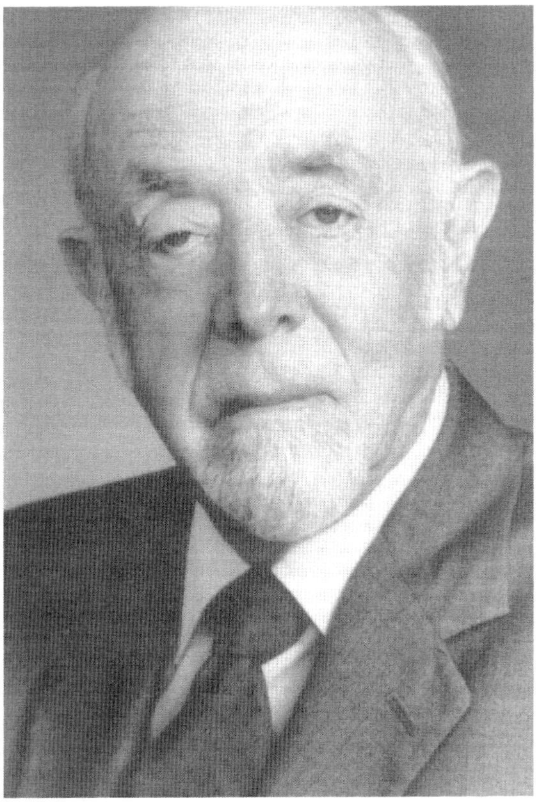

John Nelson, Golden Gem
A third-generation citrus grower, John "Jack" Nelson spent 42 years at Golden Gem Growers, which was founded in 1946 by his father. Nelson served on the Florida Citrus Mutual Board. He developed the citrus pallet box and recognized "pounds solids" as a basis for valuing a grove's production. He was inducted into the Florida Citrus Hall of Fame. (Courtesy of the Florida Citrus Hall of Fame.)

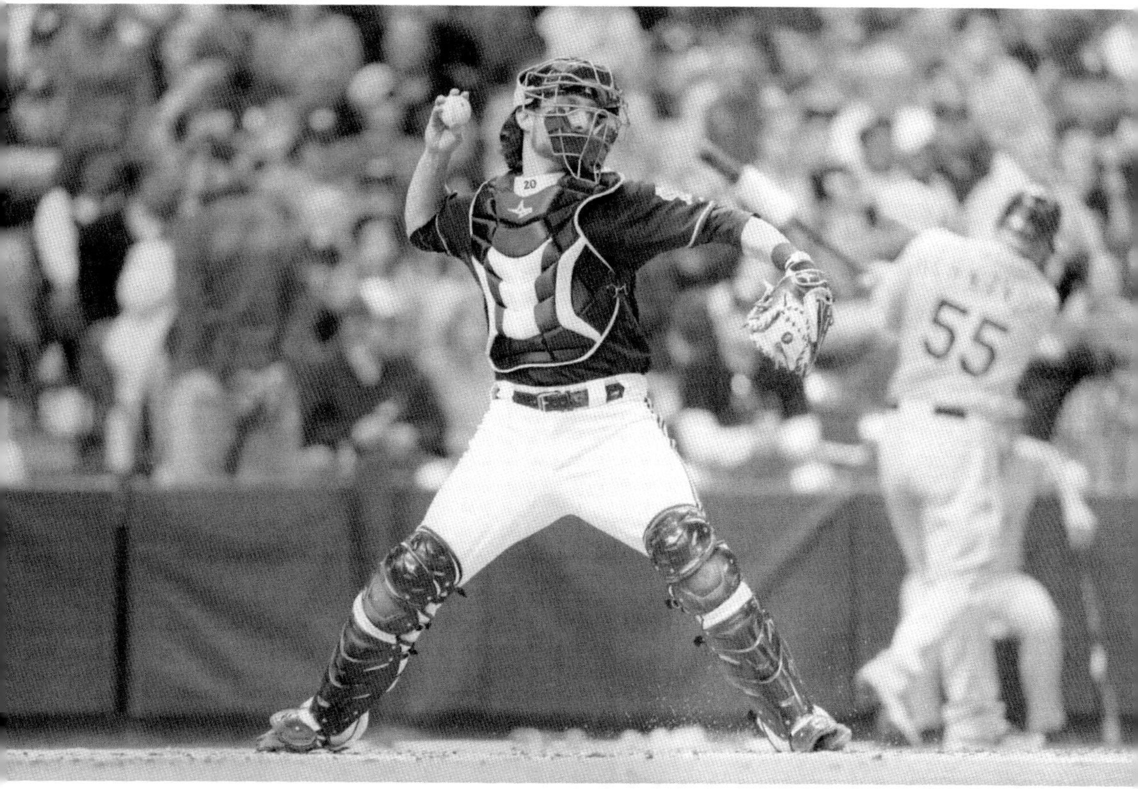

Jonathan Lucroy

Umatilla High School retired its No. 6 baseball jersey in 2011 to honor alumnus Jonathan Lucroy, a talented catcher for the Milwaukee Brewers. At the University of Louisiana at Lafayette, he set school records for doubles, runs batted in, and total bases. He was drafted by the Brewers in 2007 and was a postseason all-star. Lucroy finished the 2011 season with 12 home runs. He is the first catcher in Major League Baseball recorded history to have two games in a single season with seven or more RBIs. His father, brother, and cousin were also standout baseball players. (Courtesy of the Milwaukee Brewers.)

Albert Sharp "A.S." Matlack

In 1875, A.S. Matlack settled in Sorrento. He was the town's first railroad station agent and postmaster, operating the post office out of his general store. When Sorrento was part of Orange County, Matlack was the deputy tax collector. A surveyor and draftsman, he also platted and mapped the city. Matlack wrote newspaper articles published throughout the United States. (Courtesy of the Lake County Historical Society.)

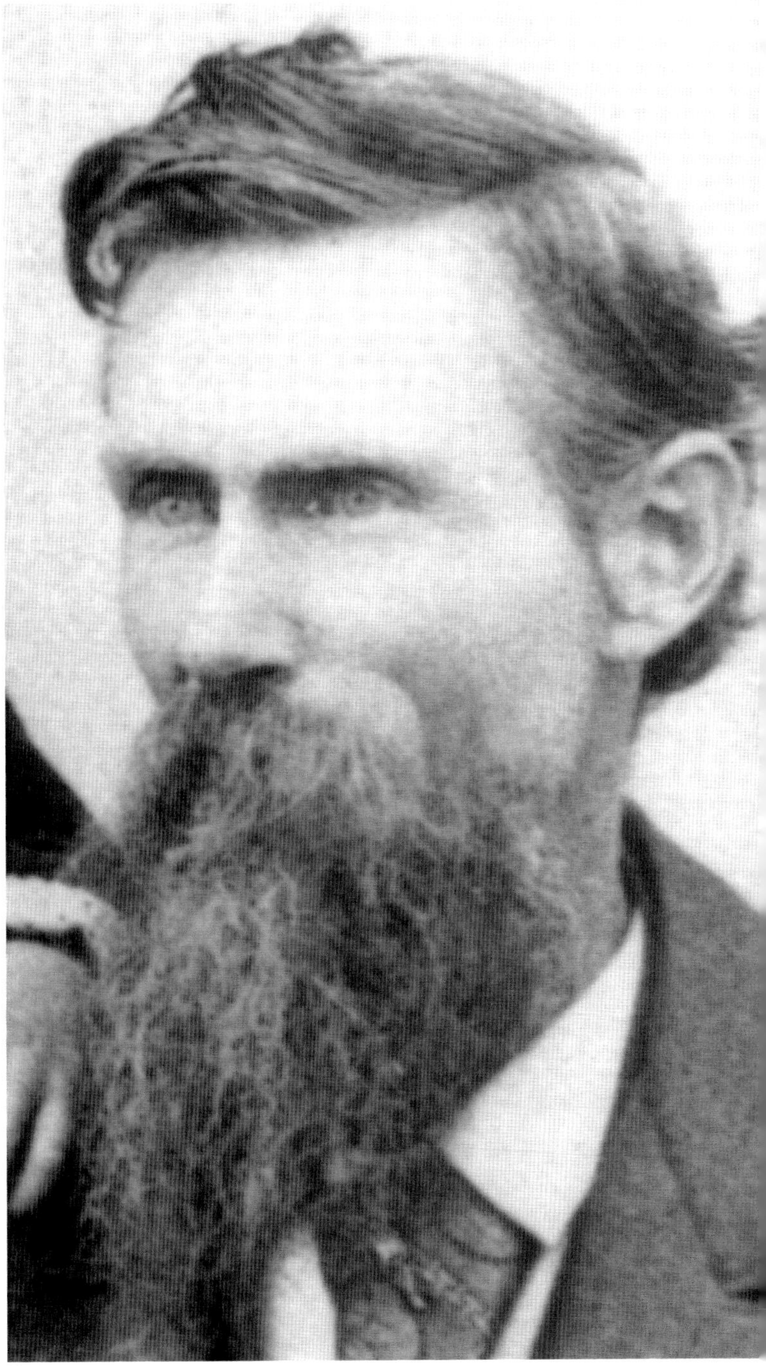

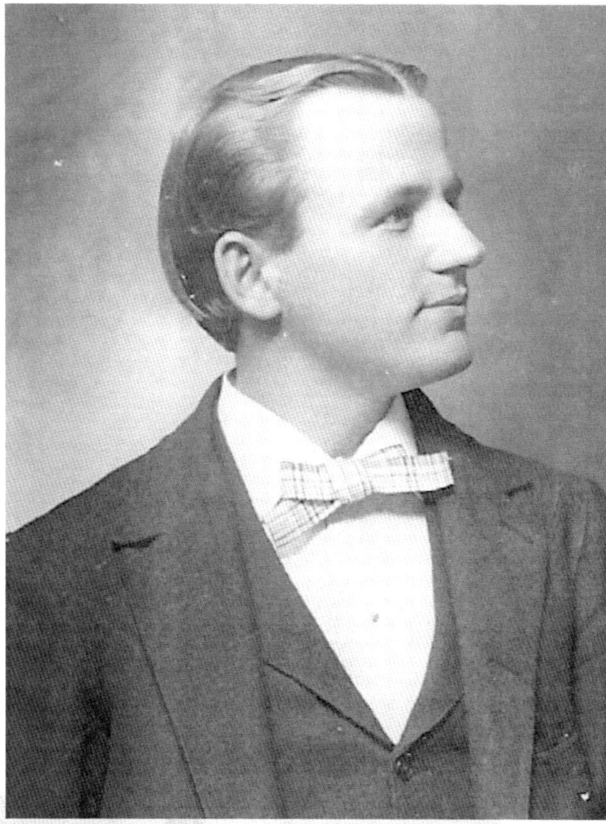

Sam Stoltz, Builder with Imagination
Self-taught architect Sam Stoltz spread his innovative style throughout the Mount Plymouth community in a series of houses he built called "Plymouthonians." Pictured here is Plymouthonian No. 1. The Tudor revival–style homes are recognizable by their high-pitched roofs, soaring chimneys, and coquina-rock fountains. Stoltz was born in 1876 on a Nebraska farm. He studied commercial art in Chicago and worked at advertising companies. He and his wife, Patti, moved to central Florida in 1925 and were drawn to the Mount Plymouth community, where he created his signature homes. One of the Plymouthonians was supposedly owned by the bookkeeper of gangster Al Capone, who enjoyed playing golf at nearby Mount Plymouth Golf Club. (Right, courtesy of Patti Dilldine; below, courtesy of Scott Amey.)

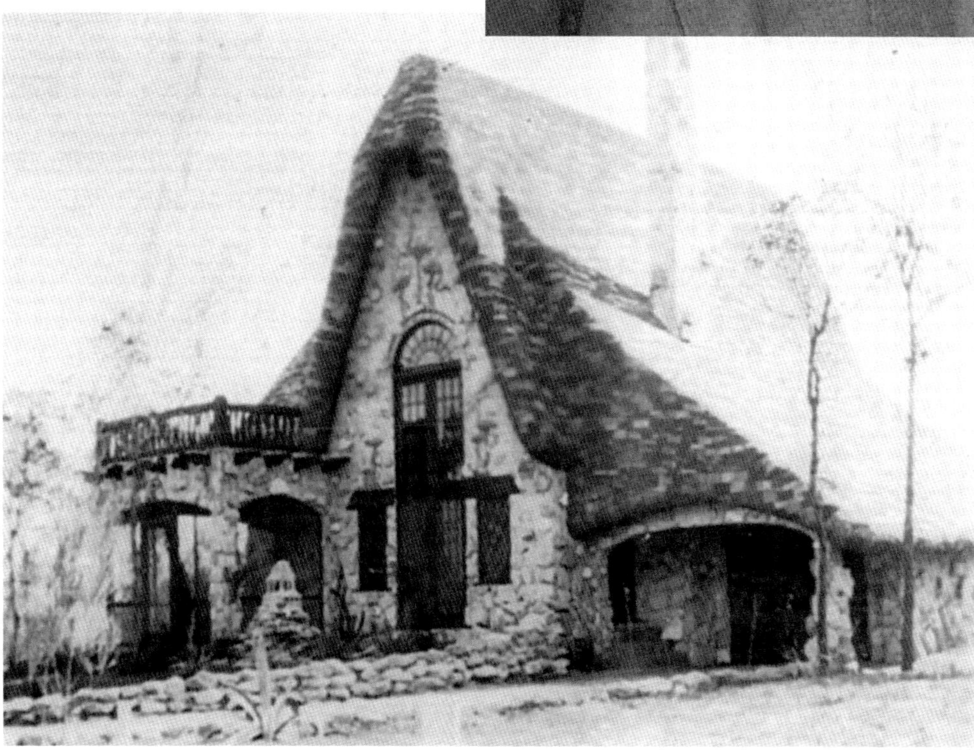

Catherine Hanson
The pride of east Lake County, Catherine Hanson served from 1990 to 2006 as Lake County's first female county commissioner. She was commission chairman three times. Hanson initiated the county's first economic summit and State of the County Address. She is most proud of her creation of the Land Acquisition Program that preserves natural lands for parks, trails, and wildlife. Hanson was inducted into the Lake County Women's Hall of Fame. She was awarded Florida Business and Professional Women's Glass Ceiling Award and the East Chamber of Commerce Founders' Award. She was named Realtor of the Year and was president of the East Lake Chamber of Commerce. Hanson's career includes serving as a teacher and manager of a large family dairy farm. She currently serves on the Workforce Central Florida Board and the North Lake Hospital Board. (Courtesy of Catherine Hanson.)

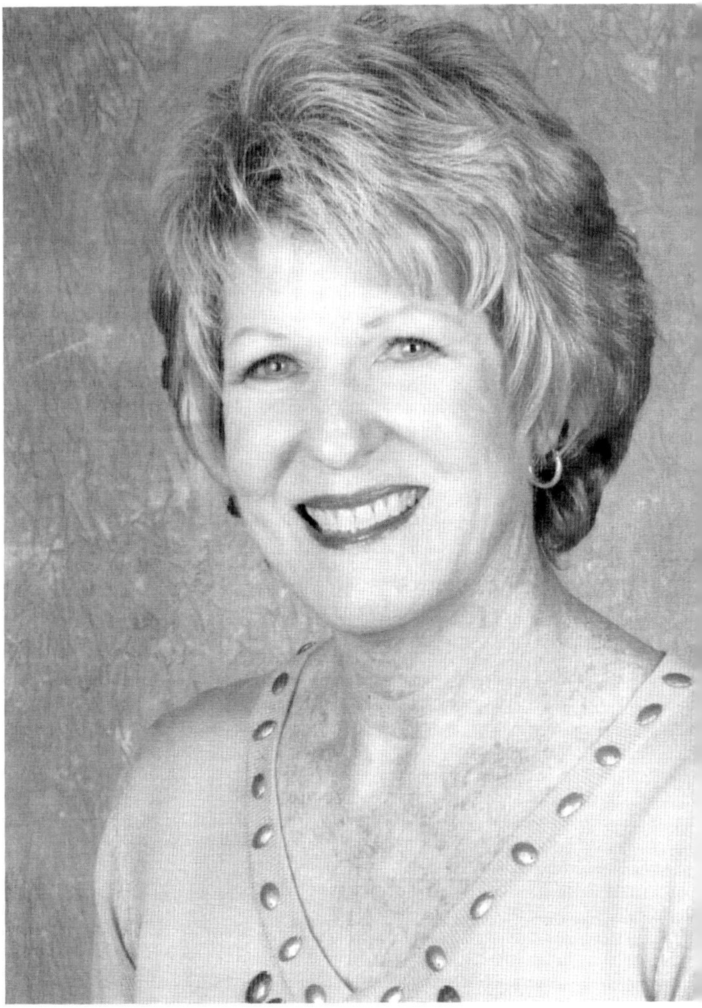

Moses Levy and John Jacob Astor IV

Astor was once home to Indian tribes and a 1562 French Huguenot colony that was wiped out by Spanish explorers in 1566. Centuries later, Moses Levy (shown here) wanted to establish a colony for oppressed European Jews. He built a mansion on a hill and raised indigo and citrus before moving to Virginia. He sold his Florida property to William Astor in 1874. Astor built a hotel, and the town flourished. After Astor died, his son, John Jacob Astor IV, inherited the land, but he died on the *Titanic* in 1912. Today, the northeast Lake County town is popular for its bass fishing and charming atmosphere. It is called "the Jewel of the St. John's River." (Right, courtesy of the State Archives of Florida; below, courtesy of RMP Archive/Library of Congress.)

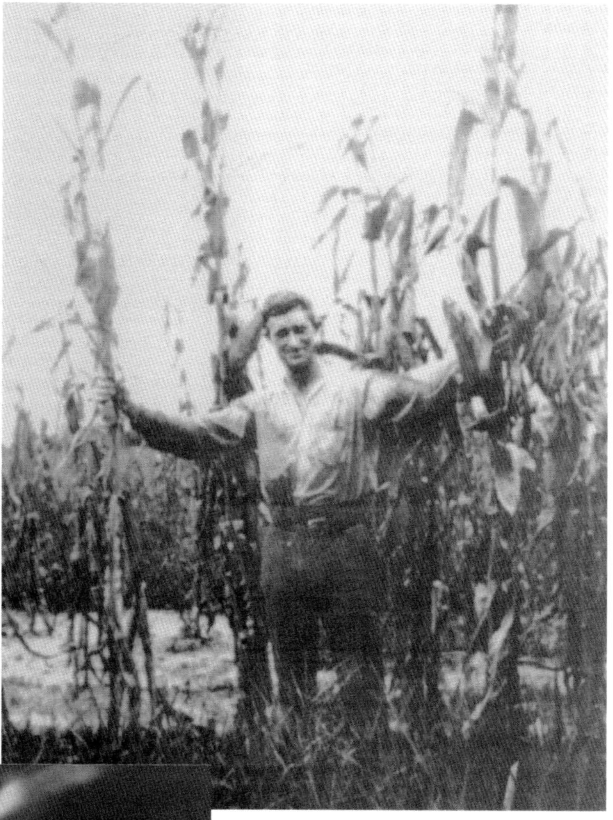

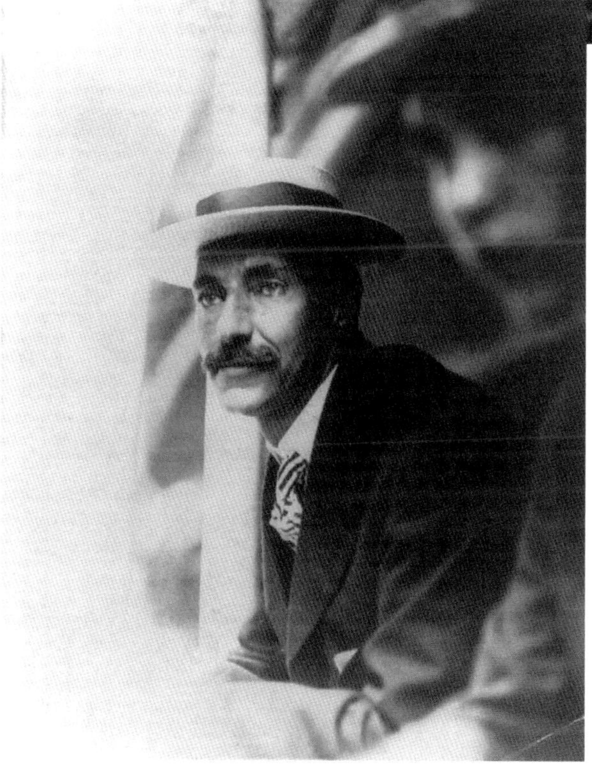

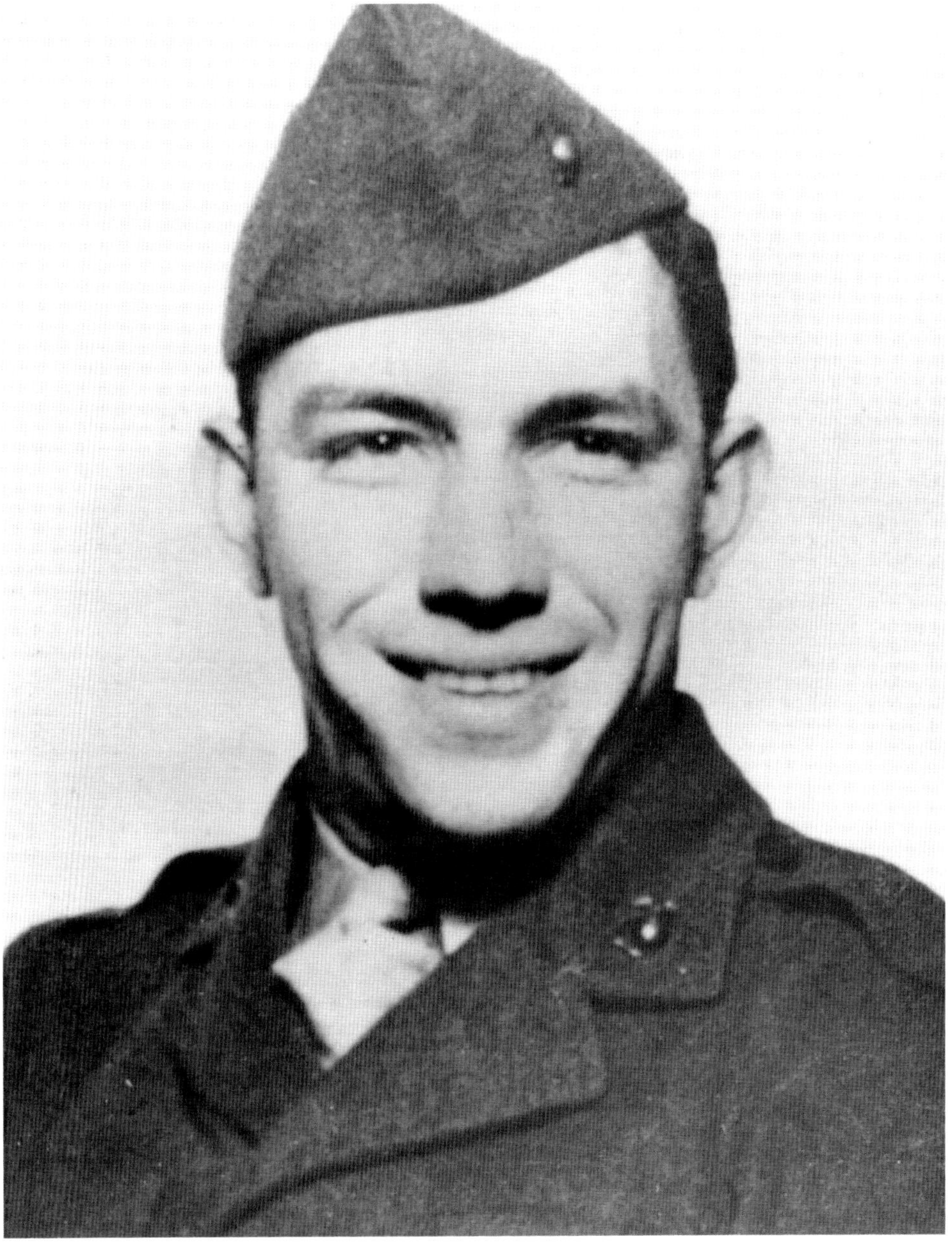

Robert McTureous, Medal of Honor Hero

When Robert McTureous was rejected by his local draft board during World War II, he saved his money to have two hernia operations so he could serve. In 1944, he joined the Marine Corps. At Okinawa, his rifle company suffered several casualties, and his platoon was pinned down by heavy enemy fire. The 5-foot, 8-inch Marine filled his pockets and jacket with grenades, then charged up the hill, tossing grenades into the Japanese positions so that his wounded comrades could be removed. McTureous was badly wounded, but crawled 200 yards to shelter before asking for aid. His bravery enabled his company to capture the hill. He died on a hospital ship a few days later. The Medal of Honor was presented to his parents on August 7, 1946. (Courtesy of Lake County Historical Society.)

CHAPTER THREE

Central Lake County and Ghost Towns

Howey-in-the-Hills, Astatula, Okahumpka, Yalaha, Kismet, Conant, Villa City, and Mohawk

The heart of Lake County was once the center of the Seminole Indian nation. Okahumpka, as Chief Micanopy called his home, became a bustling center of trade and transportation, thanks to Hubbard Hart's stagecoach and steamship lines connecting Atlantic coast tourists to Florida's interior and west coast.

Today, central Lake County draws visitors from around the world. Golf enthusiasts flock to Mission Inn, a resort featuring two top-notch golf courses and fine dining amid Spanish mission–style architecture. The delightful Yalaha Bakery has given the town national exposure on the Food Network and draws visitors from across the state. Astatula is the kind of hometown where everyone knows their neighbor. Everyone certainly knows "Miss Ollie," who, as the longtime town clerk, was so beloved that she got a street named in her honor.

No Lake County history would be complete without mention of some of the ghost towns, where dreams once lived and died. Some of the more colorful include Conant, settled by a group of wealthy British men who enjoyed horse racing; Villa City, founded by a Baltimore salesman who dreamed of a city of European-style villas; Mohawk, home to a world-famous hunting lodge; and tiny Kismet. The whimsically named town was the honeymoon destination of Elias and Flora Disney, one of the first couples to get married in the newly formed Lake County. Their famous son, Walt, would create the world's most popular tourist destination just 50 miles away.

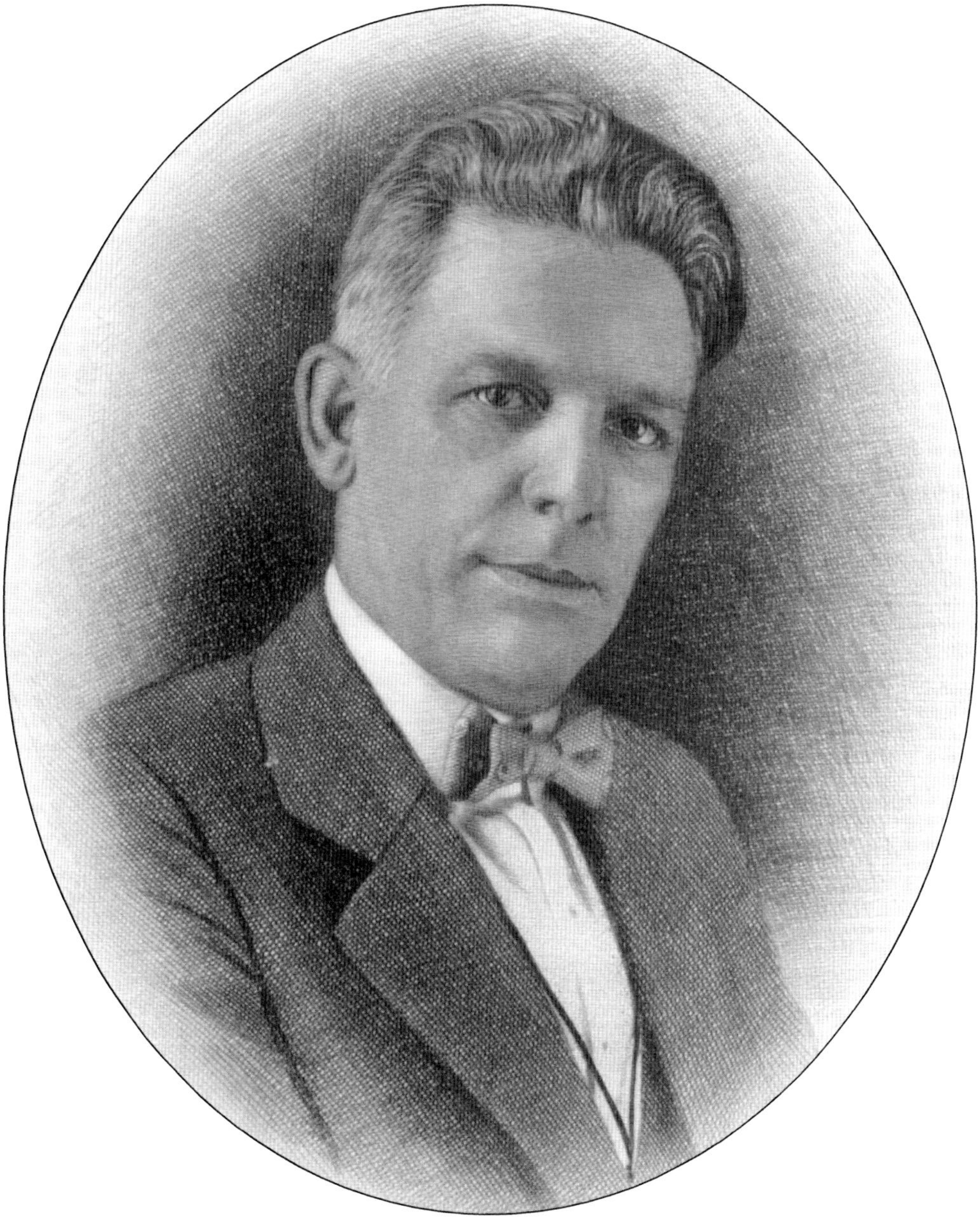

William J. Howey

Born in 1876, Illinois native William J. Howey was possibly Florida's greatest citrus developer. He sold insurance, automobiles, and pineapples in Mexico before founding Howey-in-the-Hills. He learned the citrus business near Winter Haven before a visit to Lake County drew him to the beauty of the rolling hills. He bought property and made a fortune promoting his vision of a town surrounded by citrus groves. By 1925, when the town was incorporated and Howey became mayor, a stunning half-million mature trees stretched as far as the eye could see. Howey opened the state's first citrus juice bottling plant and was one of the first to pasteurize the juice. Ambitious, Howey ran a failed campaign for governor, hoping to ride the coattails of Herbert Hoover with the slogan, "Hoover, Howey and Happiness." (Courtesy of the Lake County Historical Society.)

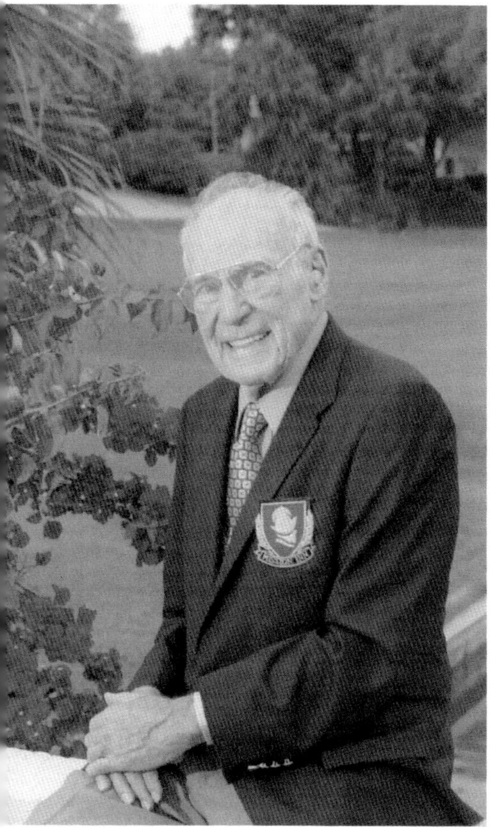

Nicholas Francis "Nick" Beucher

Beucher (left), a Chicago native and former top Morton Salt salesman, was a successful commodities broker before he turned the weed-choked Floridan Country Club into the internationally renowned Mission Inn Resort and Club. In 1964, Beucher saw a *Wall Street Journal* advertisement for a languishing golf course developed by William J. Howey. Intrigued by the hills, lakes, and climate, Beucher purchased the 168-acre property for $160,000. He shared his vision with his wife and six children, who continued the patriarch's legacy after his death in 2005. Mission Inn includes two 18-hole golf courses, along with guest and dining rooms. The Beucher family, pictured below, are, from left to right, (first row) Michelle Beucher Purser, Carol Beucher Kelsey, Donna Beucher Line, Nick Beucher, and historian and author Peggy Beucher Clark; (second row) Bob Beucher and Bud Beucher. (Courtesy of Britt Runion Photography.)

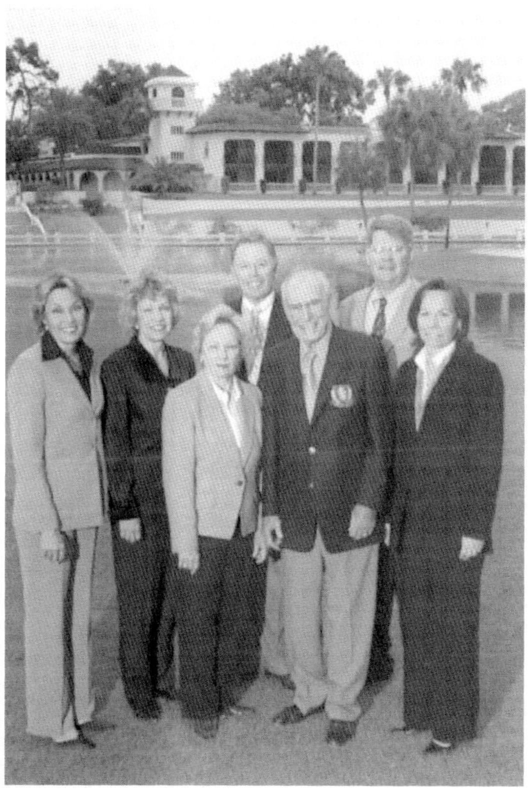

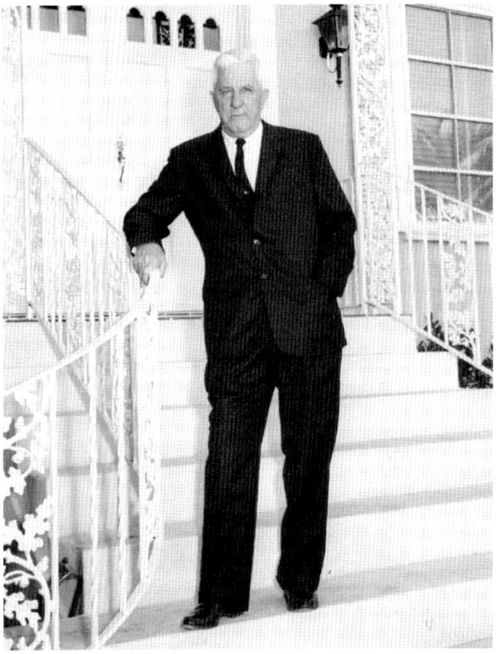

Clarence Vaughn "C.V." Griffin Sr.
In 1928, William J. Howey offered 25-year-old C.V. Griffin Sr. a contract to build a packing house in Howey-in-the-Hills. Within five years, the Vaughn-Griffin Packing Company was the second-largest fresh-fruit shipper in Florida. Griffin helped elect his former University of Florida classmate Fuller Warren governor in 1948. Griffin also associated with presidents Harry Truman and John Kennedy. (Courtesy of the Lake County Historical Society.)

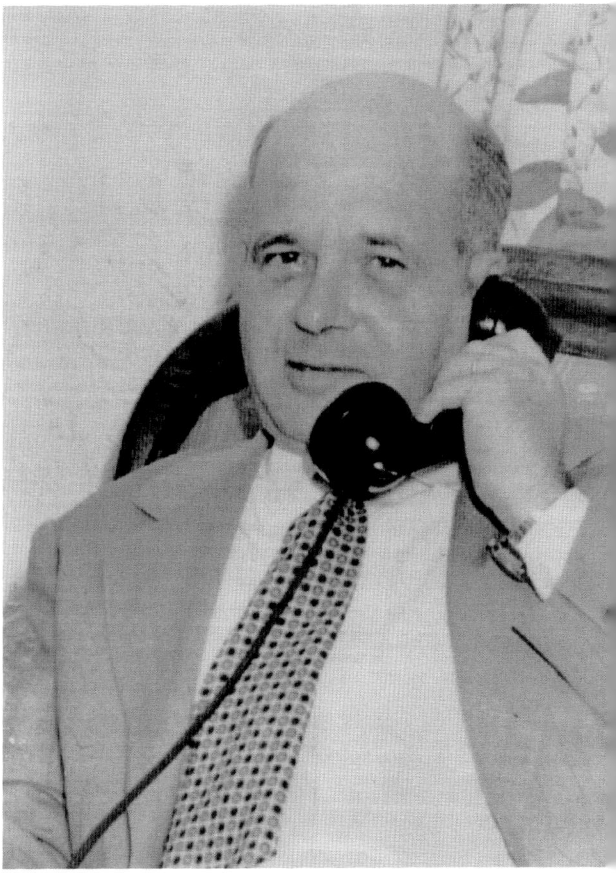

Dodge Taylor
Referred to as "Mr. Citrus," Dodge Taylor came to Howey-in-the-Hills in 1923 as sales manager for the W.J. Howey Company until Howey's death in 1938. Taylor continued as sales manager until 1940, when Howey's wife, Grace, sold the company assets and town to Dodge Taylor and C.V. Griffin. Taylor was instrumental in developing the Florida Citrus Code of 1949. (Courtesy of the Lake County Historical Society.)

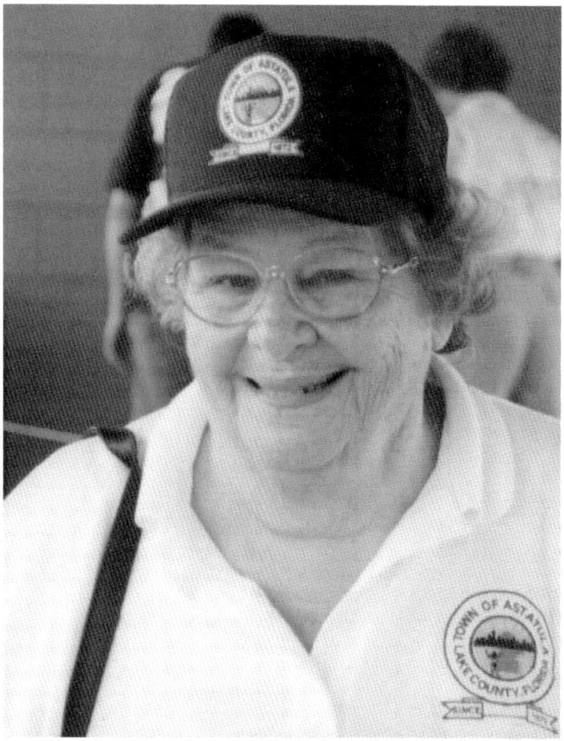

Olive Ingram, "Miss Astatula"
Olive "Ollie" Ingram is known to her friends as "Miss Astatula." She was born at home on April 4, 1919, to Mattie Lovell Reaves and Benjamin Franklin Reaves, a direct descendant of Astatula founder Thomas Asbery Hux. After graduation from Tavares High School, Ingram worked in packinghouses and at the Astatula Post Office. After her husband's death, she worked with her mother at the Astatula Train Depot until it closed in 1960. The Astatula City Council offered Ingram a position as town clerk, a job she held for 42 years. In appreciation for her many years of dedicated service, the town named a street Miss Ollie Drive (below), and named the community building in her honor. (Courtesy of Olive Ingram.)

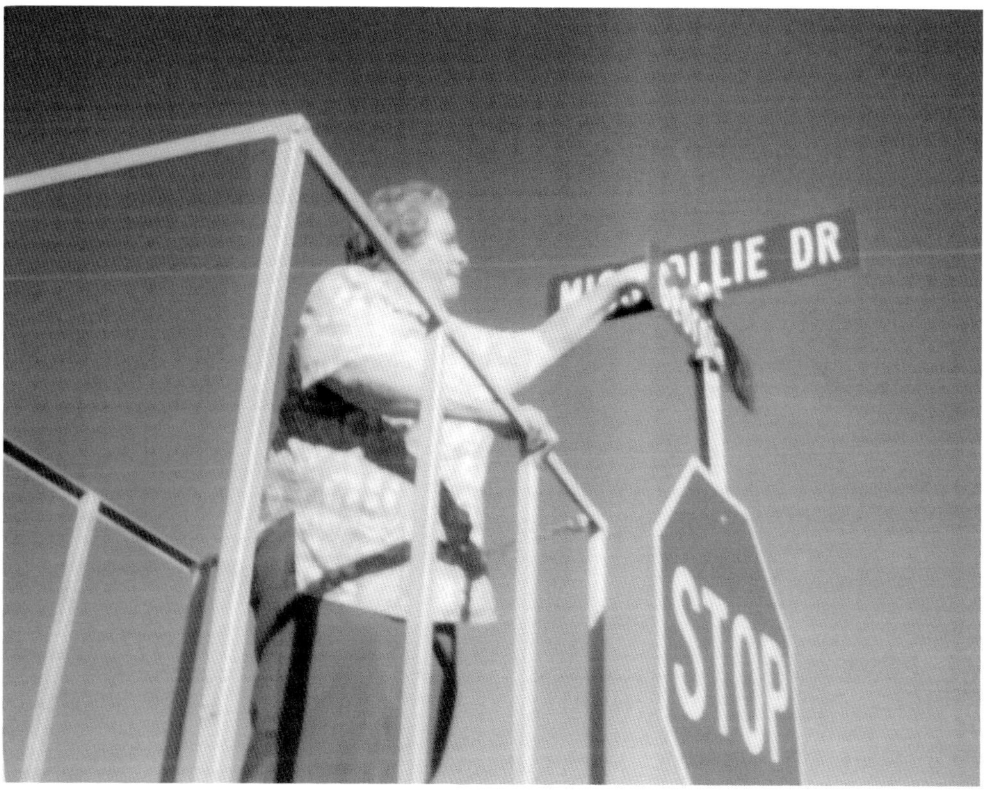

Mattie Lovell Reaves

For 30 years, Mattie Lovell Reaves served as Astatula's postmaster before becoming a railway agent for 18 years. Reaves was born in 1890. She married Benjamin Franklin Reaves, a citrus grower, deputy sheriff, and town councilman. Her father-in-law, Franklin Reaves, was appointed Astatula's first town clerk in 1927. (Courtesy of Olive Ingram.)

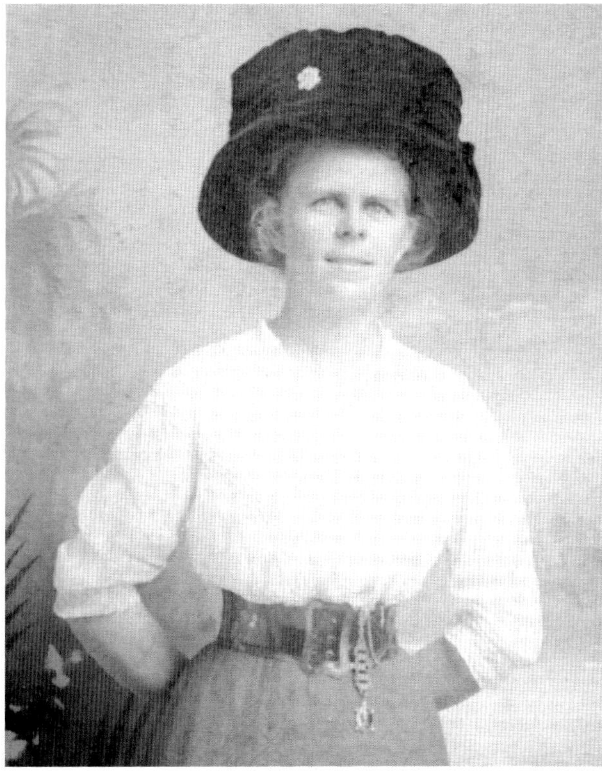

Bruce Lee

Twin brothers Bruce Lee (shown here) and Bernice Lee, of Astatula, served in World War II. Upon their return, Bruce Lee married his high school sweetheart, Lillie Mae Scott. He was concerned that Astatula Baptist Church had padlocked its doors while he had been away. Lee used bolt cutters to cut the padlock and made arrangements to hire a preacher. (Courtesy of Bruce Lee.)

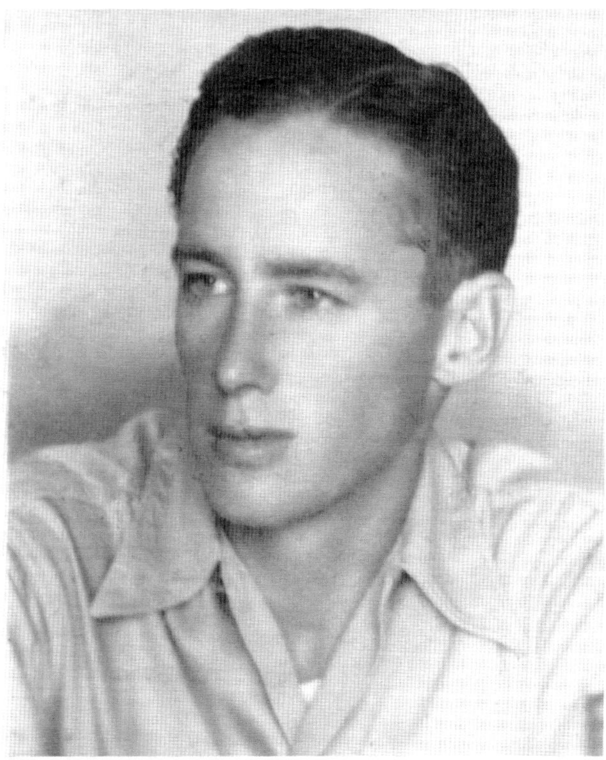

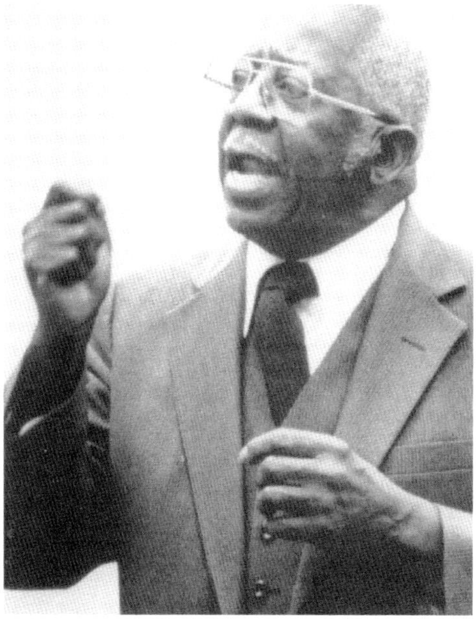

Virgil Hawkins
In his efforts to earn a law degree, Virgil Hawkins, an Okahumpka preacher's son, helped desegregate Florida's universities. The former Bethune-Cookman College teacher went before the Florida and US Supreme Courts, petitioning to enter the University of Florida's law school. He eventually earned a degree in Massachusetts. After his 1988 death, the University of Florida posthumously awarded Hawkins a law degree and named a legal clinic after him. (Courtesy of the University of Florida.)

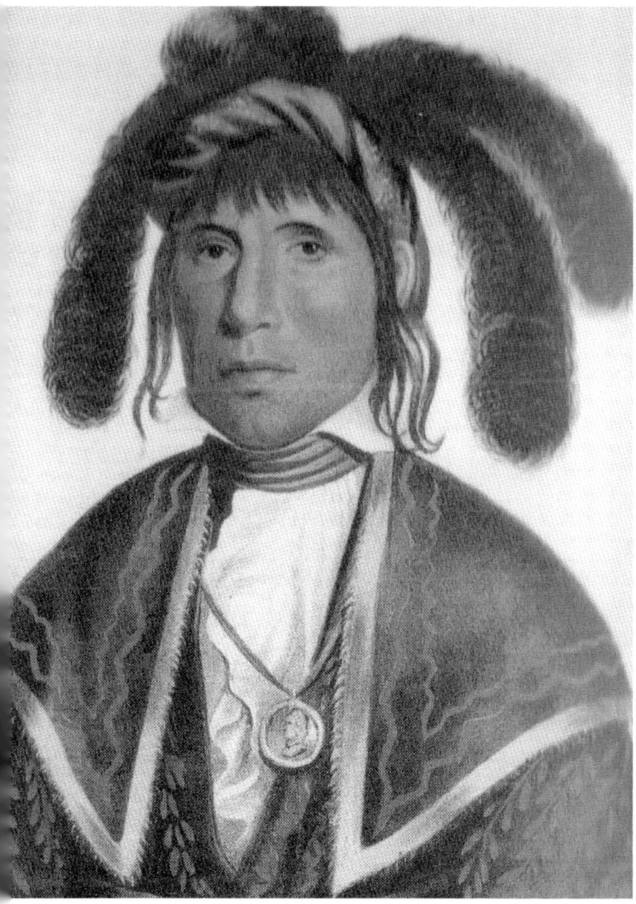

Chief Micanopy
When the English sent a surveyor into Florida's central interior in the early 1800s, they found a thriving population near present-day Okahumpka led by Chief Micanopy, whose name means "king of kings." The settlement included several thousand Seminoles and African Americans who had fled slavery. They had cattle and grew corn, among other crops. Most of the farming was done by women. (Courtesy of State Archives of Florida.)

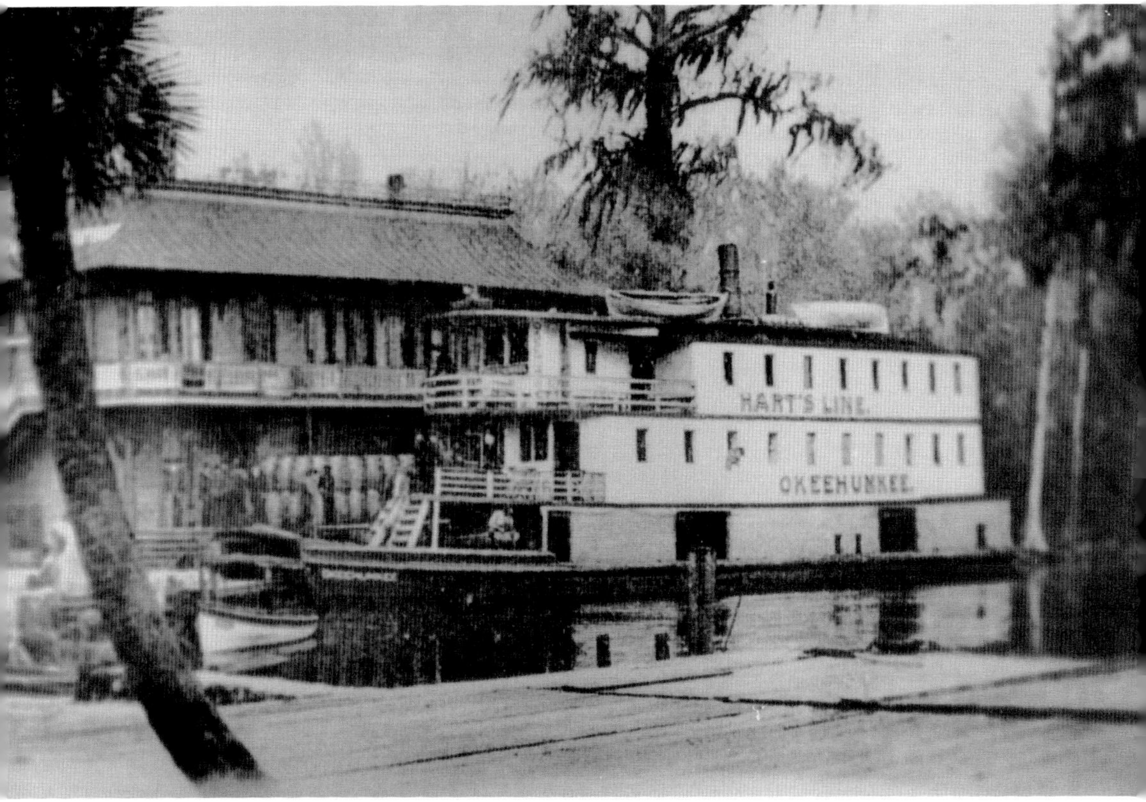

Hubbard Hart's Steamboats

Before the Civil War, Okahumpka was a bustling center that included a stagecoach line to Tampa and two steamboats—all run by Hubbard Hart. During the Civil War, Hart's transportation system carried supplies for the Confederacy. The steamship line prospered into the 1920s, carrying passengers and goods from as far away as Palatka along the crooked Ocklawaha River and a chain of lakes connected by canals dug by Hart. Travelers enjoyed the scenery and shot alligators along the way. Hart is credited with being one of the first to recognize and promote Florida as a tourist destination. He also invented the first inboard paddle boat, which was showcased at the 1893 Chicago World's Fair. He died in 1895 after he fell from a trolley in Atlanta. (Courtesy of the State Archives of Florida.)

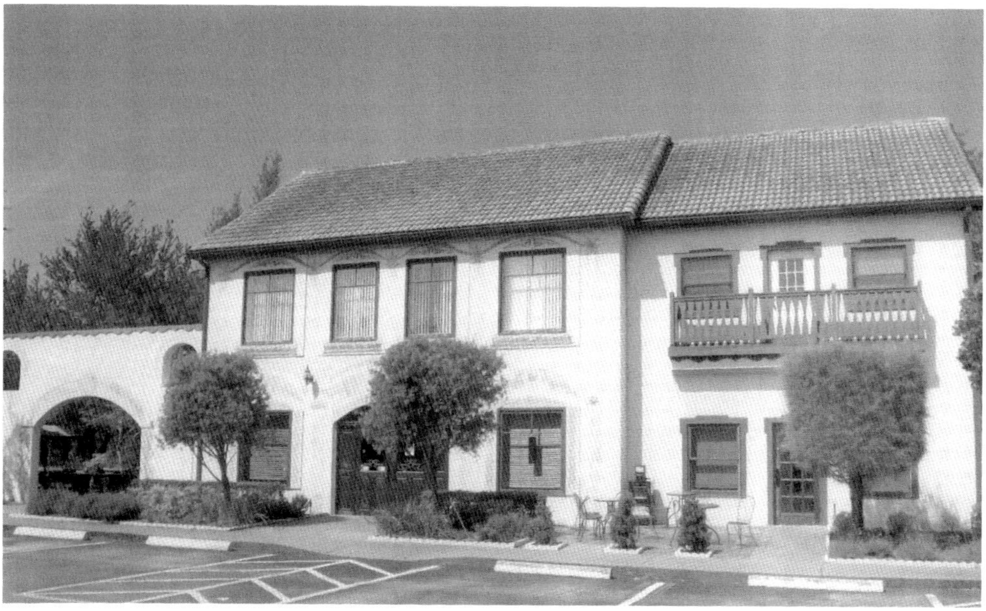

Juergen and Anne Marie Klumb—Yalaha Bakery
Juergen and Anne Marie Klumb were customers of the Yalaha Bakery for 12 years before they became owners of one of Lake County's most popular eateries. The bakery is housed in a European-façade building on rural County Road 48. Customers travel for many miles to enjoy authentic German cooking and the countless variety of pastries, Bavarian pretzels, breads, and rolls. Among the most popular pastries are Stollen and the bakery's signature bee sting pastry, which is filled with Bavarian cream and topped with orange blossom honey and almonds. The bakery has been featured on the Food Network and in national publications. Orders for the Stollen come from as far away as Hawaii and Canada. The Klumbs regularly feature musical entertainment, but it's the eye-popping desserts that are the main attraction. (Courtesy of Doris Bloodsworth.)

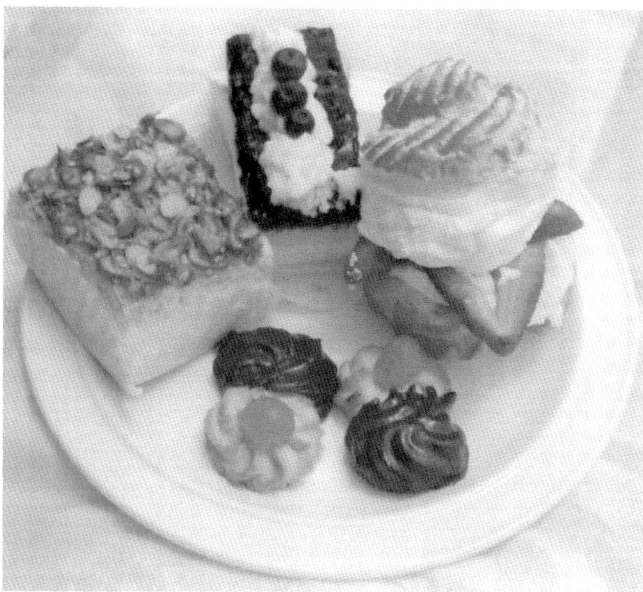

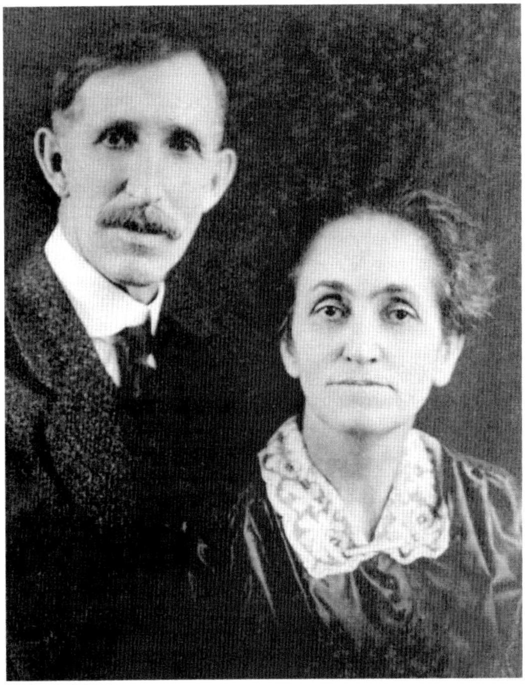

Elias and Flora Disney
One of the first marriage licenses issued in newly formed Lake County was to Elias Disney and Flora Call, on December 27, 1887. The couple honeymooned in Kismet, which became a ghost town. They lived for a short time in nearby Acron before moving to Chicago. Their son, Walt, would return to build the world's No. 1 tourist destination just 50 miles away. (Courtesy of Diane Disney.)

Conant
Historians dispute whether the man in this photograph is W.P. Pool or Major Sherman Conant, for whom the town in the background is named. Conant was founded in 1884 by wealthy English settlers who named the community after a Florida Southern Railway financier. After the Great Freeze of 1894–1895, Conant became a ghost town. Today, the site is known as The Villages. (Courtesy of the Lady Lake Historical Society.)

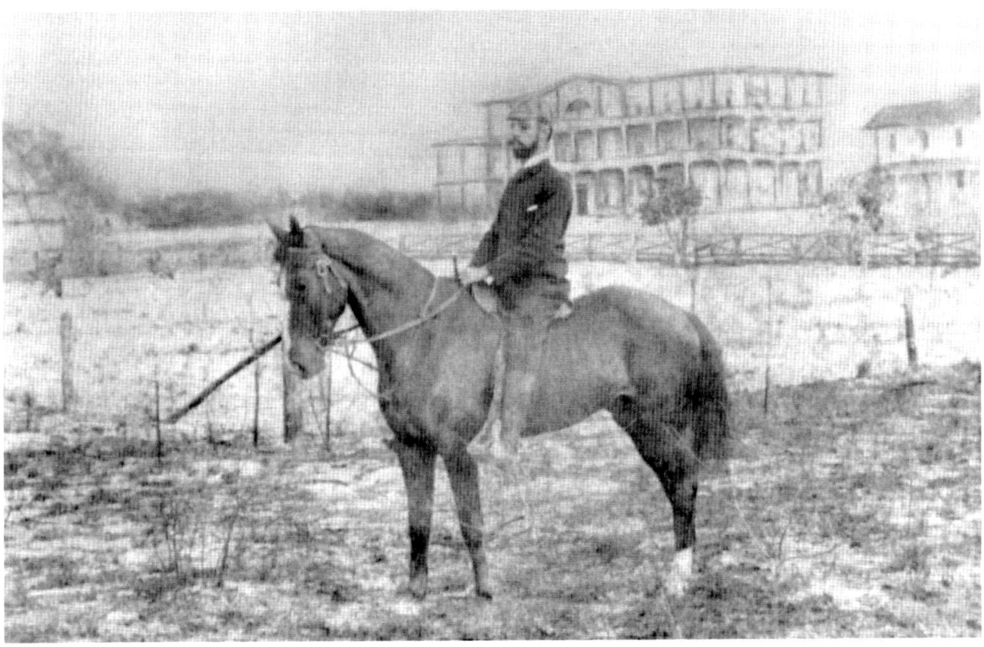

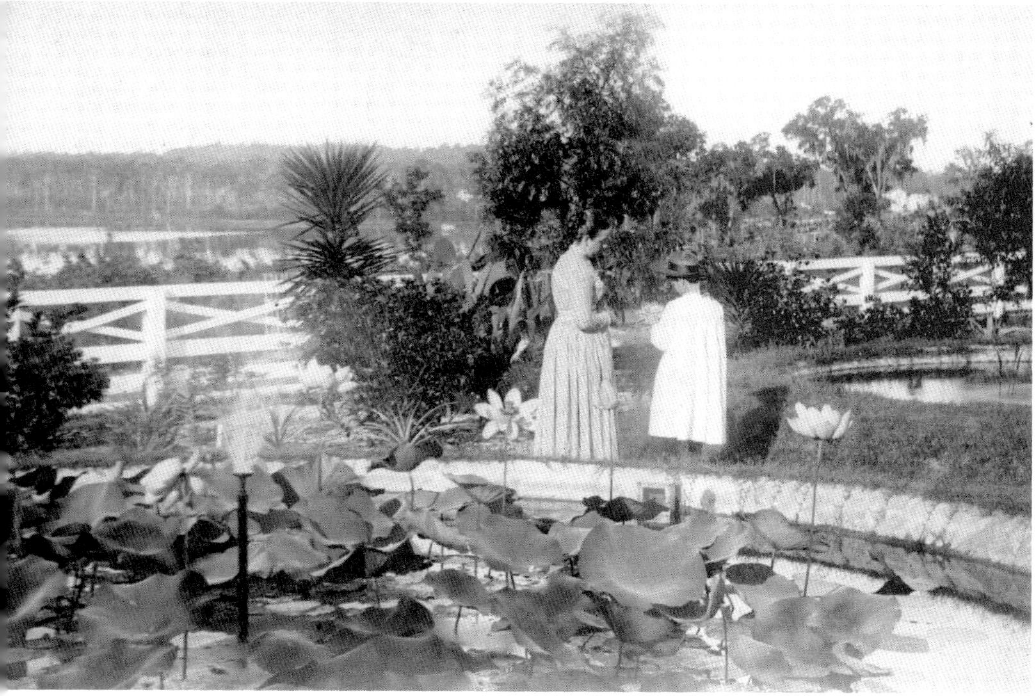

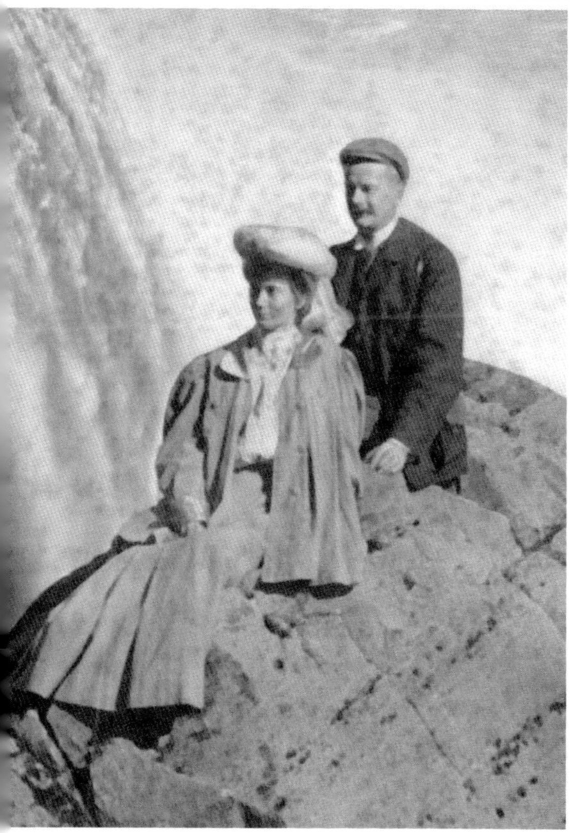

Villa City

Colgate salesman George King dreamed of a community of European-style villas when he founded Villa City, an idyllic, hilly property surrounded by lakes. Baltimore relatives and friends created a town with lavish gardens and a hotel, general store, and church. King named five surrounding lakes after family members, including his wife, Emma (above left), and daughter Desire (above right). Villa City became a ghost town overnight after the Great Freeze of 1894–1895. (Courtesy of Howard King.)

Chetwynd

In 1886, a young Cambridge graduate named Robert Francis Edward "Frank" Cooke joined a group of British friends in Chetwynd, Florida, known today as Fruitland Park. While many of those settlers fled after the Great Freeze of 1894–1895, Cooke stayed and became a successful banker. Cooke is pictured with his wife, Margaret Hopkins, on their honeymoon at Niagara Falls, on April 3, 1923. (Courtesy of the Leesburg Heritage Museum.)

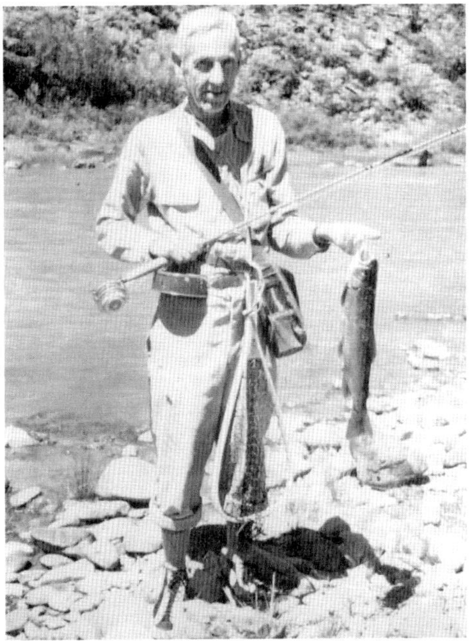

Harry Stokes

In 1888, New York native Charles Stokes settled on Plum Lake near present-day Minneola. He was joined by his brother Harry (pictured), who took over his brother's popular Jolly Palms hunting and fishing lodge after Charles moved away. Harry Stokes became a respected Clermont banker and county commissioner, serving from 1928 until his death in 1956. (Courtesy of the Stokes family.)

Mohawk, Florida

After Charles Stokes arrived in Florida, he opened a post office in his home and called the new settlement Mohawk after Mohawk Valley, New York. Stokes had a thriving mail-order business for a root thought to have medicinal value. Though Mohawk did not survive, descendants of the Stokes family continue to live in the home shown here. (Courtesy of the Stokes family.)

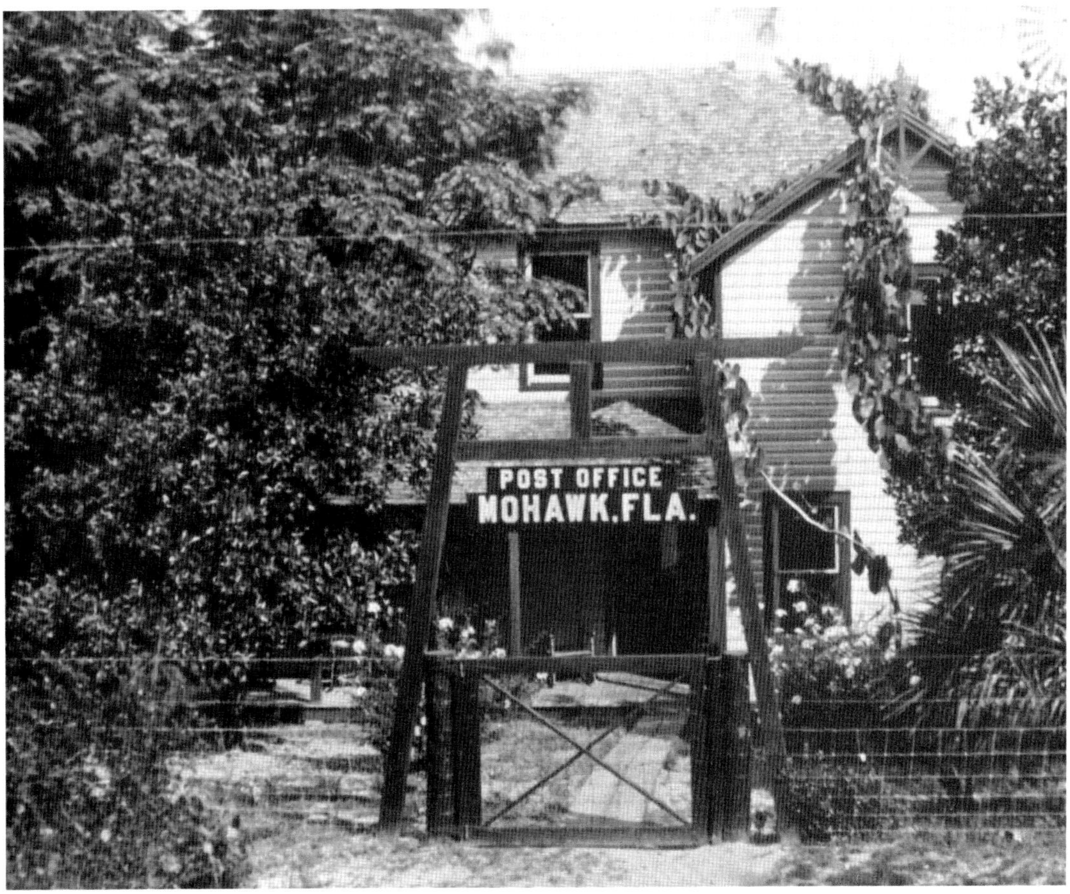

CHAPTER FOUR

South Lake County

Clermont, Groveland, Mascotte, Minneola, Montverde, and Stuckey

Once a mostly agricultural area, south Lake County now is home to the largest city in the county, Clermont, and the second-fastest-growing city, Groveland. The two cities, and the neighboring towns of Mascotte, Minneola, Montverde, and Stuckey, are often referred to as one community: South Lake.

Clermont is proud of its "Gem of the Hills" reputation. The city was founded by four New Jersey men who methodically created a "model town." With its rolling hills and chain of lakes, Clermont attracts families, retirees, and numerous professional athletes, including Olympic medalists.

Groveland flourished in the 1920s, when it was home to the largest sawmill in the Southeast, and again in the post–World War II era, when citrus was king. Groveland pioneers included some of the most influential men of their day, such as E.E. Edge and his son, L.D. Edge, and sawmill operator J. Ray Arnold, who made quality education a priority.

Mascotte is one of the oldest communities in the area, and today includes a large Hispanic population as well as families whose roots go back to the Civil War.

Minneola was founded the same year as Clermont. The two cities hug the shores of Lake Minneola and are bound together, like ribbons, by busy US Highway 27 and the Florida Turnpike.

Montverde may not share a busy highway, but that's just fine to the residents who call it home and the students who attend the internationally acclaimed Montverde Academy. The small town also boasts the beautiful Bella Collina gated community, whose private residences house Hollywood stars and golf celebrities.

Stuckey was built around an early turpentine still. Many of the families in the historically African American community are descendants of the turpentine workers who came in the late 1800s from the Carolinas and Georgia. Stuckeyfest has become an annual homecoming event for the tight-knit community.

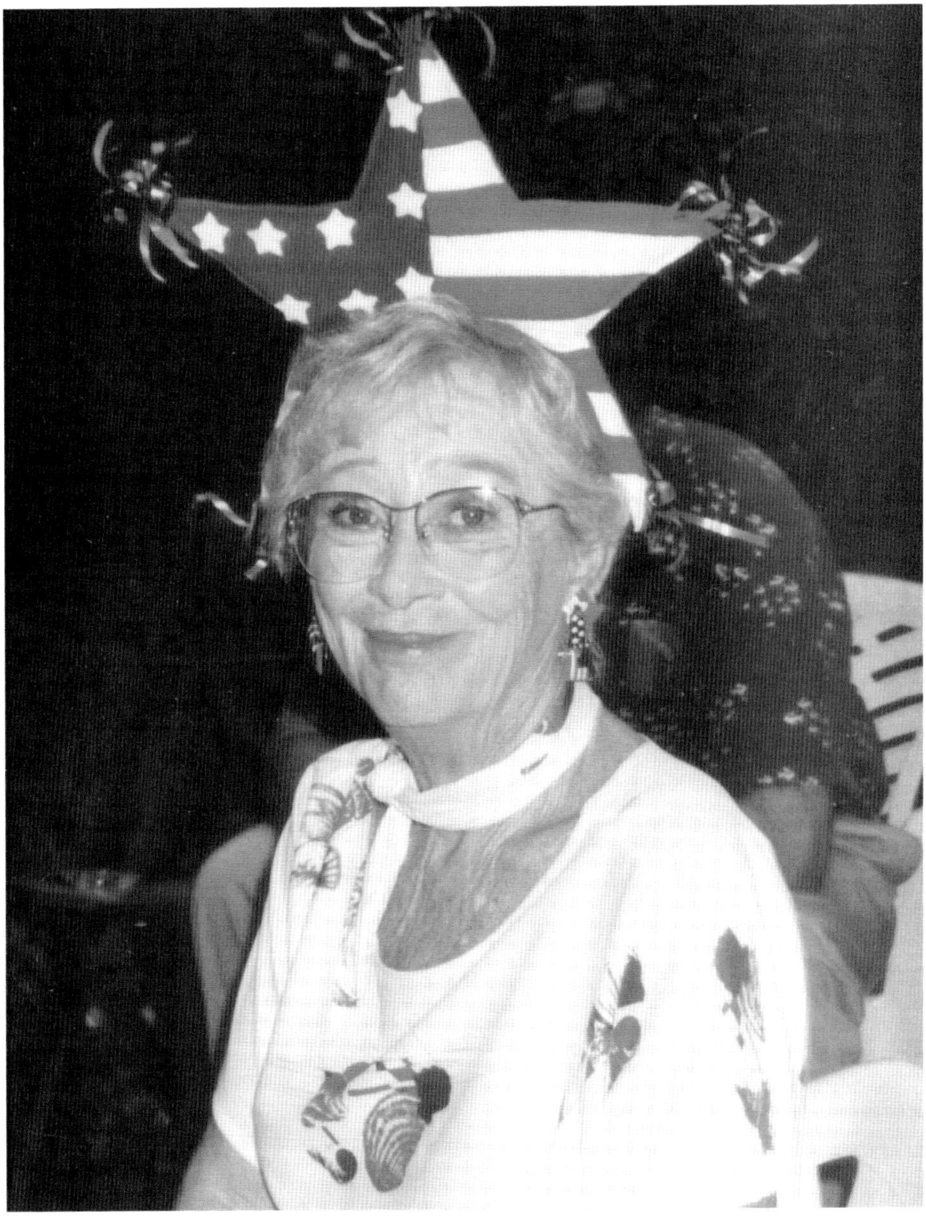

Ann Dupee, Journalist and Civic Activist

Ann Dupee is one of Lake County's most recognized and respected leaders. Her early career included working with the Ice Capades. She and her husband, George Dupee, a former *Wall Street Journal* executive, came to Clermont in late 1967 after purchasing the *South Lake Press*. After her husband's death, Ann Dupee served as publisher and editor. She continues to write a weekly column, "Remember When." Her many accomplishments include being inducted into the Lake County Business Hall of Fame and Women's Hall of Fame. She served on Clermont's city council and was president of the South Lake Chamber of Commerce, South Lake Kiwanis Club, and Beta Theta ESA. She is a member of the Cooper Memorial Library Association Board. She is known for her signature themed headpieces. (Courtesy of Ann Dupee.)

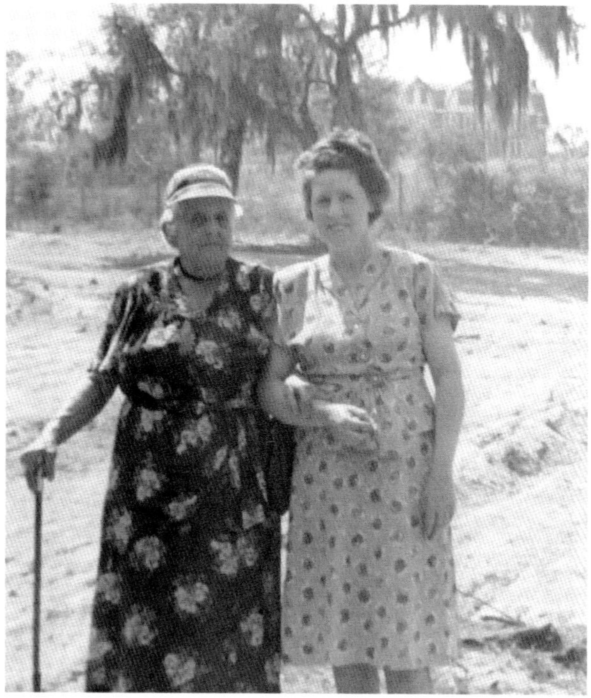

Hattie Millholland and Miriam Johnson, Clermont History-Makers
Miriam Johnson (right) was president of the Lake County Historical Society and wrote a definitive history of Clermont with coauthor Rosemary Young titled *Clermont: Gem of the Hills*. Johnson is seen here with the legendary Hattie Daggett Millholland, who supervised the digging of a canal and built the historic Log House seen in the background. (Courtesy of the Lake County Historical Society.)

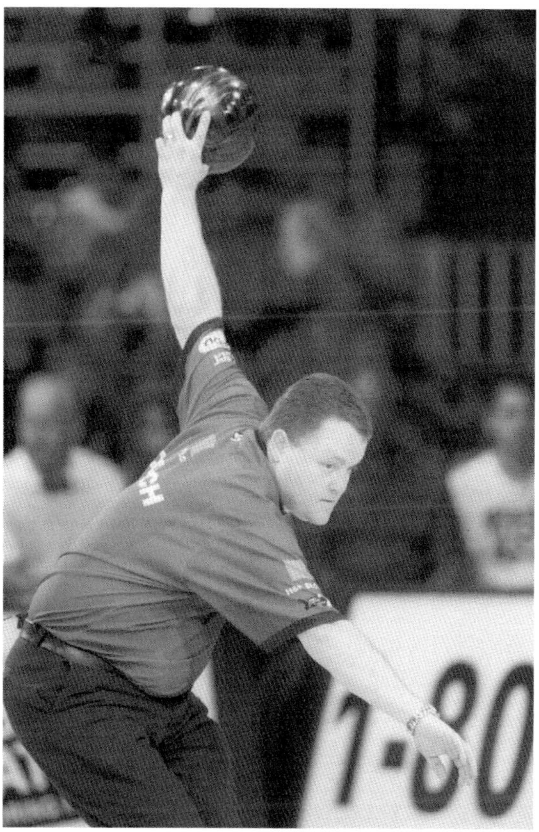

Jason Couch
In 2012, Clermont native Jason Couch was inducted into the Professional Bowlers Association Hall of Fame. The 16-time PBA Tour titlist is the only bowler to win three straight PBA Tournament of Champions titles. He was the 1992 PBA Rookie of the Year. Clermont also is home to PBA champions Norm Duke and Randy Pedersen. (Courtesy of Jason Couch.)

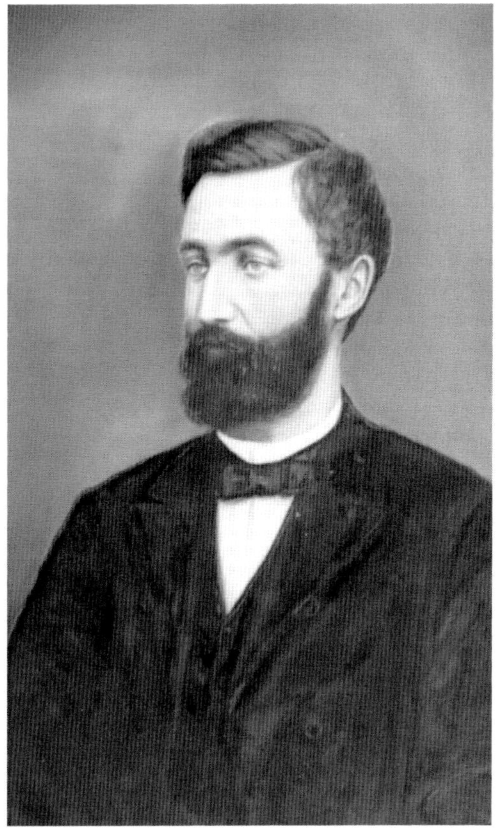

William House
Before he became president of the Clermont Improvement Company and created the "model town" in south Lake County, William House was a Pennsylvania senator and justice on New Jersey's Supreme Court. The Vineland, New Jersey, resident and his family moved to Clermont in 1884 and built a five-story home overlooking Lake Minnehaha. (Courtesy of the Cooper Memorial Library Association.)

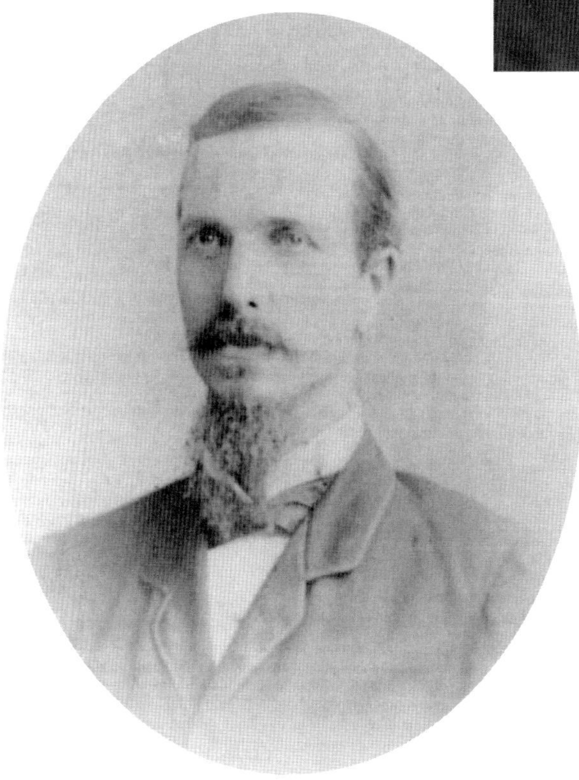

Arthur Wrotnowski
Civil engineer Arthur Wrotnowski was general manager and treasurer of the company that founded Clermont. He surveyed and mapped the city, skills he had developed while serving in the Union Army's Engineering Corps. He was the town's first postmaster before moving to Mexico and New Orleans. (Courtesy of the Lake County Historical Society.)

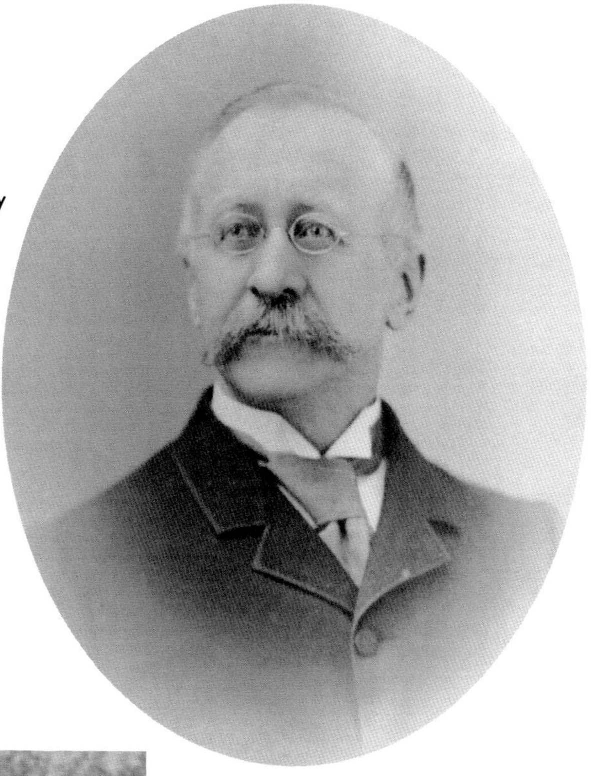

Thomas Steele
Clermont Improvement Company secretary Thomas Steele (shown here) brought his son, Charles Steele, to help start the new model community in south Lake County in 1884. After the elder Steele returned to Vineland, New Jersey, his son stayed on and married Laurette Bishop Pollard. (Courtesy of the Lake County Historical Society.)

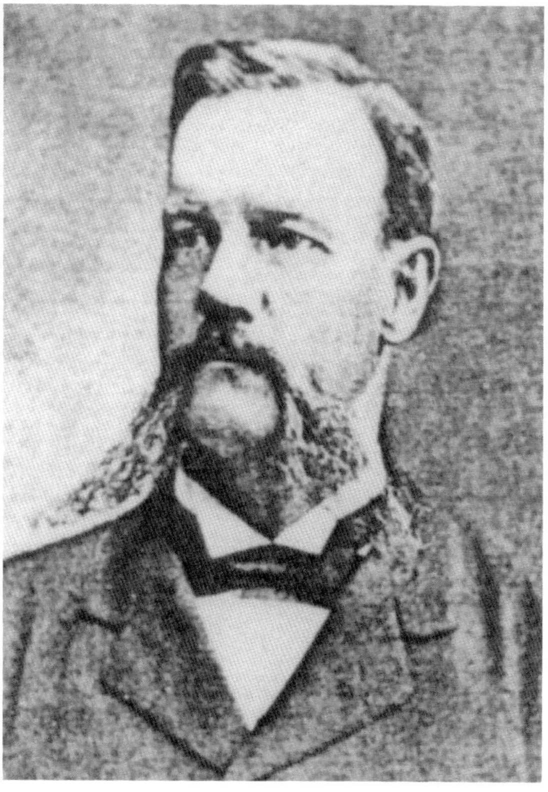

Judge Alfred Beers
The fourth member of Clermont's founders was Judge Alfred Beers, who served as legal counsel for the enterprise. A Union Army veteran, he returned to Bridgeport, Connecticut, where he became active in the Grand Army of the Republic, a charitable organization that won approval for the annual observance of Decoration Day, or Memorial Day, as it is now called. (Courtesy of the Lake County Historical Society.)

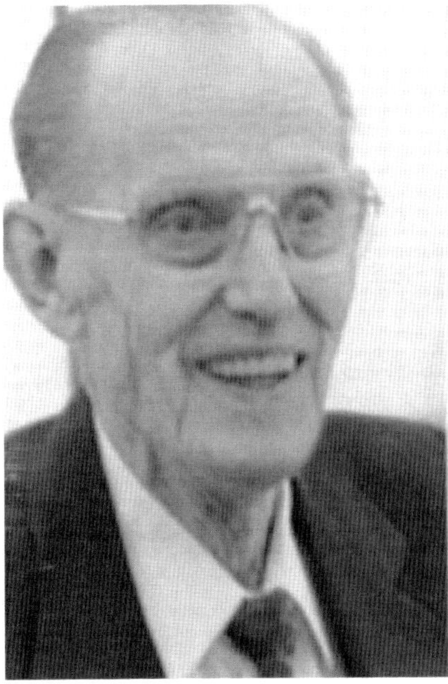

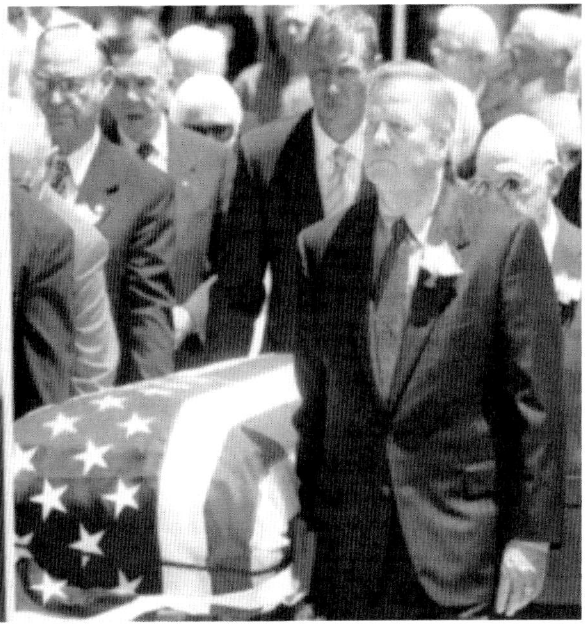

Robert Oakley Seaver, "Mr. Clermont"

Robert "Oakley" Seaver's ancestors include Clermont's earliest pioneer, Herring Hooks. Seaver was the Clermont postmaster for 32 years and was known as "Mr. Clermont" for his many civic contributions, including founding the Clermont Kiwanis Foundation and Friends of Cooper Memorial Library. He also served as president of the South Lake County Historical Society, and was a charter member of the South Lake Chamber of Commerce. His death in 2006 was front-page news, with the headline "Farewell, Mr. Clermont." (Courtesy of the Oakley Seaver family and *The Daily Commercial.*)

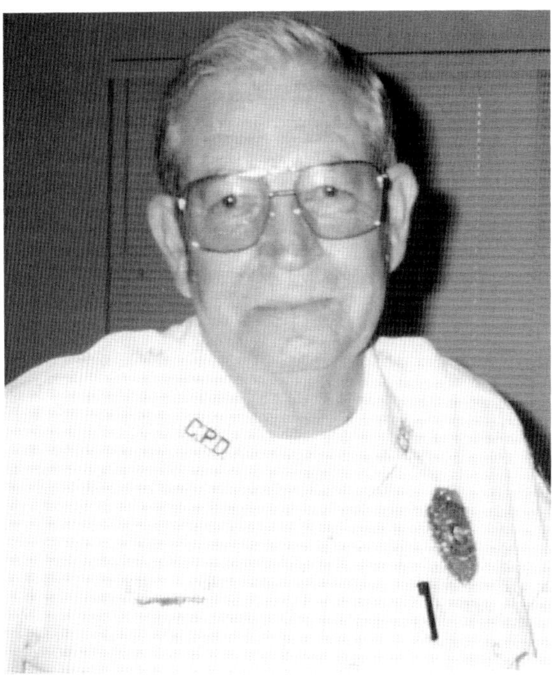

Prentice Tyndal

Pres. Bill Clinton and Gov. Lawton Chiles were among those who congratulated Clermont police chief Prentice Tyndal when he retired in 1996 after 37 years of service. Tyndal was the longest-serving police chief in the nation. City officials thanked the chief by giving him the 1992 Crown Victoria police car he had driven prior to retirement. (Courtesy of Ann Dupee.)

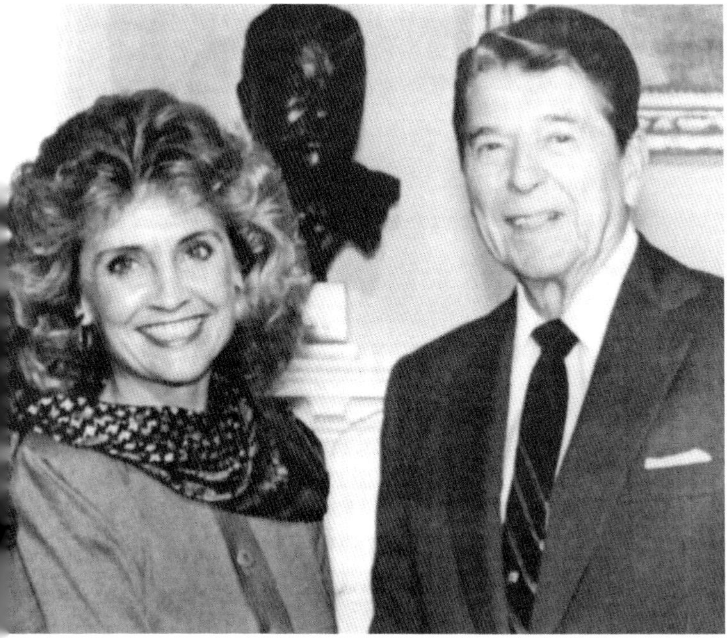

Micki Blackburn Nagel
Former schoolteacher turned successful realtor Micki Blackburn Nagel has won countless awards for her civic and philanthropic contributions. She was the driving force behind the South Lake Historic Village, is a member emeritus of the Cornerstone Hospice Foundation Board, helped fund mammograms for women without insurance, and served on numerous charity boards. Nagel was on Florida's electoral board during the election of President Ronald Reagan. (Courtesy of Micki Blackburn Nagel.)

James and Sally Townsend
James Townsend (right) and his wife, Sally, were Clermont's first African American settlers, arriving in 1887. He was a farmer and teacher. She established a maternity clinic for African American mothers. "Aunt Sally" was the town midwife, delivering thousands of babies. The couple founded the first school for African American children. Their home is preserved in the Historic Village. (Courtesy of the South Lake County Historical Society.)

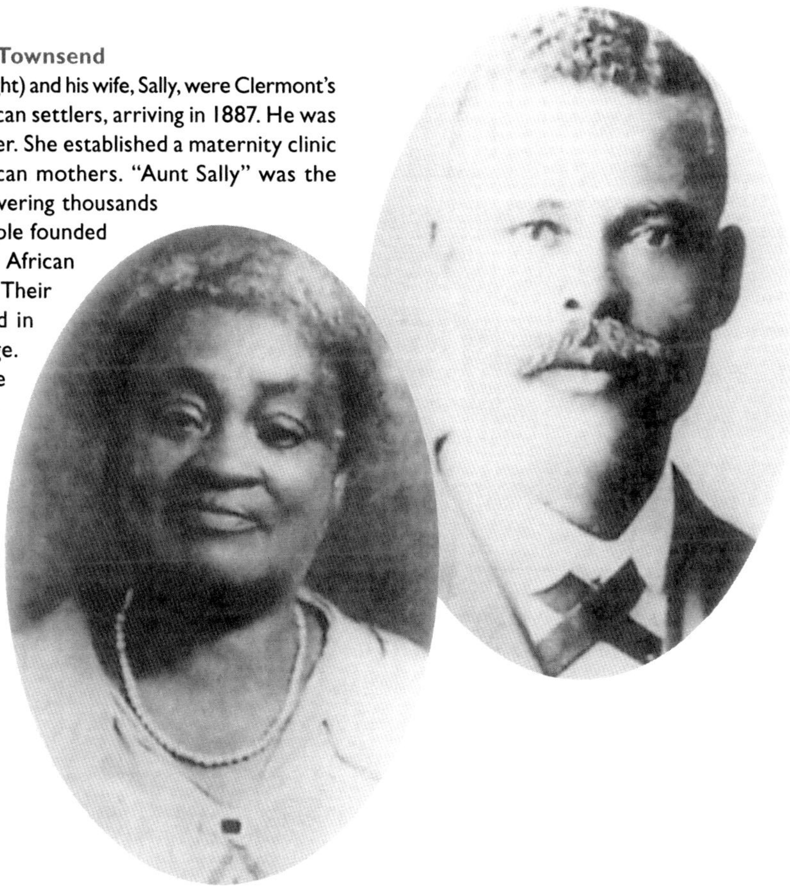

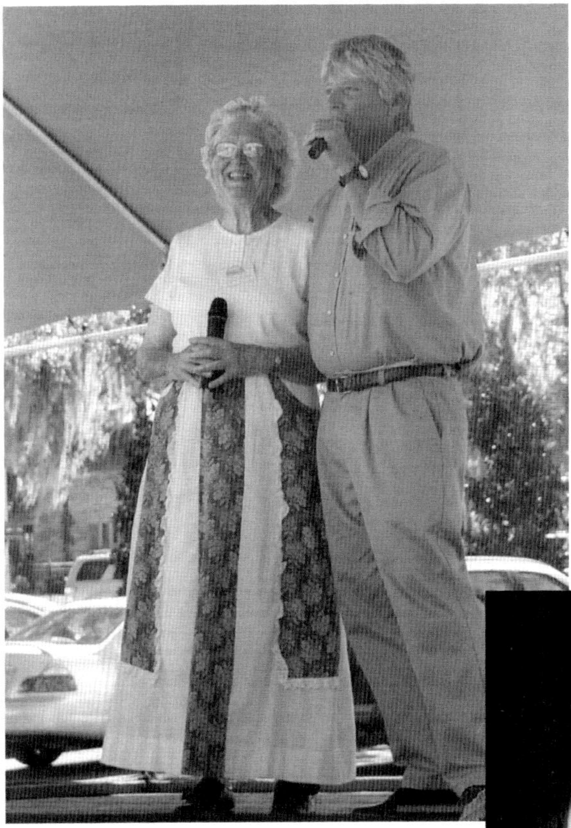

Dolores Walker, Honorary Historian
Dolores Gano Walker (pictured with Clermont mayor Hal Turville) is not only Clermont's official historian, she is the granddaughter of two south Lake County legends: Archibald Gano, a sawmill operator who helped incorporate Clermont; and George Myers, Mascotte's first mayor. Walker is active in several historical societies. (Courtesy of Linda Charlton.)

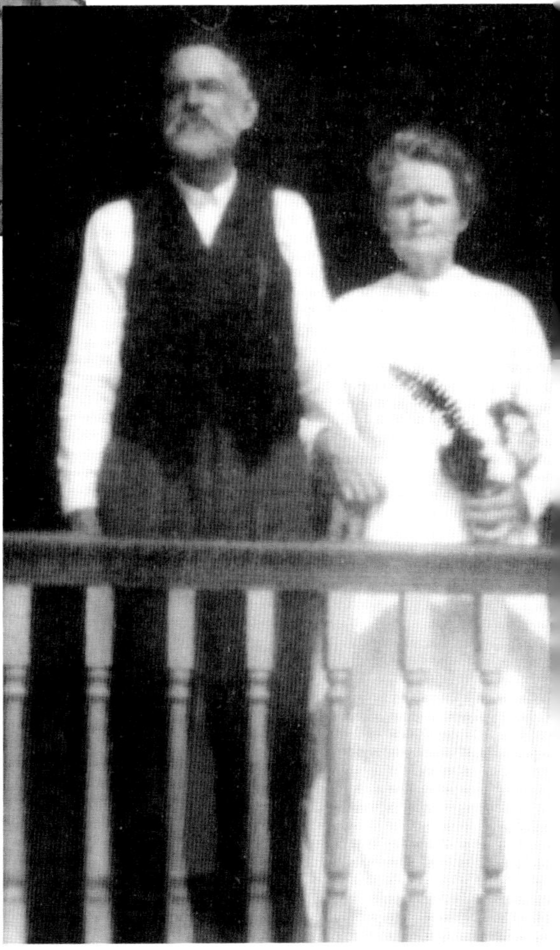

Archibald Gano
An expert sawmill operator who provided lumber for many of the oldest homes in south Lake County, Archibald Gano is one of the area's most important pioneers. He built a tomato-packing plant, and his Clermont home, built in 1891, serves today as a shelter for women and children. His Villa City sawmill was dynamited by neighbors upset by the dam he built to generate power. He is pictured here with his wife, Sallie. (Courtesy of Dolores Gano Walker.)

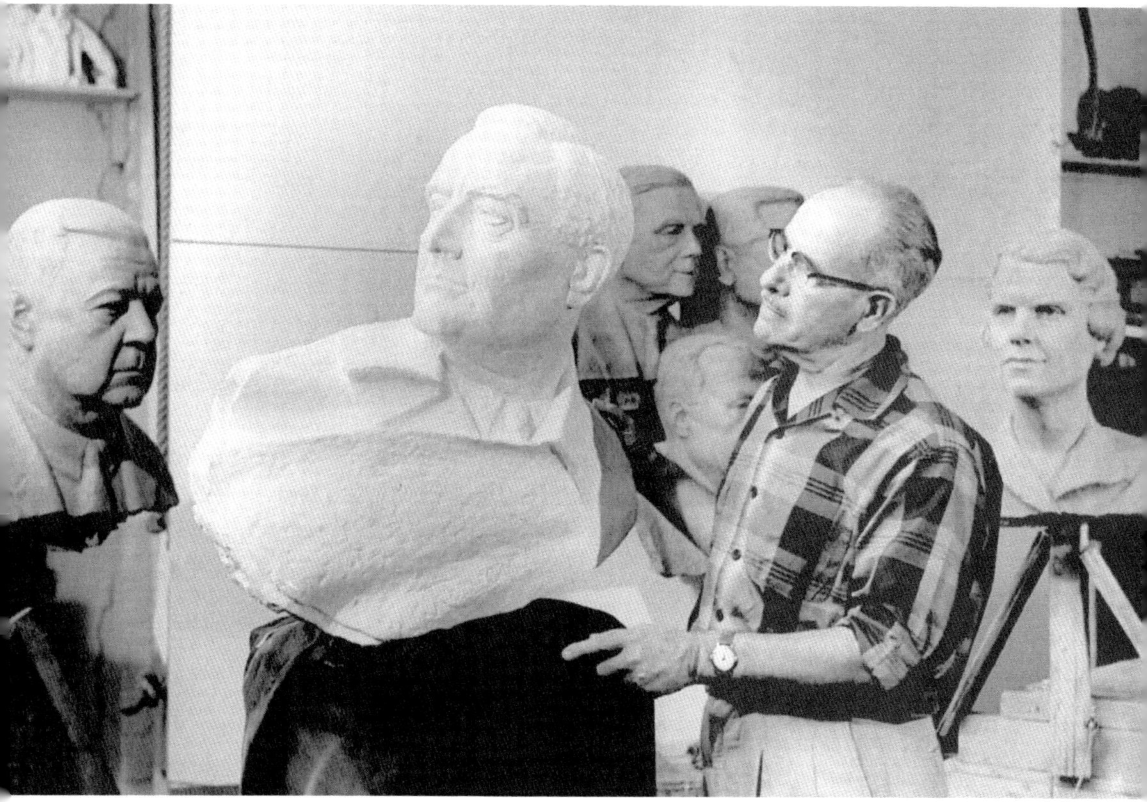

Edmond Amateis, Sculptor and Philanthropist

Few patrons of Clermont's Cooper Memorial Library know that the books they read may have been paid for by one of the city's most talented and thoughtful residents, Edmond Amateis. The sculptor, born in Rome in 1897, was commissioned to create busts for the Polio Wall of Fame. Other major works include the Department of Labor building in Washington, DC, and the Baltimore War Memorial. After moving to Clermont, he enjoyed gardening and developed the Dorothy Amateis rhododendron, named after his wife. He created a foundation that generously supports the Cooper Memorial Library in Clermont. (Courtesy of the National Sculpture Society.)

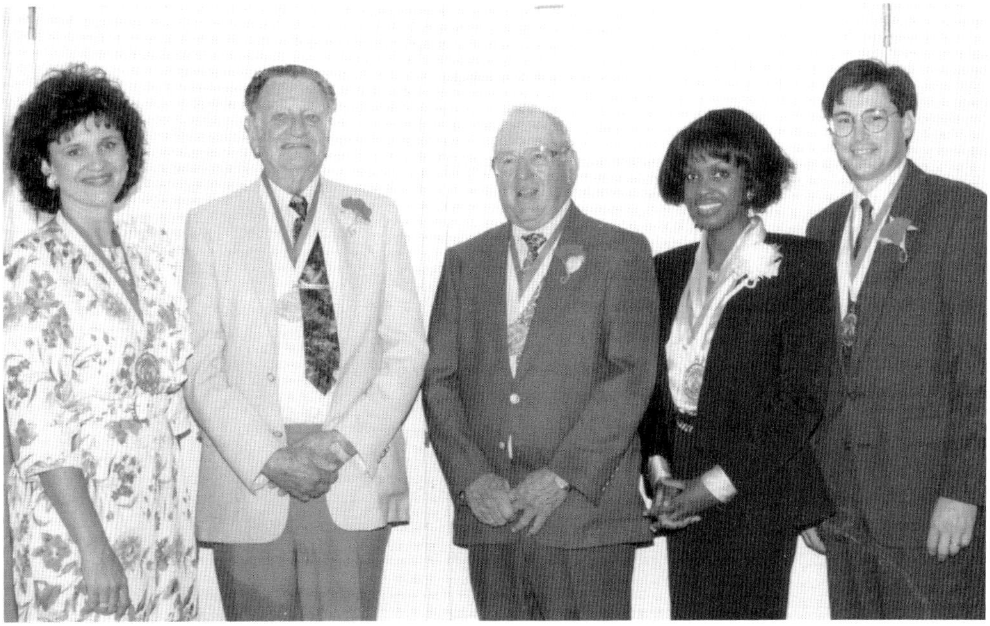

CHS Alumni Hall of Fame

In 1993, Clermont High School graduated its last class and inducted its last hall of fame members. Pictured above are, from left to right, Carmen Schoolcraft Arnold (retired Lake County educator), E.T. Brantly (standing in for his son, inventor Thomas Brantly), Jack Gaines (Clermont High School coach), Julia Johnson (Public Service commissioner), and Dean Saunders (state representative). (Courtesy of Toni Bell.)

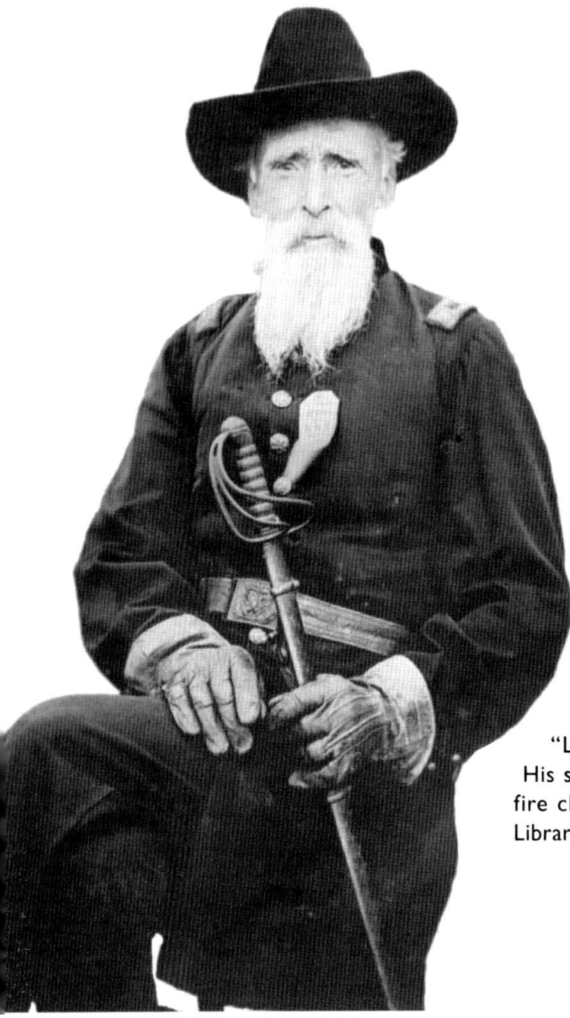

Capt. Montgomery Cooper

After the Civil War, Iowa native Montgomery Cooper moved his family to Clermont, where he held picnics that reunited Union and Confederate soldiers. He and his wife, Alice, donated land for the original Cooper Memorial Library. The building, affectionately called "Little Cooper," is preserved at the Historic Village. His sword is treasured by great-grandson and Clermont fire chief Carle Bishop. (Courtesy of Cooper Memorial Library Association.)

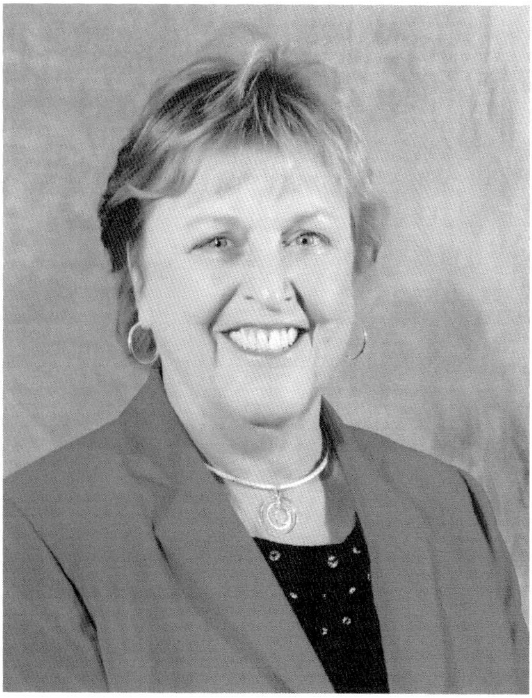

Leslie Longacre
Clermont Citizen of the Year Leslie Longacre touched many lives in her 35-year career. The former nurse retired in 2011 as chief executive officer of South Lake Hospital. She served as president of Cornerstone Hospice's board of directors and was chair of the South Lake Chamber of Commerce. *Orlando Business Journal* named her its 2011 Lifetime Achievement Hero. (Courtesy of South Lake Hospital.)

Tyson Gay, Champion
Clermont's National Training Center is home to numerous world-class athletes. Six NTC athletes have earned eight Olympic medals. Among the medalists is Tyson Gay (pictured), who won a silver medal in the 2012 Olympics for the men's 4x100 meter relay. Gay previously held the American record for the 100-meter dash. Other NTC Olympians include Justin Gatlin and Kellie Wells. (Courtesy of Adidas.)

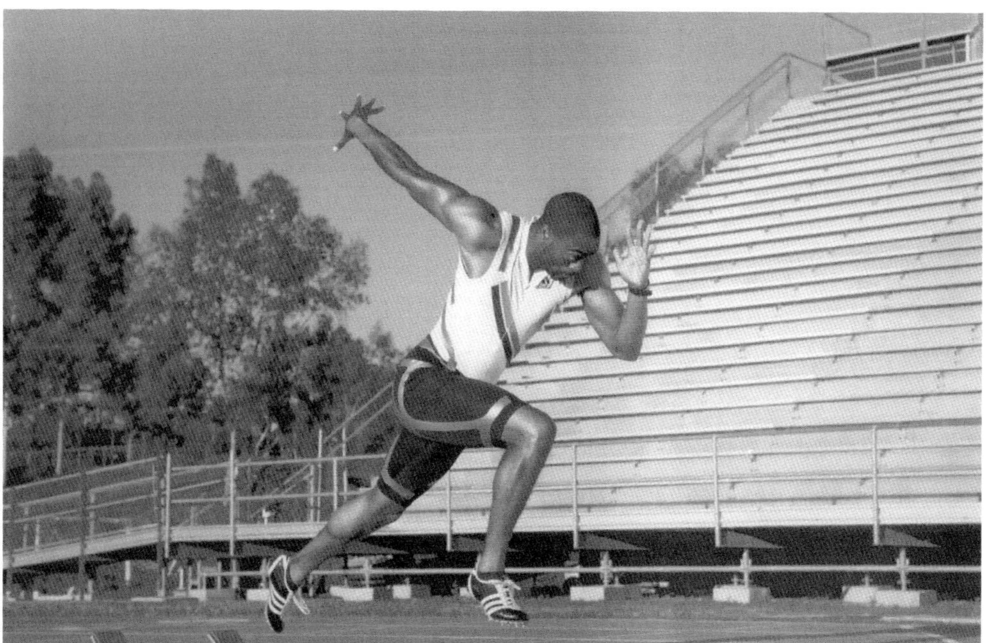

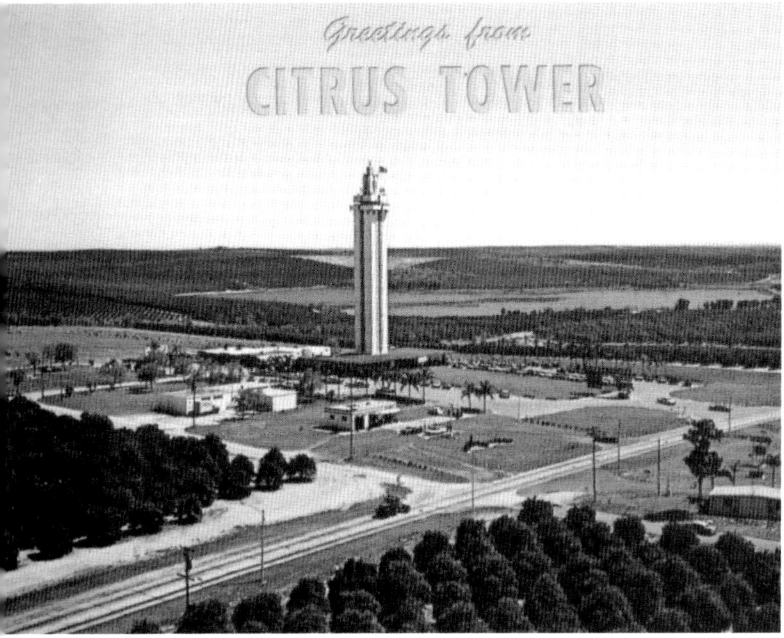

Citrus Tower
The iconic Citrus Tower was one of Florida's most popular attractions after it was built in 1956 by A.W. Thacker and Jack Toole, both formerly from Pittsburgh. The Citrus Tower, on US Highway 27, is currently owned by Greg Homan. It is the state's highest observation point and includes observation decks and a 360-degree view of more than 2,000 square miles. (Courtesy of Clayton Bishop.)

John Zweifel, Miniaturist
After he visited the White House in 1956, John Zweifel dreamed of building a miniature replica. The detailed model became part of Zweifel's Presidents Hall of Fame attraction in Clermont. Showing their replica to Pres. Gerald Ford are, from left to right, John Zweifel, Jan Zweifel, and Jack Zweifel. The *Guinness Book of World Records* calls the replica the world's largest dollhouse. (Courtesy of John Zweifel.)

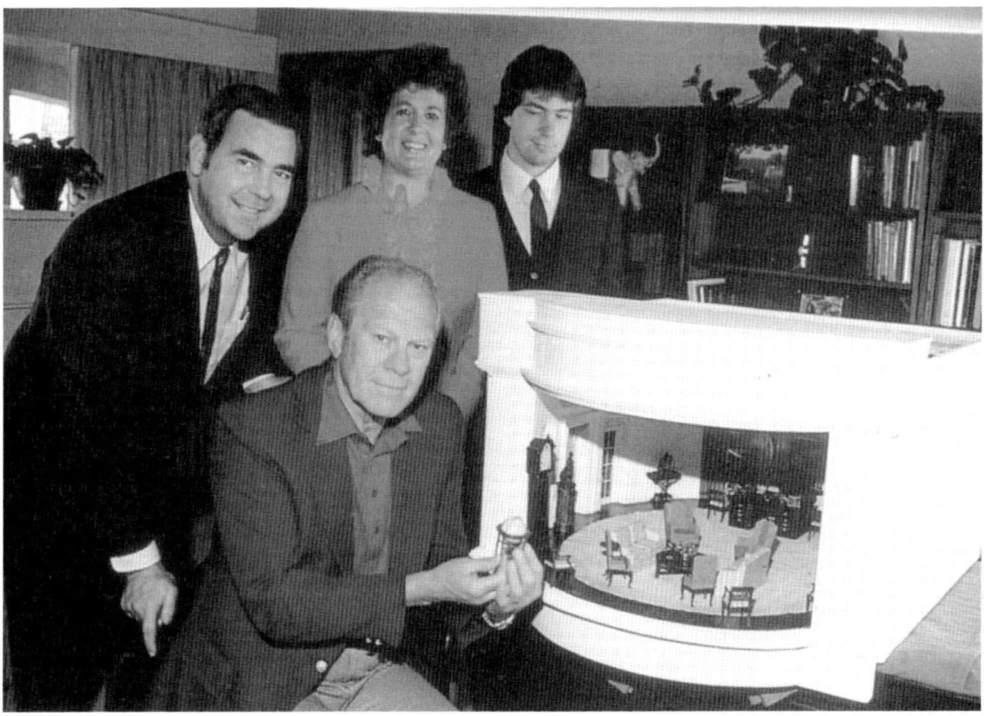

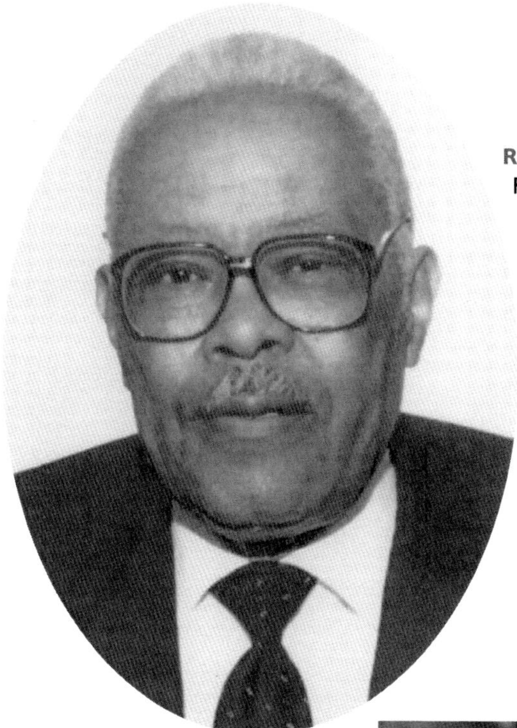

Rev. William McKinney
Few people are remembered more fondly than the Reverend William McKinney, former principal of Lincoln Park High School. His motto was "Anybody can be a quitter. Don't quit." His daughter, Aurelia Cole, is a longtime educator in Lake County schools. Her father also served as pastor of New Jacob's Baptist Church. A park was named in his honor. (Courtesy of Aurelia McKinney Cole.)

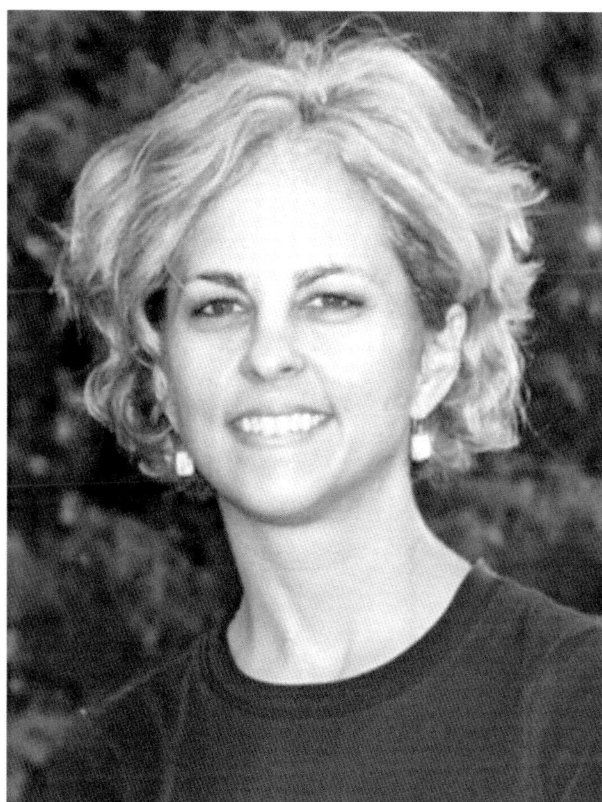

Kate DiCamillo, Author
Newberry Award–winning author Kate DiCamillo loved books and writing from the time she was a child in Clermont. She is the author of *Because of Winn-Dixie* and *The Tale of Despereaux*. Both of the popular children's books were made into movies. She currently lives in Minneapolis, but has many family members still residing in Clermont. (Courtesy of Winding Oak and Candlewick Press.)

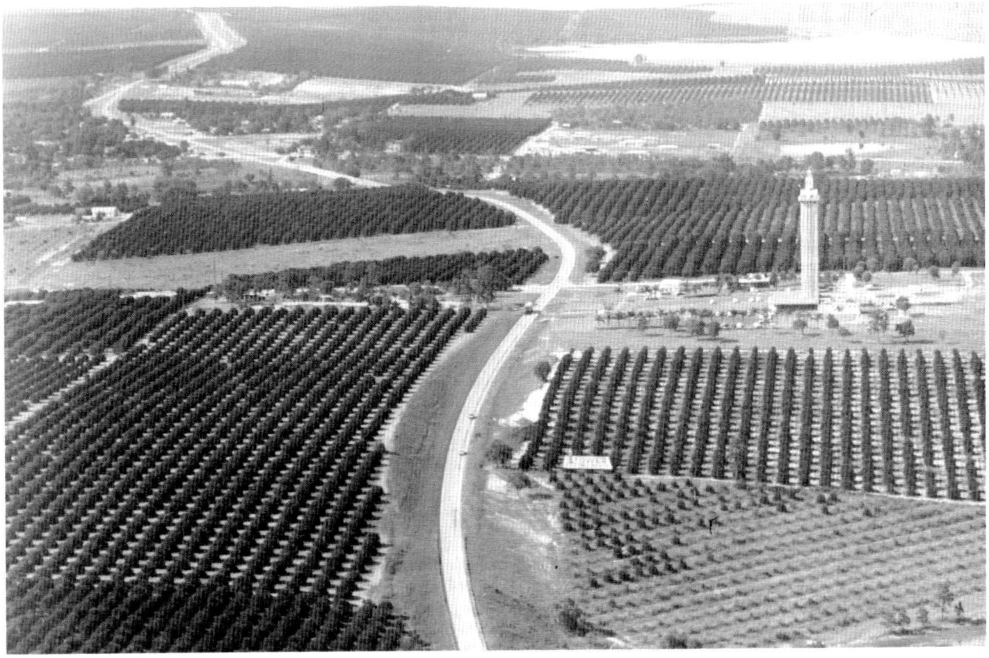

When Citrus was King
Before devastating freezes in the 1980s, south Lake County was blanketed with orange groves. Citrus was king, driving much of Lake County's economy. Historic grove-owning names include Langley, Leininger, Crittenden, Viti, Micheloni, Wynn, Minute Maid, Blue Goose, and Clermont's Postal Colony. The Kuharske family invented a root stock that continues to be popular throughout the citrus industry. (Courtesy of the State Archives of Florida.)

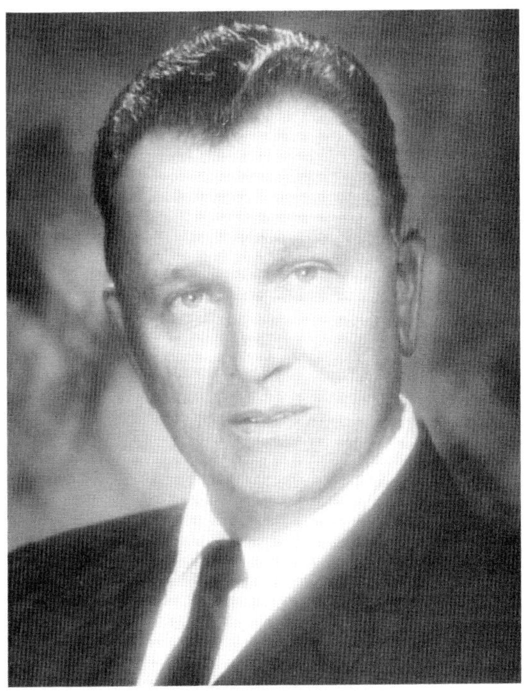

Eugene Busbee
In 1944, business partners Eugene Busbee, William Bolin, and Norton Wilkins entered the citrus business in Groveland, forming B&W Canning Company. B&W was the largest employer of its kind in the state of Florida, with more than 500 employees. Severe freezes during the 1980s decimated the citrus industry, including B&W. The plant was demolished in 2009. (Courtesy of Barbara Busbee Sealy.)

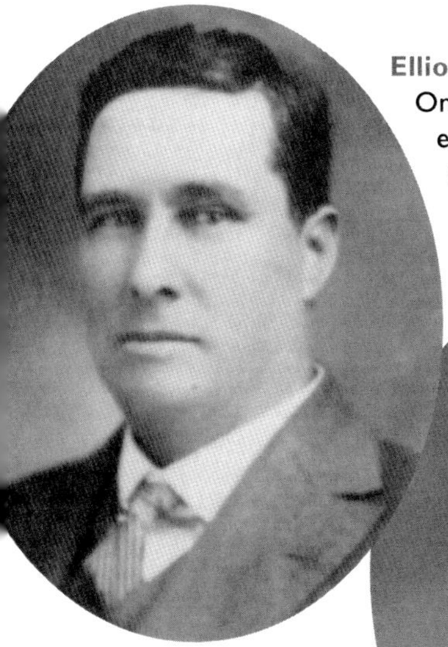

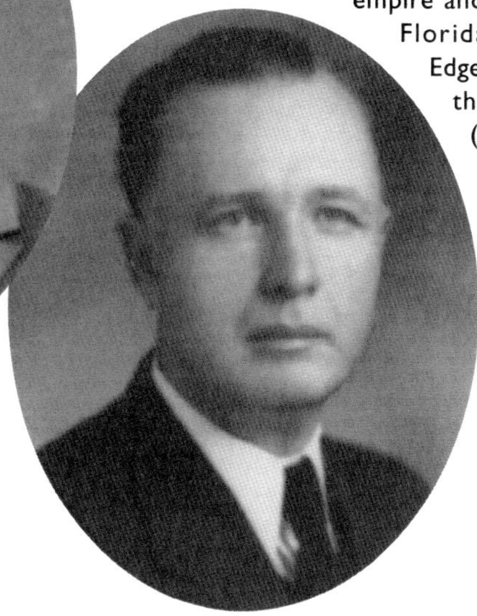

Elliott E. Edge and Lacy D. Edge

One of Lake County's most successful father-and-son teams was the entrepreneurial E.E. Edge (left) and his politically savvy son, L.D. Edge (right), who was the youngest-ever speaker of the Florida House of Representatives. The Edges ran a large business and agricultural empire and started what evolved into the Florida Telephone Company. L.D. Edge, Groveland's first mayor, drove the construction of Highway 50. (Courtesy of the Groveland Historical Society.)

Joe Fairchild Sr., Visionary Leader

Third-generation banker Joe Fairchild Sr. not only earned a reputation for integrity while establishing People's State Bank, but he also was instrumental, as Groveland's mayor, in bringing residential mail delivery and street lights to the city. He supported many school, church, and civic programs. Fairchild (right) is shown in 1959 accepting the first residential mail delivery from Stanley Koss. (June Fairchild.)

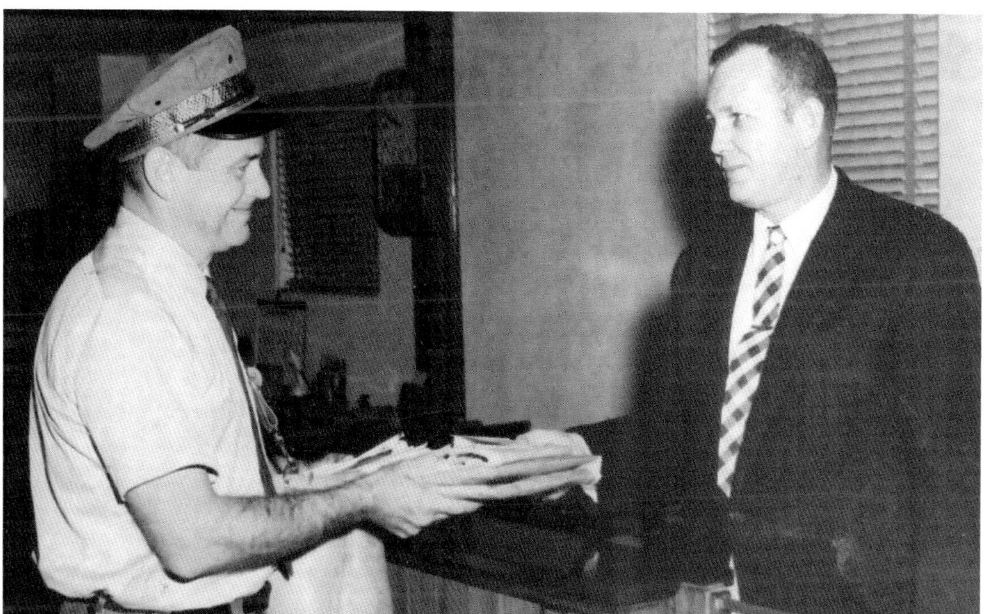

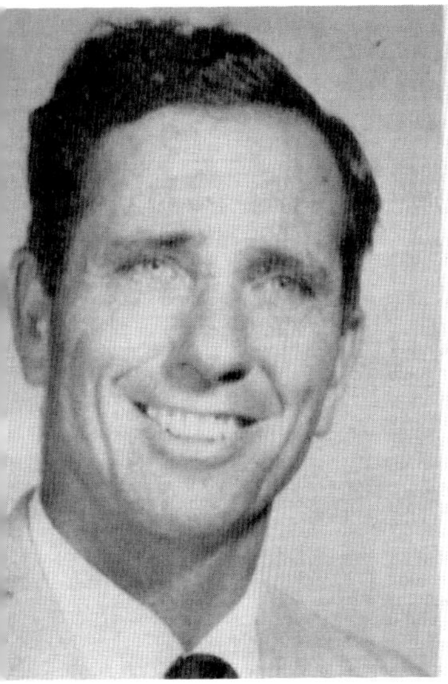

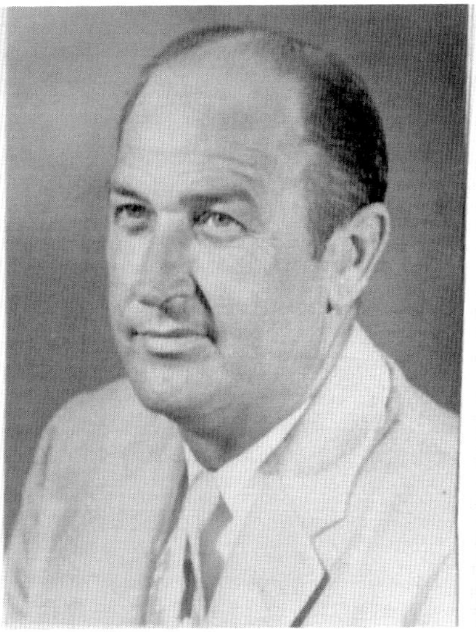

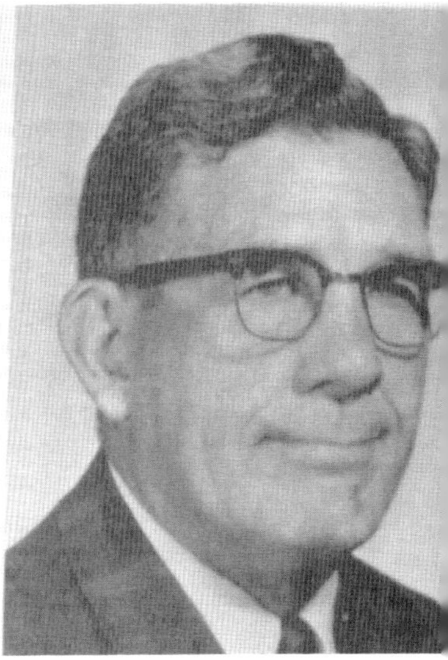

Shaw Buck, Julian Rowe, and Walter Stanfield
The Groveland High School legends pictured above are, from left to right, Shaw Buck, Julian Rowe, and Walter Stanfield. Buck was a Florida Athletic Coaches Association Hall of Fame coach known for his winning teams and for building character. He was assisted by athletic director Rowe, a Groveland postman for 50 years, and Stanfield, a popular teacher and former boxer. (Courtesy of the Groveland Historical Society.)

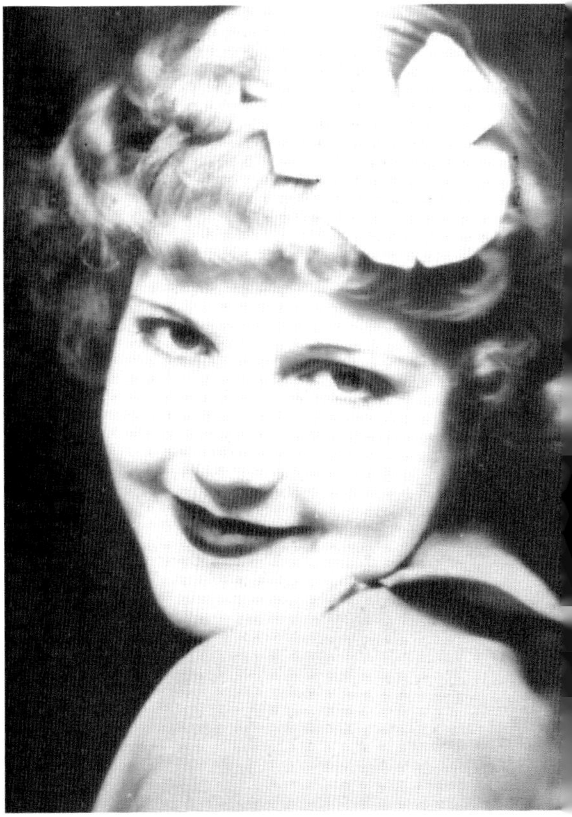

Cyleta Lee Austin, Historian Emeritus
Descended from some of south Lake County's earliest pioneer families, the Lees and Carters, Cyleta Lee Austin meticulously recorded local history and supported the Lake County Historical Society. From an early age, Groveland's historian emeritus was fascinated by history, and she maintained a rare photograph collection. Austin, born in 1917, was a contributor to *Through the Schoolhouse Doors: A History of Lake County Schools.* (Courtesy of Cyleta Lee Austin.)

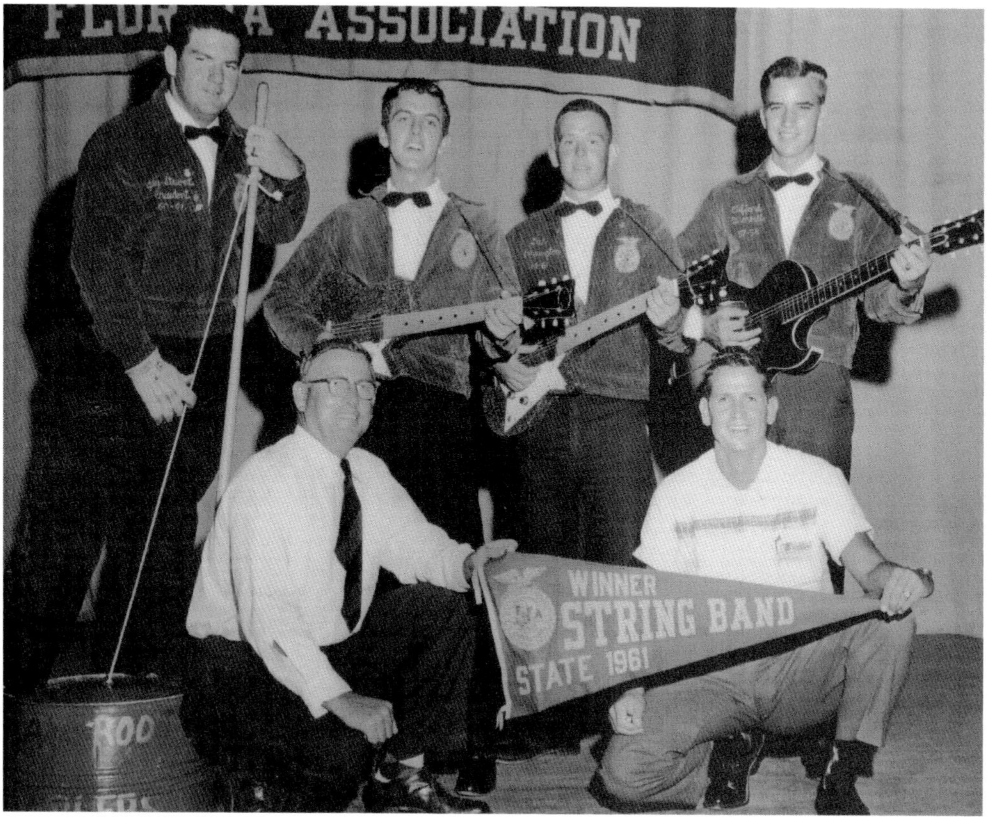

FFA Legends

Agricultural teachers Robert Campbell and Freddie Garner brought national recognition to Groveland's Future Farmers of America (FFA) program. Garner became the superintendent of Lake County schools. Many of Groveland's FFA students had successful agricultural careers, including FFA Hall of Famer Donald Bronson. Pictured here are, from left to right, (first row) Robert Campbell and Freddie Garner; (second row) Jay Stewart, Sherman McGregor, Keith Rudd, and Earl Drawdy. (Courtesy of the Groveland Historical Society.)

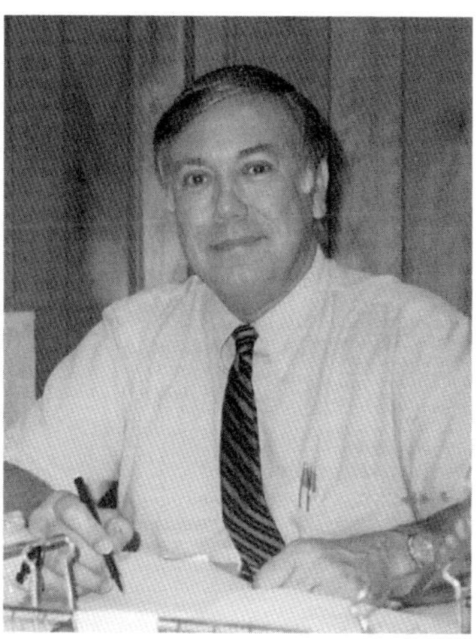

Cecil Gray, Educator

In 1960, Cecil Gray started teaching English at Groveland High School. He was adviser for many senior classes and became Groveland Middle School principal in 1987. After his accidental death from a fall 10 years later, the community sought to rename the school in his honor. Today, Cecil Gray Middle School is a $43 million, state-of-the art campus. (Courtesy of BettyAnn Gray.)

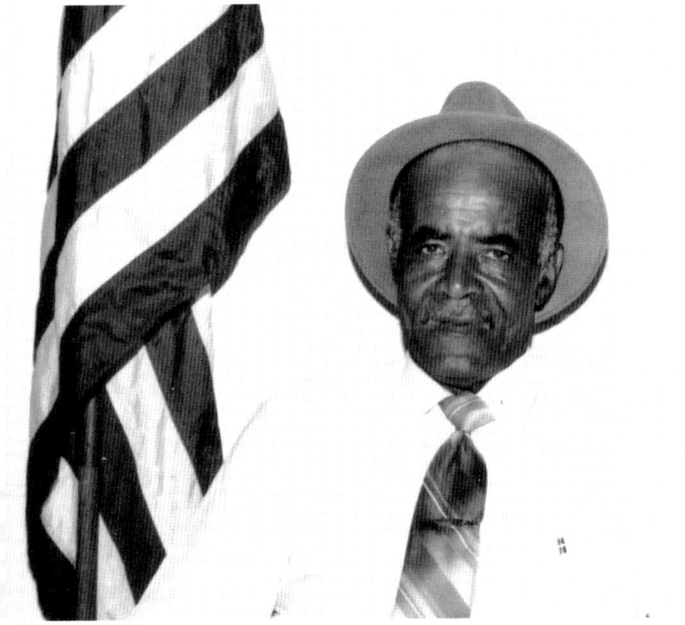

Lewis Hart, History-Maker

A former Alabama sharecropper, Lewis Hart moved to Groveland in the early 1950s to work in the citrus industry. He became a crew leader and later was a successful fruit-harvesting contractor. He bought nearly two dozen rental properties. He became Groveland's first African American city council member in 1974, a position he held for 28 years, during which time he earned a reputation for sticking up for the underdog. (Courtesy of the City of Groveland.)

James Wyche and Johnny Griffin, Community Leaders

Johnny Griffin (left) is a respected historian, entrepreneur, and Groveland city council member. He was a student of James Wyche (right), for whom the city's senior center is named. Griffin's father, John Griffin, was adviser to the Lake County School Board. Wyche was principal and teacher at segregated Edgewood Elementary School and became a school board administrator later in his career. (Courtesy of the Groveland Historical Society.)

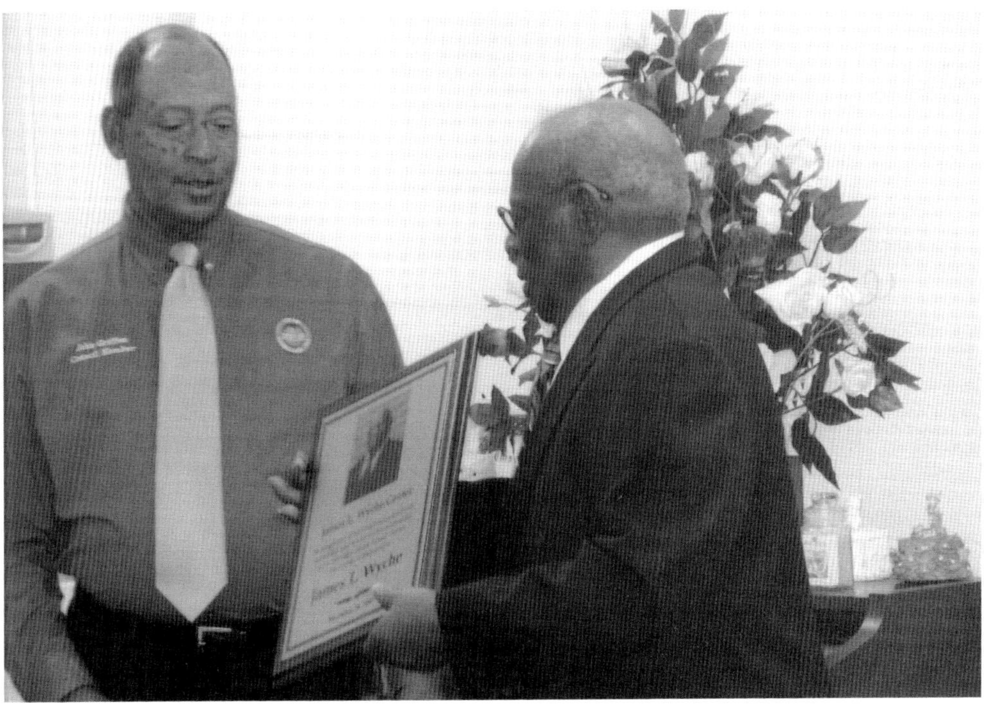

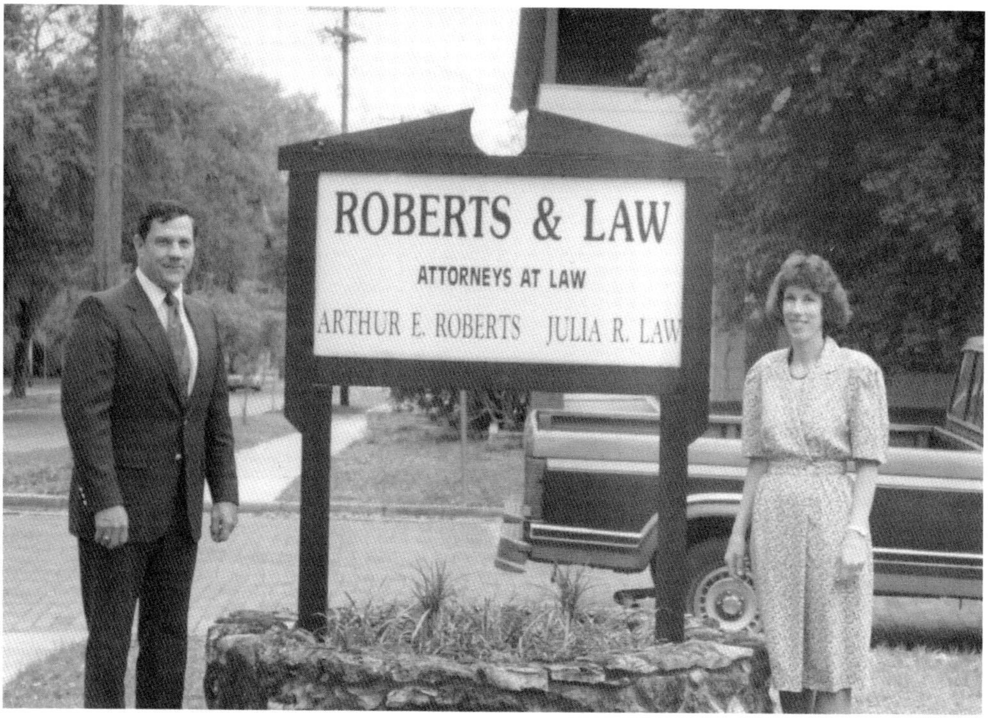

Arthur Roberts and Julia Roberts Law—A Family Affair
Groveland natives Arthur Roberts (left) and his daughter, Julia Roberts Law, practiced law together for more than a decade. They were city attorneys and shared a passion for community service. Roberts opened his office in 1961, saying he wanted to be "a country lawyer." His daughter joined the firm in 1980, along with her husband, Bill Law, who became a judge. (Courtesy of Julia Roberts Law.)

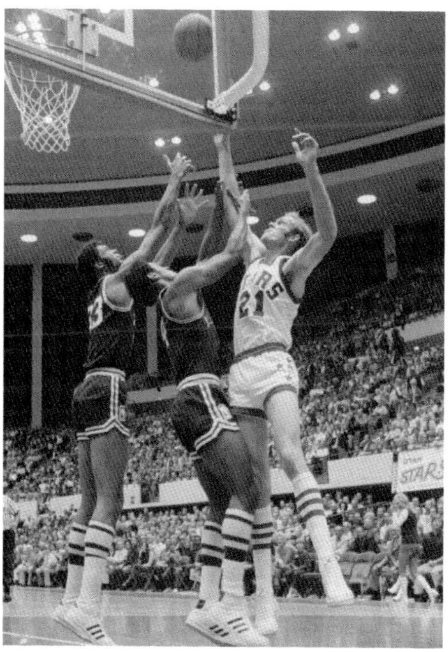

Austin "Red" Robbins, Professional Athlete
A star basketball player at Groveland High School, Austin "Red" Robbins (right) was an All-American at the University of Tennessee and led the Utah Stars to the American Basketball Association championship in 1971. He also played with the San Diego Conquistadores, New Orleans Bucs, and Kentucky Colonels. He stayed close to Groveland High schoolmates and donated memorabilia to the Groveland Historical Museum. (Courtesy of Austin Robbins.)

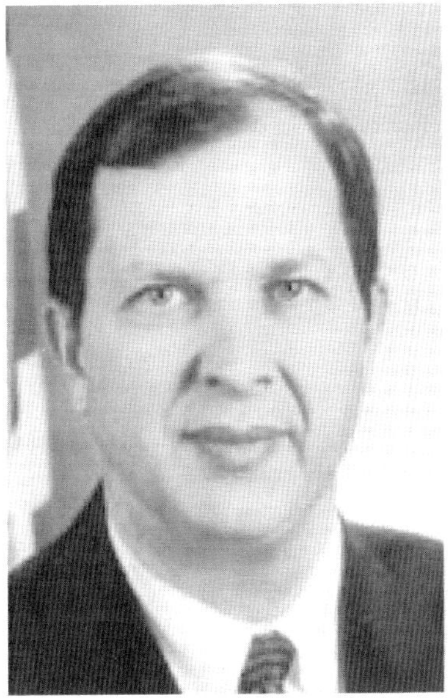

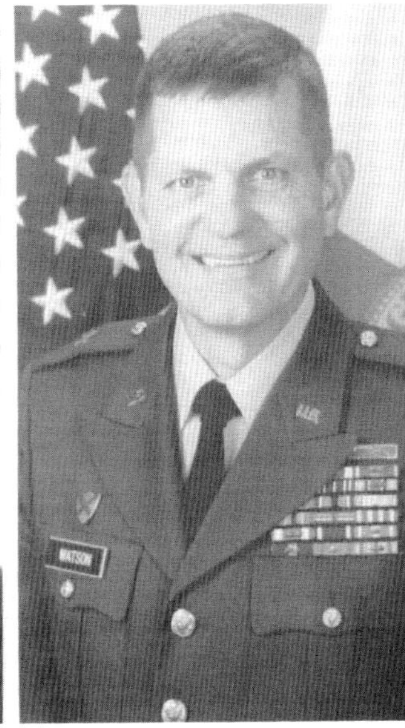

Dale and Jimmy Watson, Hometown Heroes

Sons of a Baptist minister, the Watson brothers spent their careers in public service. Dale Watson (left) was head of counterterrorism and counterintelligence for the FBI during September 11, 2001. He led major terrorist investigations and is the sole recipient of the Presidential Rank Award for the FBI. Brig. Gen. Jimmy Watson (right) oversaw the largest-ever deployment of Florida's National Guard to Iraq, among many other achievements. (Courtesy of Jimmy Watson and the FBI.)

Chief Thomas "Tommy" Merrill

As Groveland's top law-enforcement officer for 43 years, chief Tommy Merrill had the honor of being America's longest-serving active police chief. The average length of service for police chiefs in the United States is five years. In 2006, the Florida Peace Officers Association presented Merrill with the Distinguished Service Award. He retired in November 2012. (Courtesy of Groveland Historical Society.)

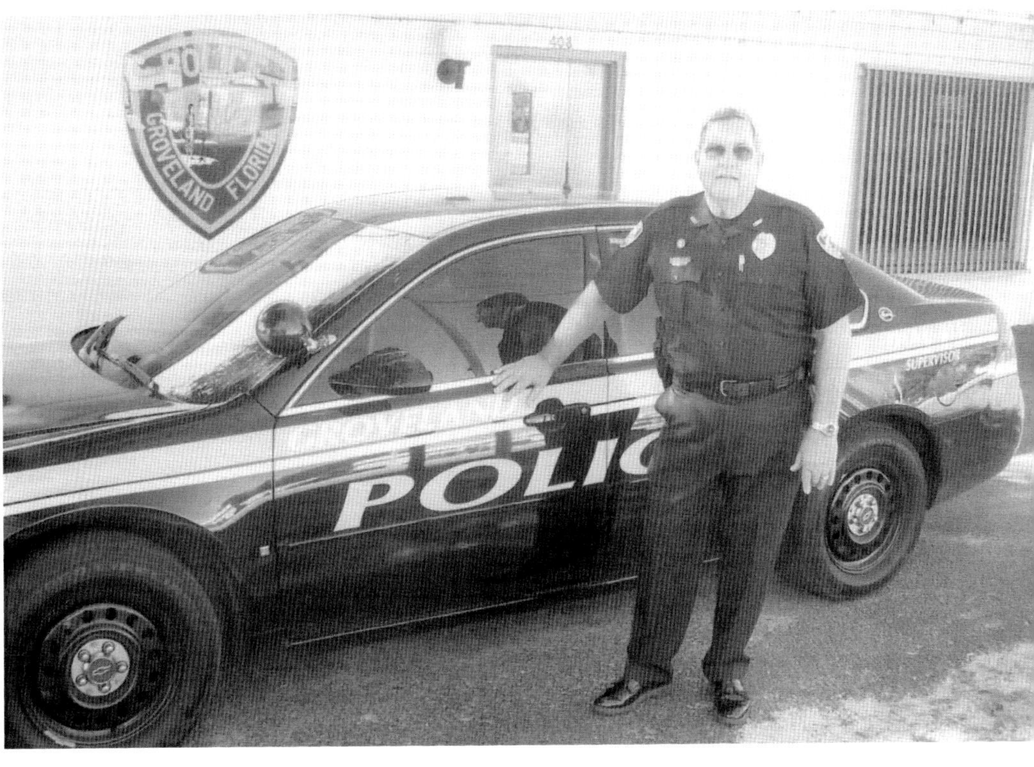

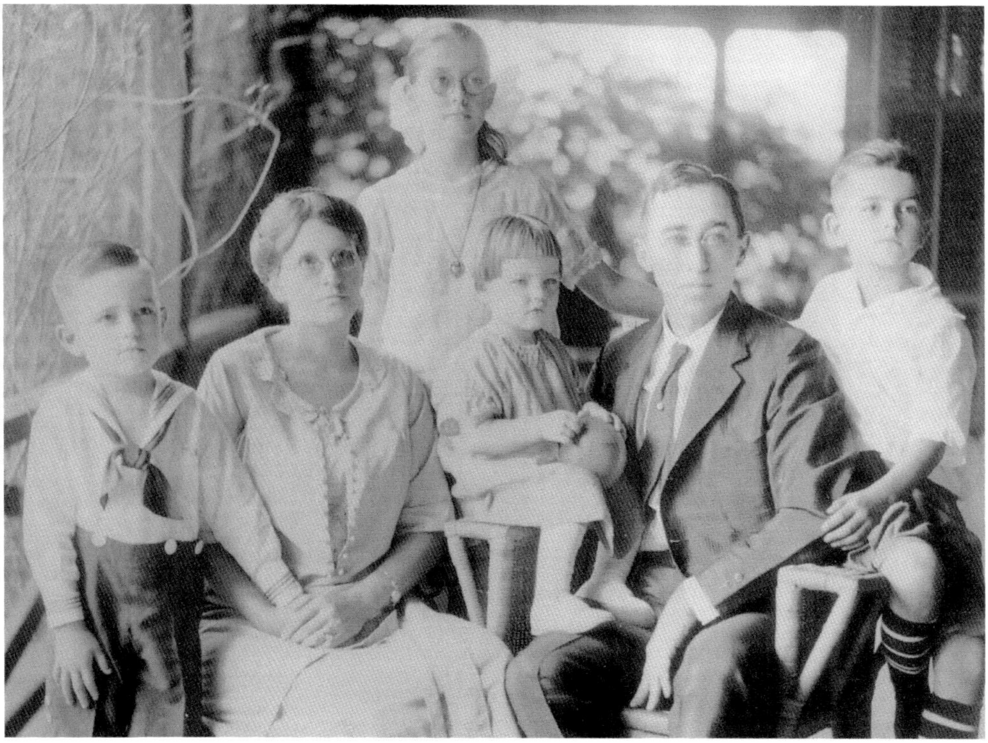

J. Ray Arnold
In 1920, an ambitious sawmill machinery salesman named J. Ray Arnold bought a mill in Taylorville, the former name of Groveland. Within a few years, it was the largest sawmill in the southeastern United States. In this photograph, the Arnold family poses for a portrait. The family members are, from left to right, Charles, Eva Lee, Frances (standing), Lucile, J. Ray, and Jeff. The Arnolds had two more children not pictured: Kathryn "Kitty" and Julian. (Courtesy of Kitty Arnold Herzog.)

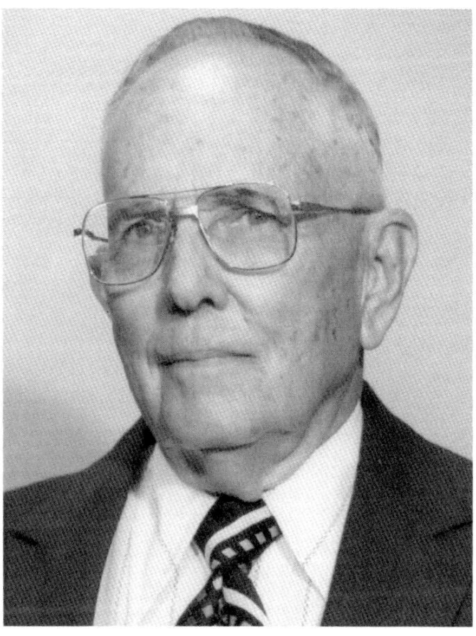

Ray Robbins
In 1937, Tuscanooga native Ray Robbins went door-to-door, encouraging residents to sign up to bring electricity to rural southwest Lake County. The next year, he became the Sumter Electric Cooperative's first employee. He rose through the ranks and retired as district manager of the Groveland office. After retirement, he served on the board of directors, including one term as chairman. (Courtesy of Mary Helen Myers.)

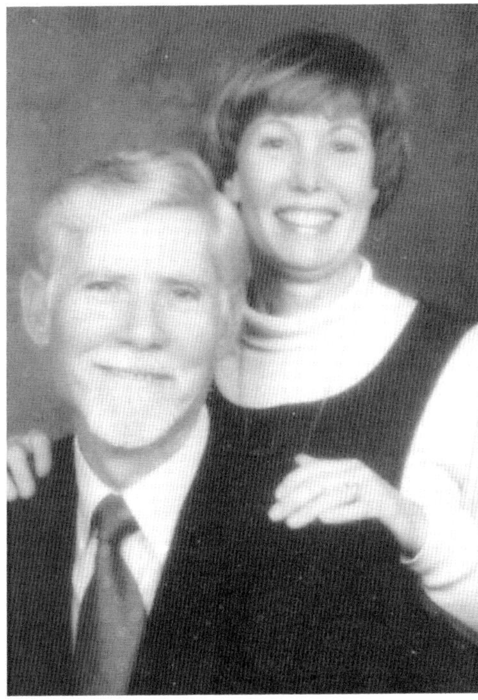

Marilyn Gammon Smith

A former homecoming queen, Marilyn Gammon Smith maintained affection for her hometown and high school throughout her life. She managed a website for Groveland High School alumni, and this led to her dying wish to start a historical museum. Shortly after her death in 2007, the new museum was dedicated to her memory. Her husband, Kemp Smith, is president of the Groveland Historical Society. (Courtesy of Kemp Smith.)

Irvin Barwick

Groveland football standout Irvin Barwick earned an athletic scholarship that took him to Chipola Junior College and an agricultural degree from the University of Florida. He was employed in the citrus industry for more than 30 years. Pictured below shaking hands with Polish leader Lech Walesa (left), Barwick was part of a Florida trade mission to Europe. A Groveland High School alumni award bears his name. (Courtesy of the Barwick family.)

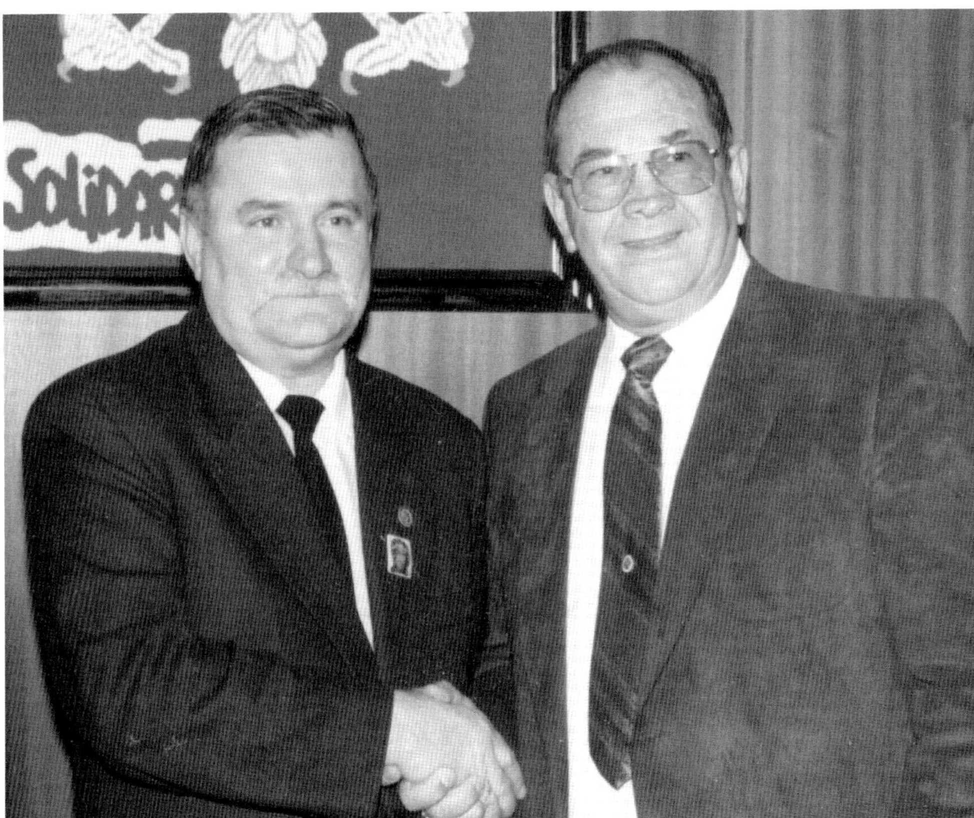

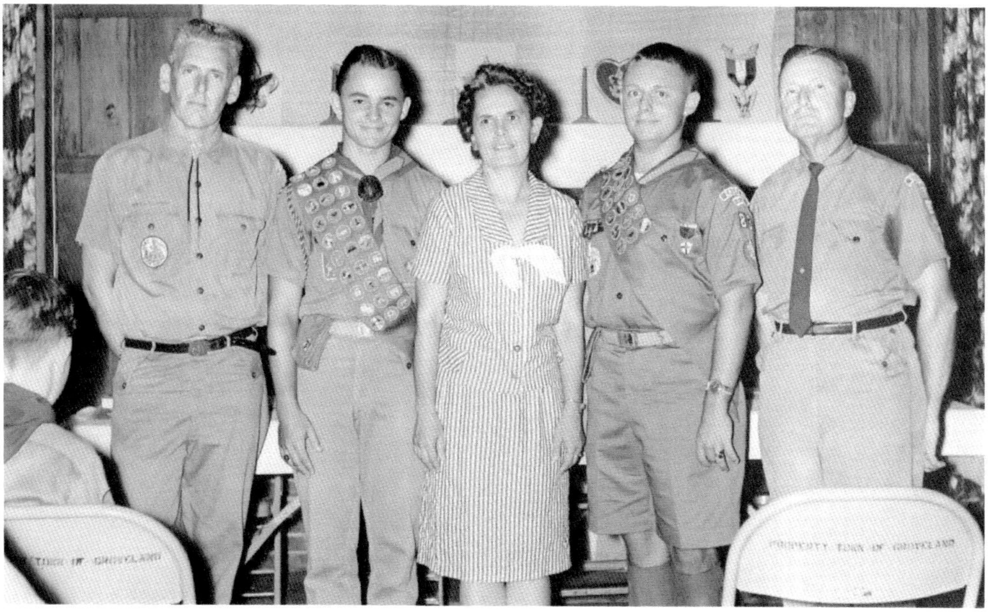

Bob and Marion Baysinger
Illinois natives Bob and Marion Baysinger were chaperones at Groveland's Teenway Club in the 1960s and were active in many church and civic activities, including the Boy Scouts. Bob Baysinger was a postman and World War II veteran. The city's library is named after Marion Baysinger, a tireless volunteer. Pictured here are, from left to right, Scoutmaster Paul Hoskinson, Ric Baysinger, Marion Baysinger, Jim Baysinger, and Bob Baysinger. (Courtesy of Ric Baysinger.)

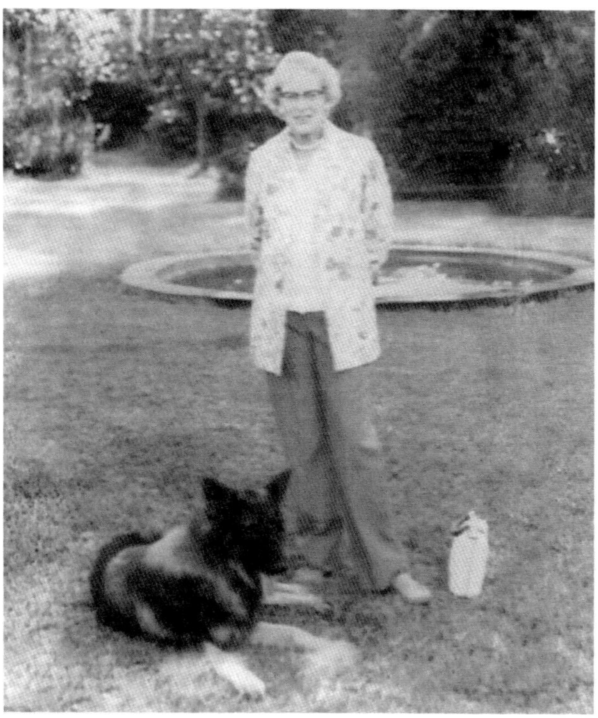

Meg Lewis
Boston native Meg Lewis and her husband, Frank, made their Tin Cup Ranch in Bay Lake the home of Girl Scout Mounted Troop 90, the only one of its kind in Florida. For more than 30 years, she organized an annual Girl Scout Rodeo. She is remembered for making each girl feel special and empowered to achieve their goals as young women. (Courtesy of Jowynn Sabin.)

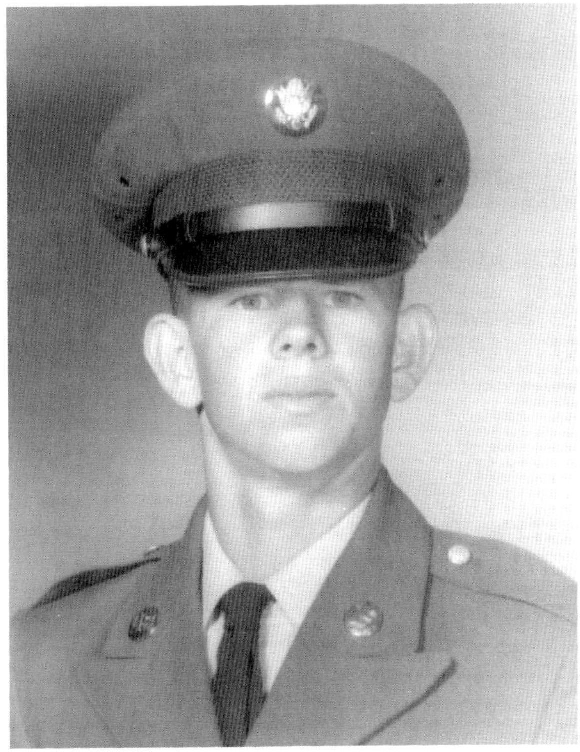

Jess Thomas

Sgt. Jess Thomas was the son of longtime Mascotte mayor Fred Thomas. Jess Thomas was drafted into the Army after graduating from Groveland High School in 1965. While on a mission in Vietnam, his unit came under heavy fire and suffered casualties. He charged enemy bunkers before he was mortally wounded. He was posthumously awarded the Bronze Star, Purple Heart, and Presidential Military Merit Medal. (Courtesy of Ila Mae Thomas.)

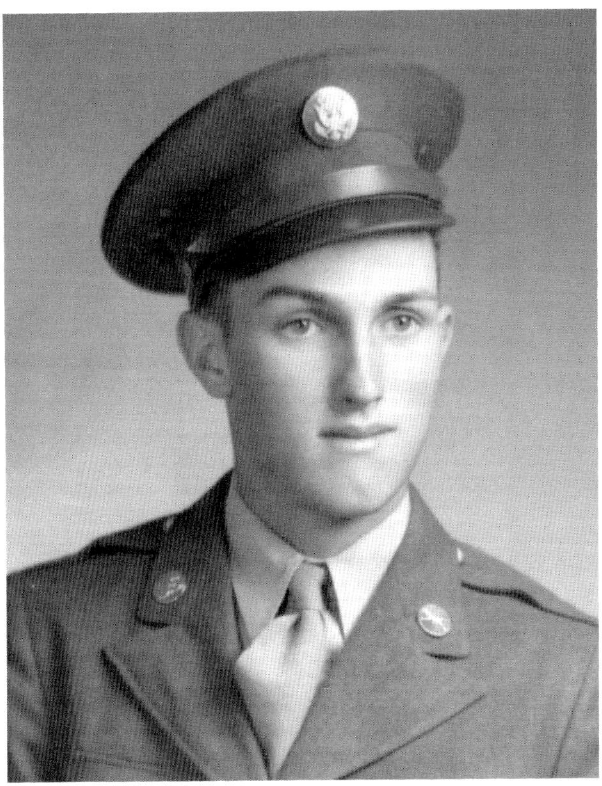

PFC Ray Tedder

Mascotte native PFC Ray Tedder was a member of the 16th Infantry, 1st Division. He took part in the Normandy invasion and died during combat in Germany on April 14, 1945. He was posthumously awarded the Bronze Star and the Purple Heart. The Mascotte civic center is named the Tedder-Thomas Memorial Civic Center to honor him and fellow soldier Jess Thomas. (Courtesy of Don and Tina Wynn.)

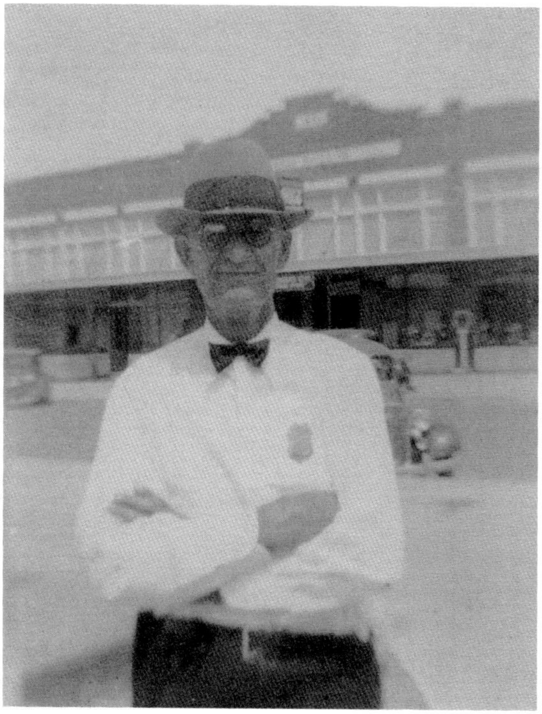

George Myers
Before George Myers became Mascotte's first mayor, he had served as a federal marshal in the Wild West, where he won a horsehair bridle from the legendary Geronimo. His wife, Susan Myers, ran the Groveland Hotel while he served as Groveland's town marshal around 1928. Part of Highway 50 is named in his honor. (Courtesy of Dolores Gano Walker.)

Bristo and James McGregor
Gospel singers Bristo (left) and James McGregor (center) spent much of their 55 years of marriage singing at weddings, funerals, and many special events. When they were in their twenties, the duo competed in a talent contest. The prize was a recording contract in Nashville. The couple tied two out of three times, finally losing to a then-unknown country singer named Mel Tillis. (Courtesy of Bristo McGregor.)

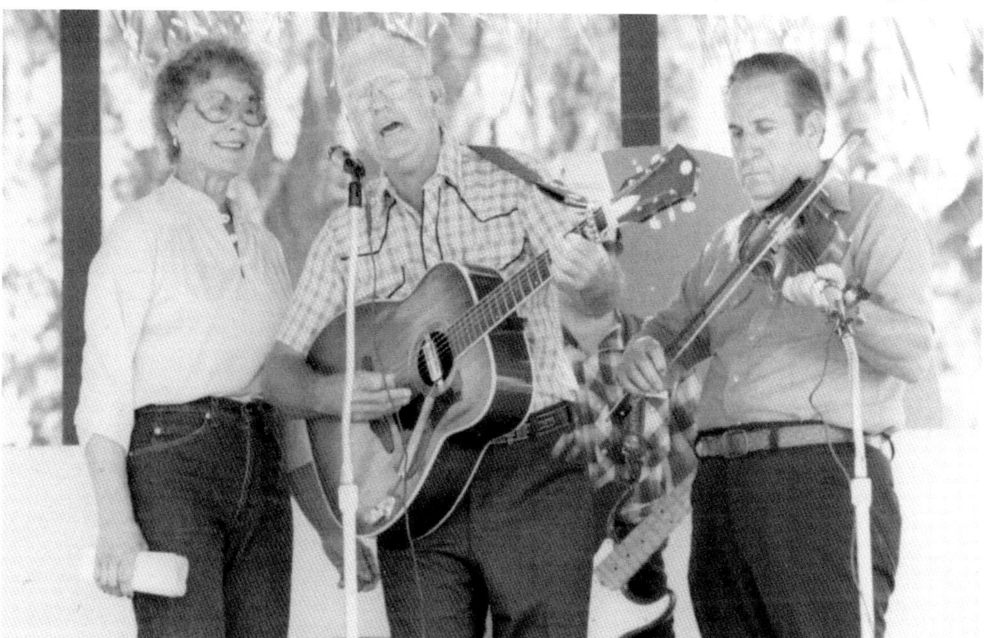

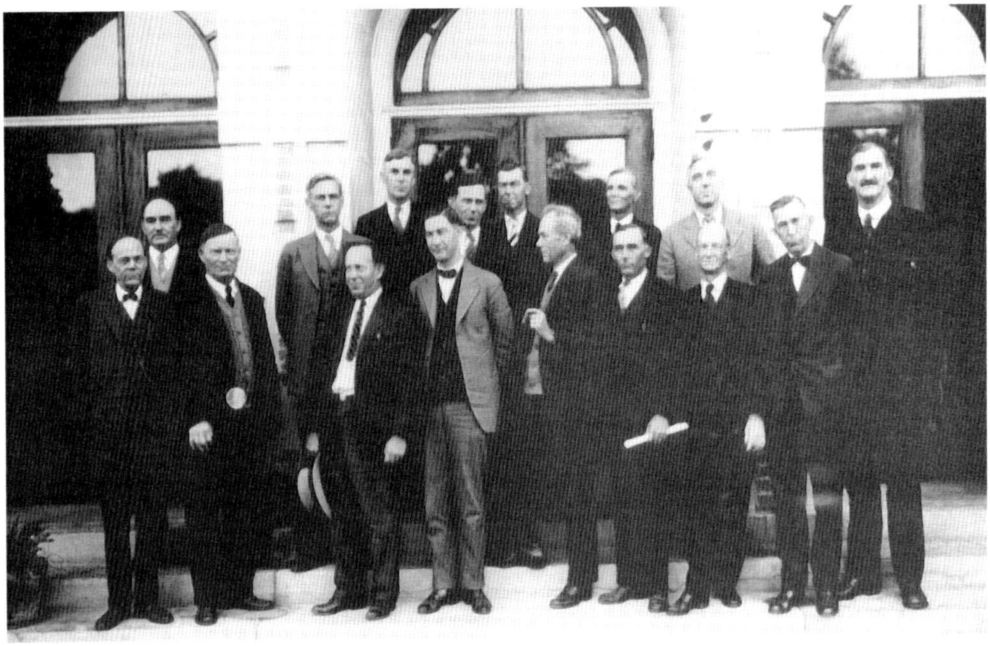

Manuel Sloan
Revered Lake County commissioner Manuel Sloan was the grandson of Groveland founder Daniel Sloan. He is remembered as someone always willing to help his neighbors. A successful cattle rancher, Sloan is pictured here (first row, sixth from left) holding plans for the Howey Bridge that spans Little Lake Harris. His son, G.P., gained national attention by becoming a Groveland city council member on a coin toss. (Courtesy of Peggy Parrish Sloan.)

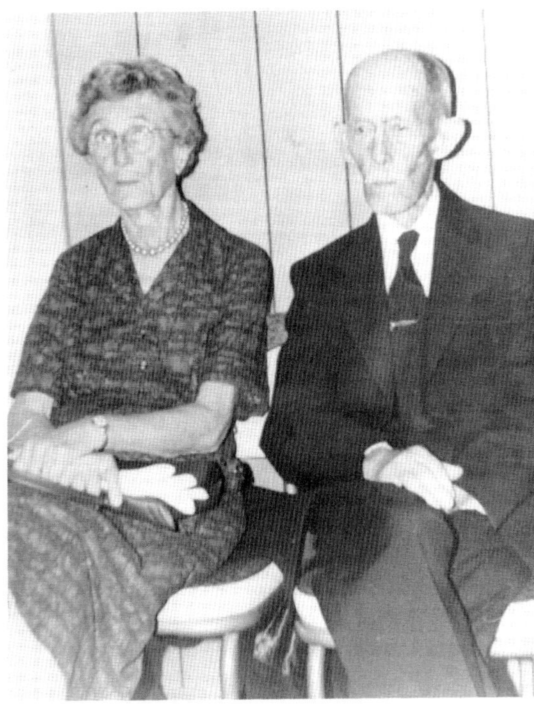

Daisy and Ollie Slone
Pioneers Daisy Merritt Slone (left), and her husband, Ollie Slone, generously shared their crops and livestock with other Slone Ridge settlers. He was the grandson of Capt. William Slone, a former Confederate soldier. She was known to crochet while hunting for squirrels with her 12-gauge shotgun. A true Florida cracker, Ollie Slone snapped his 14-foot-long whip over the heads of cattle he herded. (Courtesy of Jeanette Edmundson.)

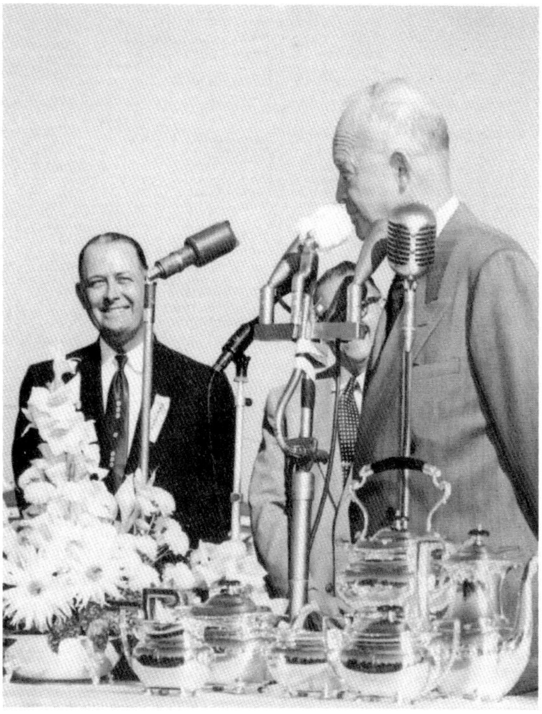

Sherman Drawdy

After graduating from Groveland High School and Tampa Business College, Sherman Drawdy became a hometown banker and then became the state's youngest bank examiner, at the age of 22. His career included working for the FDIC, the Federal Reserve Board of Atlanta, and the Georgia Railroad Bank & Trust Company, where he was chairman. In this photograph, Pres. Dwight Eisenhower honors Drawdy (left) for his outstanding work. (Courtesy of Glen Jones.)

Sheryl Williams and Jo Helen Walker, Stuckey Heroes

Lifelong Stuckey residents Sheryl Williams (left) and Jo Helen Walker devoted their lives to community service. They started Stuckey Kids Enrichment Program to serve at-risk children, among many other good deeds. Their service earned numerous accolades, including the South Lake Black Achievers Award. Williams was named Gray Middle School's Teacher of the Year in 2004. Walker portrays abolitionist Sojourner Truth and sings at nursing homes. (Courtesy of Sheryl Williams.)

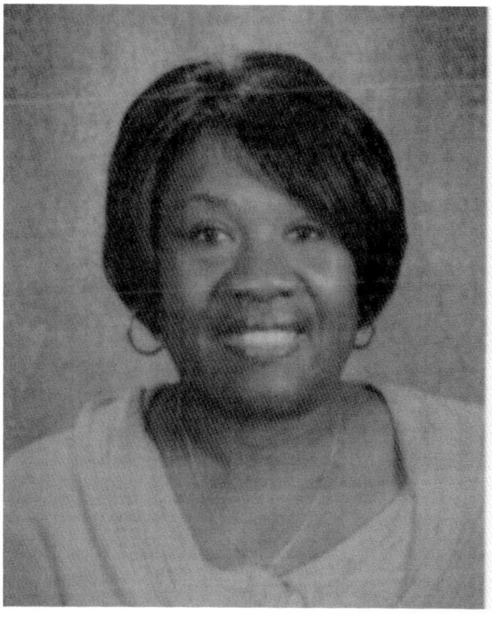

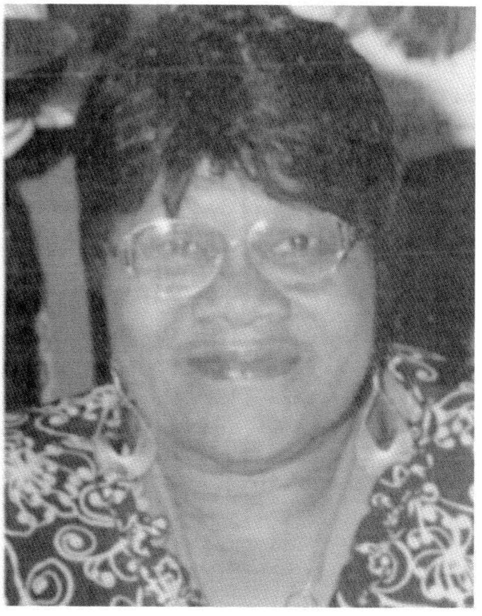

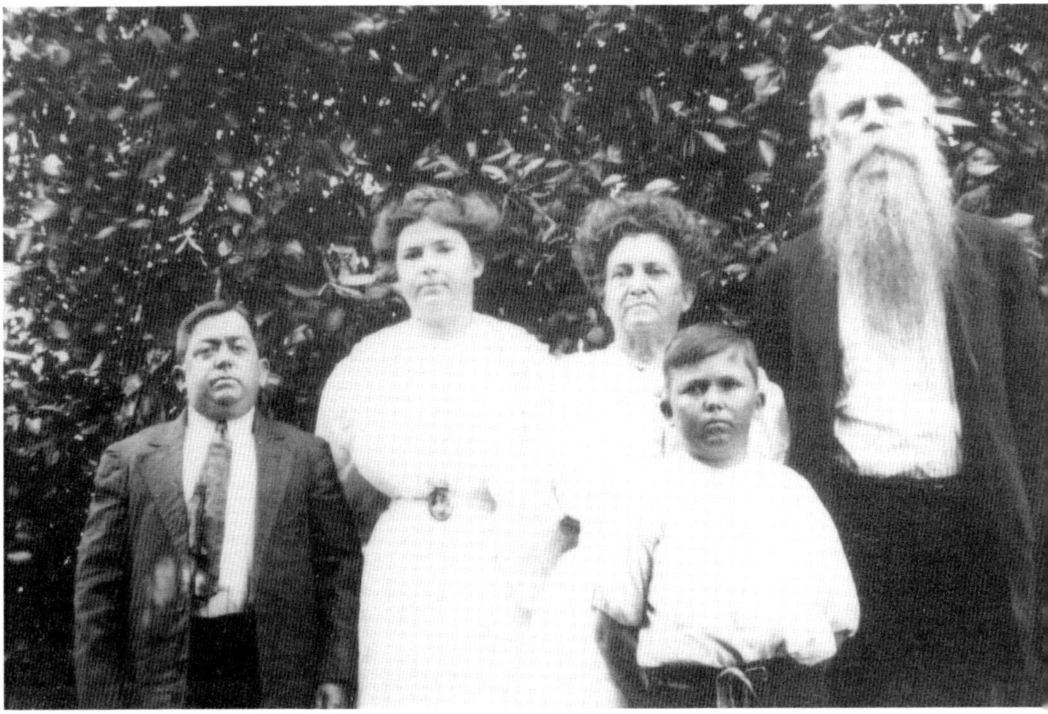

Archibald Pitt, Minneola Pioneer
Early Minneola settler Archibald Pitt came to the lakeside community in 1883. The Kentucky native was easily recognized by his long beard. He was the town's first postmaster and mayor. Pitt family members shown here are, from left to right, Allie (son, served as postmaster for 34 years), Elizabeth (daughter), Maude (daughter), Rush (son), and Archibald. (Courtesy of James Pitt.)

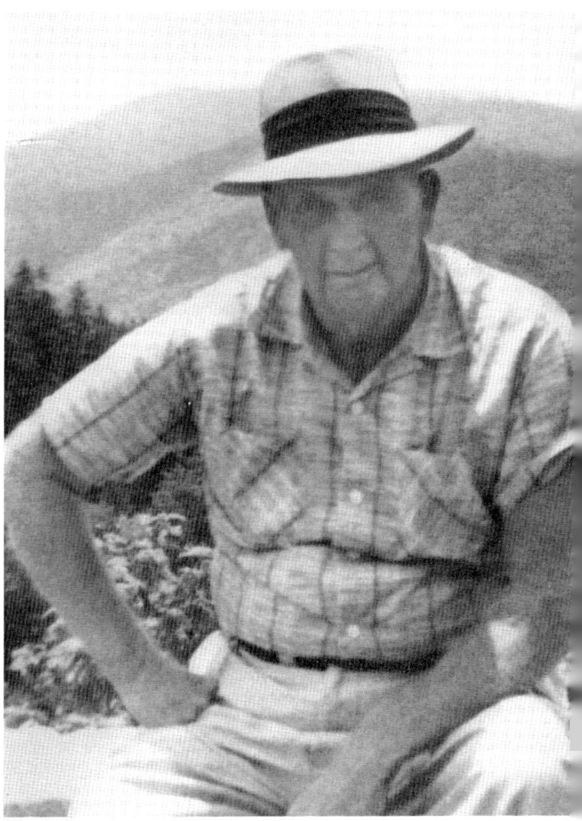

Hamp Walker
Minneola's 16th mayor, W.H. "Hamp" Walker served from 1956 until 1964, when he died unexpectedly while in office. Walker was known as a humble, honest man who loved the City of Minneola. Under his progressive leadership, the city erected a new community building, replacing a 1932 log cabin. He also led efforts to establish the waterworks department and to pave the streets. (Courtesy of Lillie Warren.)

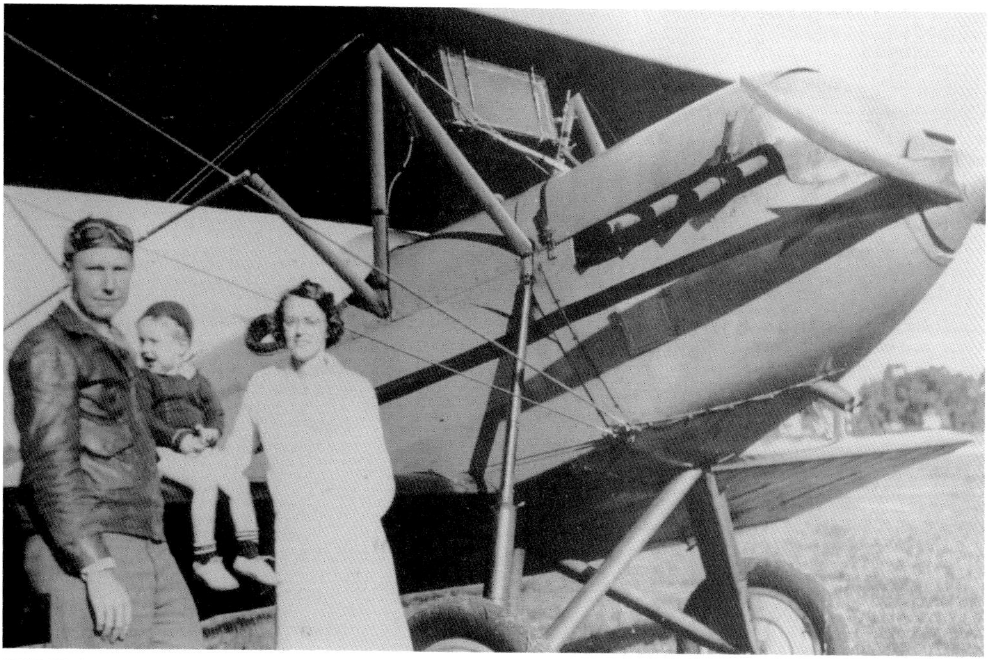

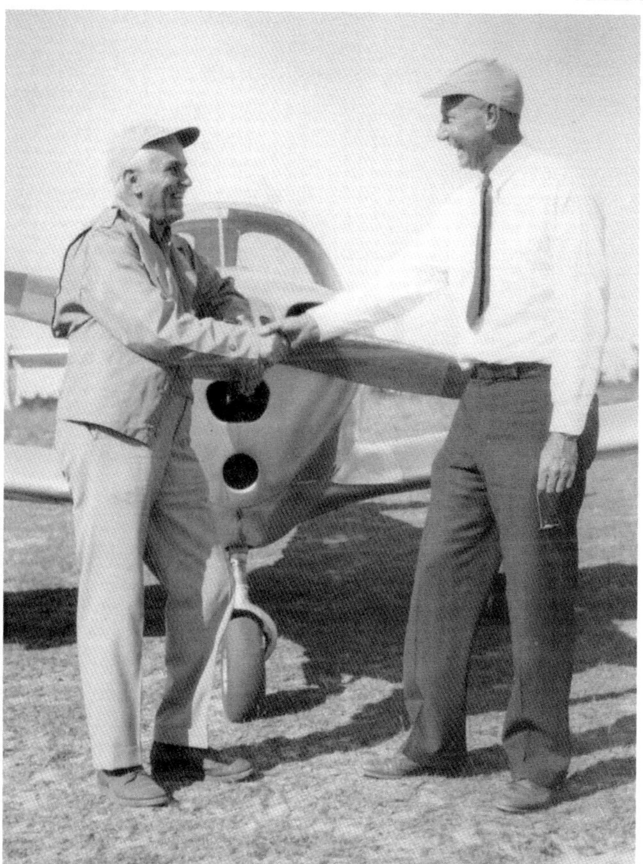

Eliot Kerlin, Aviator

In 1897, Eliot Kerlin and his family moved to Minneola. He was a teacher before going to Kansas to work at Stearman Aircraft Corporation. Kerlin became a licensed pilot and moved back to Florida with his wife and son. In 1937, he built Kerlin Airfield near Minneola. He became an instructor and trained more than 1,000 pilots. During one session, a buzzard smashed into Kerlin's Piper Cub, shattering the propeller and windshield. Kerlin landed safely on the edge of a lake and later reassembled the plane. Shown in the above photograph are Eliot Kerlin (left), his son, Eliot Eppes Kerlin (center), and the aviator's wife, Annie Kerlin. In the photograph to the left, W.B. Hunt (left) and Eliot Kerlin stand in front of an Ercoupe airplane at Kerlin Airfield. (Both photographs courtesy of Eliot Eppes Kerlin.)

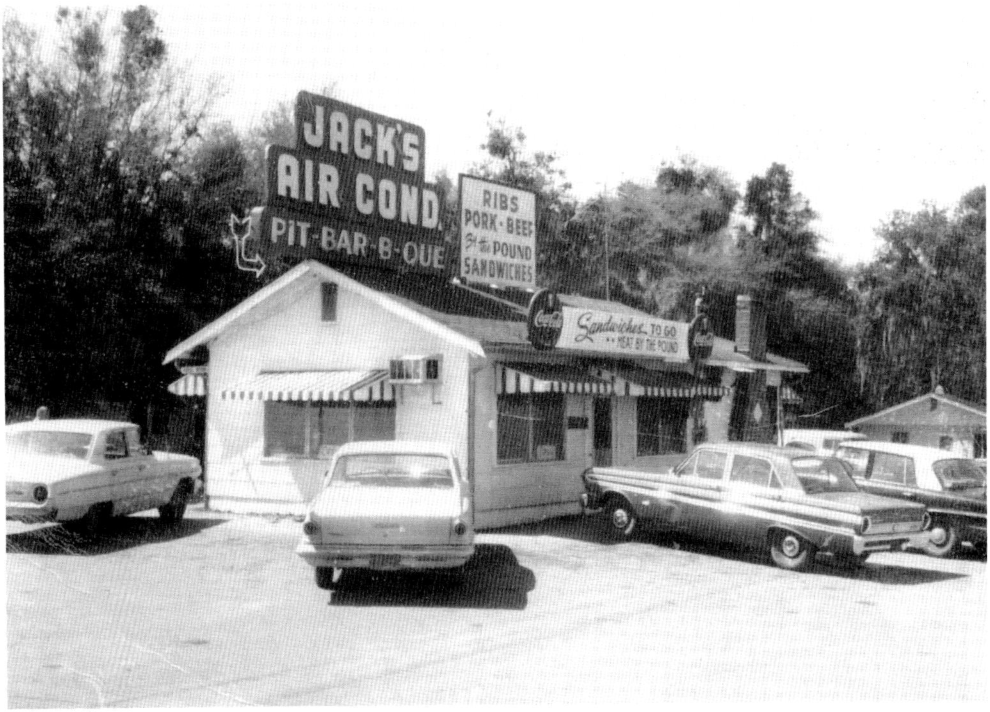

Jack's Barbeque
Jack and Lucy Underwood opened Jack's Barbeque in Minneola in 1952 and achieved a loyal following before their retirement in 1965. Their niece, Barbara Benfield, and her husband, Thomas Benfield, carried on the legacy. The restaurant, with its University of Florida memorabilia, is famous for its slogan, "When the chimney ain't smokin', we ain't open." The current owners are Charles and Eileen Costigan. (Courtesy of Thomas Benfield.)

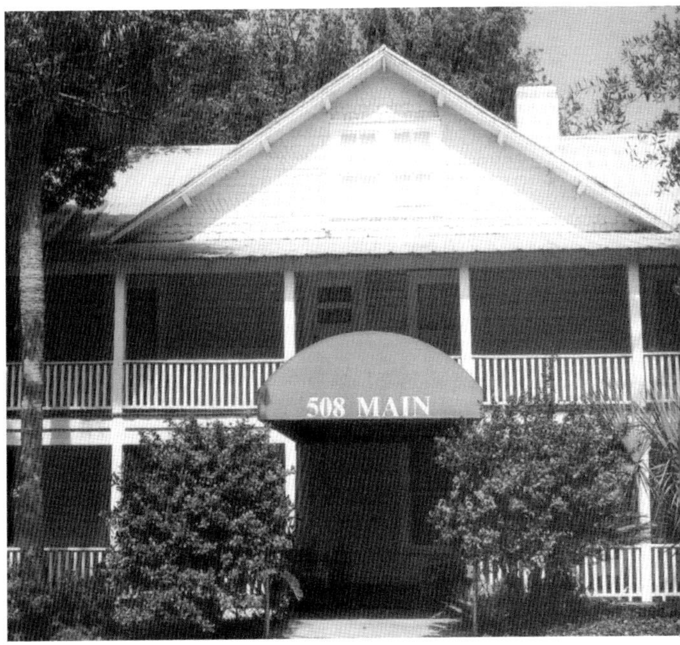

Minneola Inn
Robert and Elizabeth Straker arrived in Minneola in 1884. After he died in a mill accident, she operated a commissary and then built and operated the Straker House, known for its comfortable lodging and good food. Straker House was an especially popular destination during the 1920s land boom. The original structure burned down about 1912 and was replaced with the present Victorian-style, three-story Minneola Inn. (Courtesy of Connie Fleetwood.)

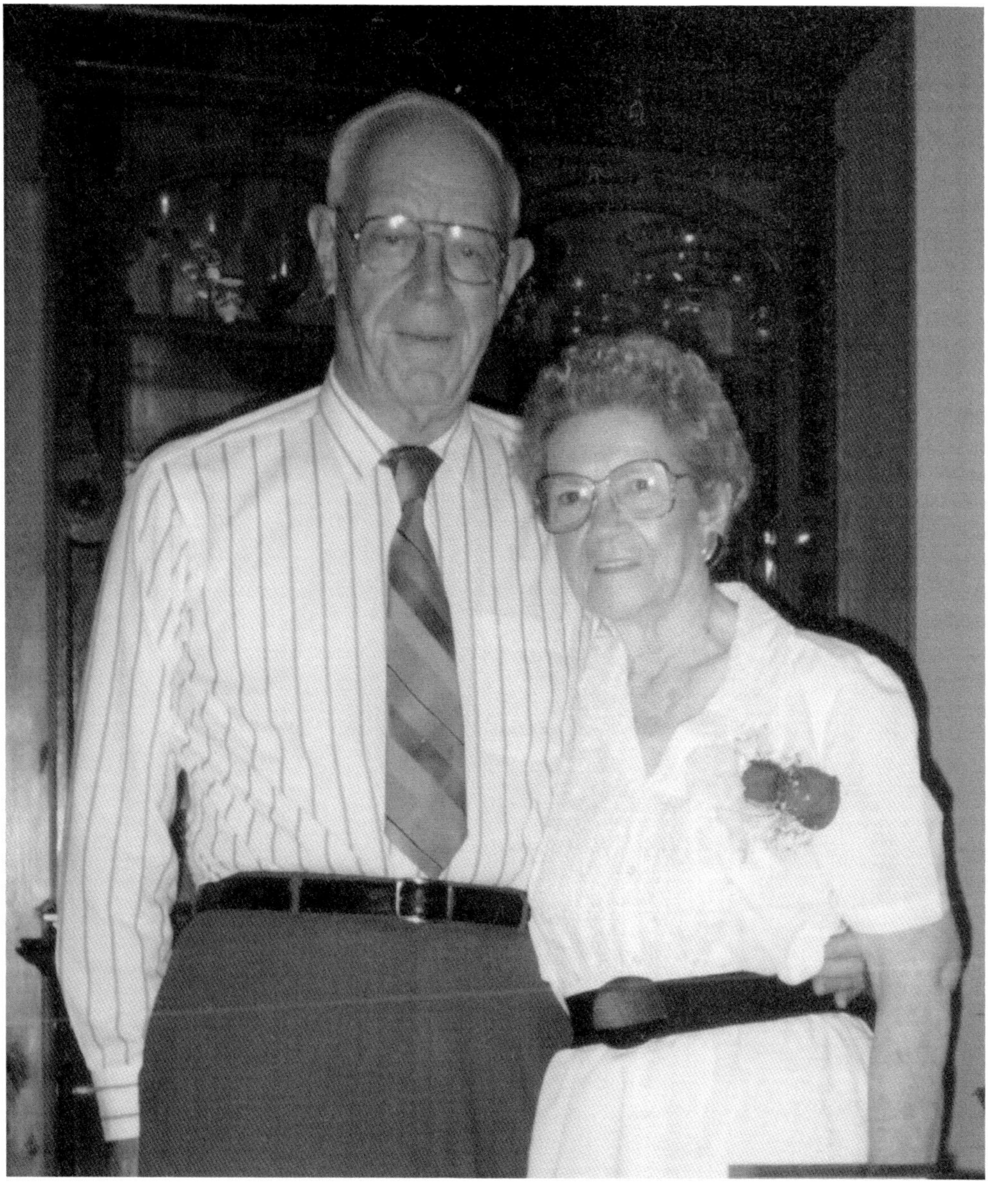

Millard Coggshall, Beekeeper and Mayor
After graduating from Cornell University in 1937, Millard Coggshall married Genevieve Predmore and became a third-generation beekeeper. The Coggshalls moved to Minneola in 1941 to produce orange blossom honey. They were active in the state beekeepers association, and he received the group's Pioneer Award. He served as mayor and city council member of Minneola and also served on the South Lake Hospital Board for 25 years. His community service included the South Lake Rotary Club, where he received the Paul Harris Fellow Award, and the local Sons of the American Revolution. Her community service included work with the Woman's Club, Pilot Club, Garden Club, and as a Girl Scout leader. She was honored with the Lake County Historical Society's President's Award. Their son, David Coggshall, was a well-respected Lake County teacher and principal. Their daughter, Carol Coggshall, worked at Sprint. (Courtesy of the Coggshall family.)

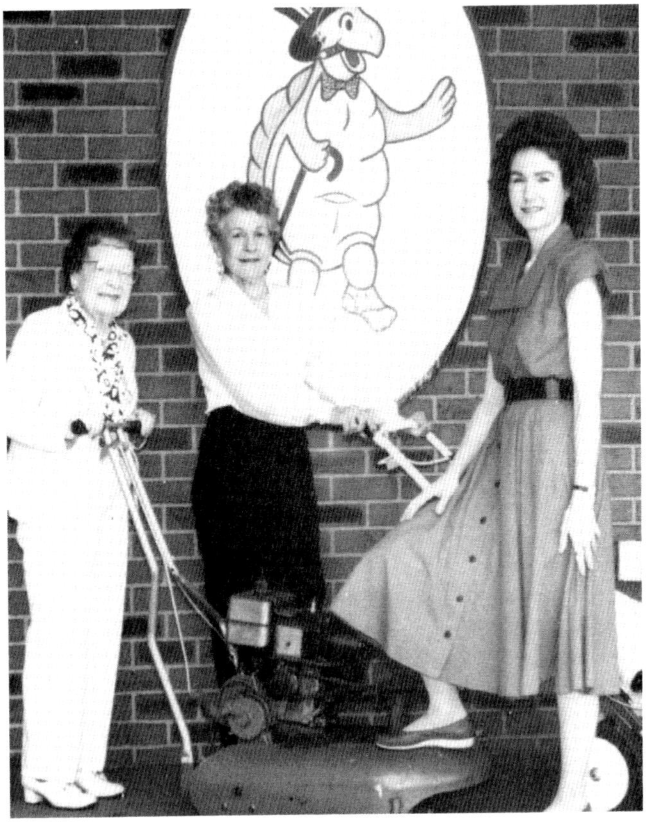

Snappin' Turtle's Founding Family

L. Neal Smith, a respected rancher, developer, and former president of Montverde Academy, was best known for inventing the world-famous Snappin' Turtle lawn mower. After he sold the self-propelled mower's patent, his son-in-law, Hoyt J. Franklin, retained distributorship of the renamed Snapper in Montverde. Shown here are, from left to right, Bessie Smith (the inventor's wife), Doris Franklin (daughter), and Gee Gee Franklin (granddaughter). (Courtesy of *Central Florida*.)

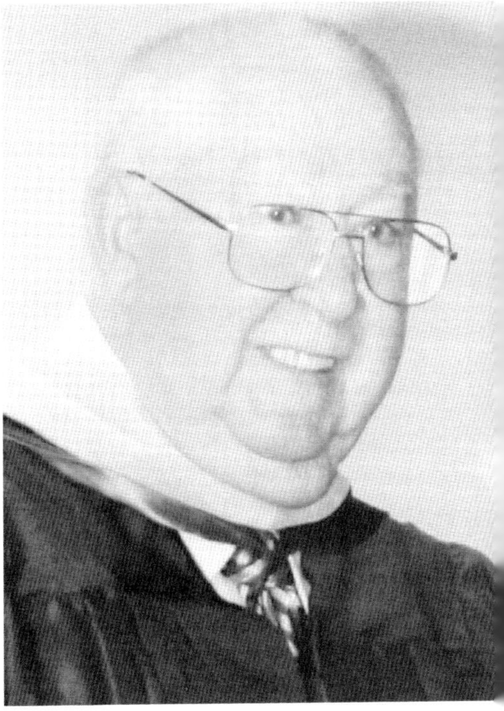

Walter Stephens, Montverde Legend

Under the leadership of Walter L. Stephens from 1968 to 1999, Montverde Academy flourished into an internationally recognized private school, which celebrated its 100th anniversary in October 2012. In the 1960s and 1970s, Stephens helped institute nondiscrimination policies that continue to shape the top-20 school, where enrollment is made up of 43 percent international students. The current headmaster is Kasey Kesselring. (Courtesy of Montverde Academy.)

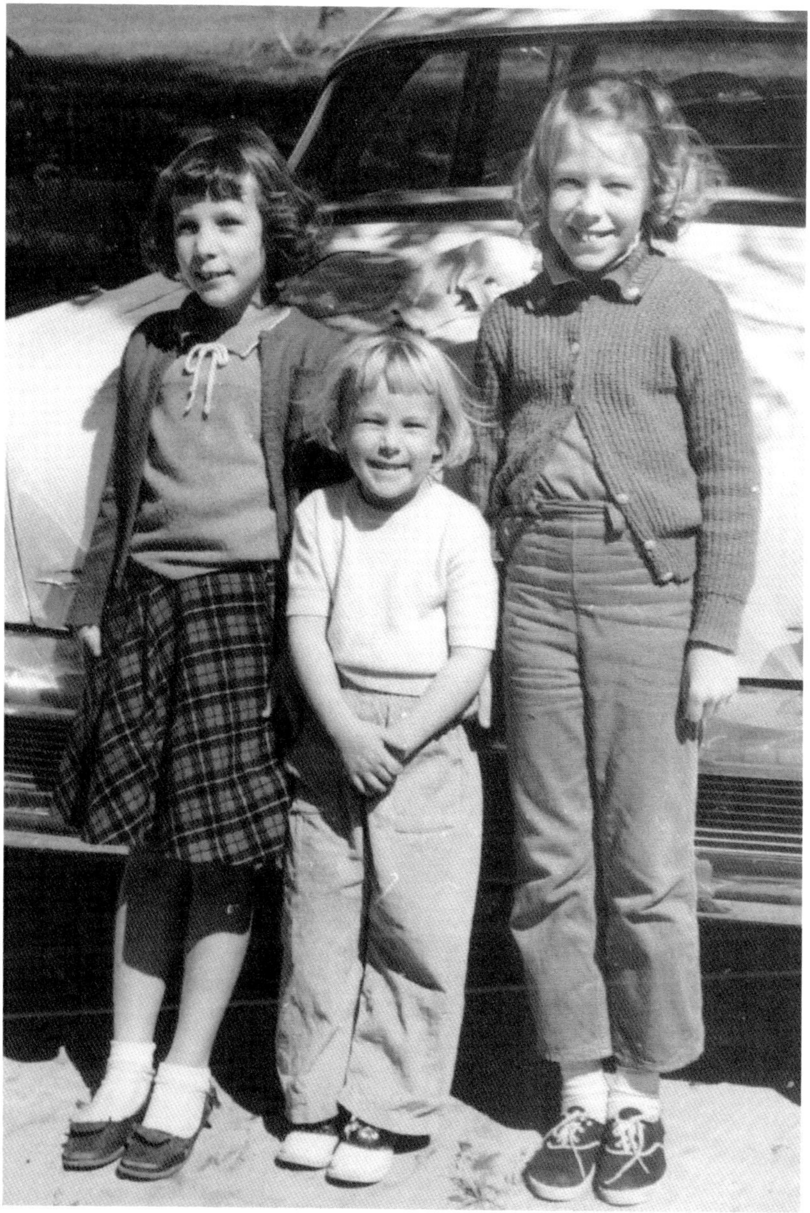

The Woolum Girls

They were known as the "Woolum girls" and came from West Virginia with their parents, Everett and Doris Woolum, in 1959 to start a new life in Lake County. The rolling hills and small-town atmosphere in south Lake County seemed ideal to raise a family. The Woolums were like many others who came to the beautiful heart of Florida seeking a better life for their children. He became part of the country's space race at Martin Marietta. She sewed her daughter's school clothes and made meatloaf that tasted gourmet. Shown here are, from left to right, Connie Woolum Fleetwood (former Groveland mayor and head of Groveland Elementary School's after-school program), Susan Woolum Pegram (lifelong educator and principal at Sorrento Elementary School), and Doris Woolum Bloodsworth (award-winning writer and historian). (Courtesy of the Woolum family.)

INDEX